Religion and Global Order

Religion, Culture and Society

Series Editors:
Oliver Davies and Gavin Flood,
Department of Theology and Religious Studies,
University of Wales, Lampeter

Religion, Culture and Society is a series presented by leading scholars on a wide range of contemporary religious issues. The emphasis throughout is generally multicultural, and the approach is often interdisciplinary. The clarity and accessibility of the series, as well as its authoritative scholarship, will recommend it to students and a non-specialist readership alike.

Religion and Global Order

Edited by

JOHN L. ESPOSITO and MICHAEL WATSON

UNIVERSITY OF WALES PRESS
CARDIFF
2000

British Library Cataloguing-in-Publication Data
A catalogue record for this book is available from
the British Library.

ISBN 0-7083-1525-9 (paperback)
ISBN 0-7083-1526-7 (hardback)

Cover Design by Olwen Fowler, The Beacon Studio
Typeset at the University of Wales Press
Printed in Great Britain by Dinefwr Press, Llandybïe

Contents

The Contributors

Editors

John L. Esposito, founding director of the Center for Muslim–Christian Understanding: History and International Affairs at Georgetown University, he is Professor of Religion and International Affairs and Professor of Islamic Studies. He has served as President of the Middle East Studies Association of North America and of the American Council for the Study of Islamic Societies and as a consultant to the Department of State as well as corporations, universities and organizations world-wide. He specializes in Islam, political Islam, and the impact of Islamic movements from North Africa to Southeast Asia.

Editor-in-chief of *The Oxford Encyclopedia of the Modern Islamic World* (4 vols., Oxford University Press, 1995), his other publications include: *The Islamic Threat: Myth or Reality?; Islam: The Straight Path; Islam and Democracy* (with John Voll); *Islam and Politics; The Iranian Revolution: Its Global Impact; Political Islam: Revolution, Radicalism or Reform?: Gender, Culture and Islam* (with Yvonne Haddad); *Islam in Asia: Religion, Politics and Society; Contemporary Islamic Revivalism* (with Y. Haddad and J. Voll); *Voices of Resurgent Islam; Islam in Transition: Muslim Perspectives; Islam and Development*; and *Women in Muslim Family Law.*

Michael M. Watson received his Ph.D. on French government from the University of Wales. He has been Dean of the Faculty of Economic and Social Studies and Chair of Political Science at the University of Wales, Aberystwyth. He has recently retired from the Department of International Politics at UWA, where he established the Centre for European Studies and was its first Director, and initiated (with James Piscatori) and directed a Masters programme on Religion, Politics and International Relations. His teaching and research interests have ranged widely, encompassing West European government and politics, economic planning and regional policy, minority nationalism, environmental politics, and religion and politics. He has published articles or books in all these areas; his preceding book (as editor and contributor) is *Contemporary Minority Nationalism* (London, Routledge, 1990)

Other Contributors

Paul Badham is Professor of Theology and Religious Studies at the University of Wales Lampeter where he is involved in teaching for an MA in Religion, Politics and International Relations. He is also editing a book with Vladislav Arzenukhin of the Herzen University, St Petersburg, on *Religion and Change in Eastern Europe.*

Rabbi Dan Cohn-Sherbok received a doctorate in philosophy from Cambridge University and a doctorate in divinity from the Hebrew Union college, Jewish Institute of Religion. He is Professor of Judaism at the University of Wales, Lampeter, and visiting Professor of Interfaith Dialogue at Middlesex University. He is the author and editor of over fifty books including *Judaism and Other Faiths, Modern Judaism* and *The Future of Judaism.*

John F. Haught (Ph.D. Catholic University, 1970) is Landegger distinguished Professor of Theology and former departmental chair at Georgetown University. His area of specialization is systematic theology, with a particular interest in issues pertaining to science, cosmology, ecology and religion. He is the author of numerous books, including *Science and Religion: From Conflict to Conversation* (Paulist Press, 1995), *The Promise of Nature: Ecology and Cosmic Purpose* (Mahwah, NJ, Paulist Press, 1993), *The Revelation of God in History* (Wilmington, Michael Glazier Press, 1988), *The Cosmic Adventure* (New York, Paulist Press, 1984) and *Nature and Purpose* (Lanham, MD, University Press of America, 1980); as well as numerous articles. He has recently established the Georgetown Center for the Study of Science and Religion.

Jeff Haynes is a Reader in Politics at London Guildhall University, where he teaches courses on Third World and International Politics. His most recent books are: *Religion and Politics in Africa* (1996), *Third World Politics: A Concise Introduction*

(1996), *Democracy and Civil Society in the Third World* (1997), *Religion in Global Politics* (1998) and (ed.), *Religion, Globalization and Political Culture in the Third World* (1998).

Simon Murden was awarded a doctorate from the University of Exeter in 1993. After working at the University of Plymouth, he became a lecturer in Middle Eastern Politics in the Department of International Politics, University of Wales, Aberystwyth. His teaching and research interests currently include security studies in the Persian Gulf, the Arab–Israeli conflict in Lebanon, and culture and hegemony in the international system. He is the author of *Emergent Regional Powers and International Relations in the Gulf 1988–91* (1995). He is currently writing a book, *Islam in the New Hegemony.*

James Piscatori is Fellow of Wadham College, Oxford, and of the Oxford Centre for Islamic Studies. He was formerly Professor in the Department of International Politics, the University of Wales, Aberystwyth, and Senior Fellow of the Council for Foreign Relations, New York (1994–6). He is the author of *Islam in a World of Nation-States* (Cambridge University Press, 1986) and co-author (with Dale F. Eickelman) of *Muslim Politics* (Princeton University Press, 1996). He is the editor of *Islam in the Political Process* (Cambridge University Press, 1983), and co-editor (with Susanne Hoeber Rudolph) of *Transnational Religion and Fading States* (Westview Press, 1997).

Sulak Sivaraksa is a graduate of the University of Wales and was called to the Bar (Middle Temple) in London. He is a leading figure in Thailand and internationally as a Buddhist and academic activist. He lectures regularly at Bangkok's four universities and has been Visiting Professor at the Universities of California (Berkeley), Cornell, Toronto and Hawaii, and is Honorary Fellow of the University of Wales (Lampeter). He was founding editor of the *Social Science Review*, Chair of the Asian Cultural Forum on Development (ACFOD), founder of the Thai Inter-Religious Commission for Development (TICD) and of the Santi Pracha Dhamma Institute, Bangkok (and still its Director). His many writings include: *Siamese Resurgence: A Thai Buddhist Voice on Asia and a World of Change* (Bangkok, ACFOD, 1985), *A*

Socially Engaged Buddhism (Bangkok, TICD, 1988), *Seeds of Peace: A Buddhist Vision for Renewing Society* (Berkeley, Parallas, 1992) and as co-editor and contributor, *Radical Conservatism* and *Searching for Asian Cultural Integrity* (Bangkok, Santi Pracha Dhamma Institute, 1990 and 1991 respectively).

Scott Thomas received his Ph.D. from the Department of International Relations at the London School of Economics and lectures in International Relations in the Department of Economics and International Development at the University of Bath. He is the author of *The Diplomacy of Liberation: The Foreign Relations of the ANC since 1960* (1996), and has lectured and written widely on the role of religion in international relations.

Michael Walsh began his academic career as a historian of the early Church, moved on to the study of hagiography, but is now particularly interested in twentieth-century Roman Catholicism. Among other publications, he has written or edited a number of books on the papacy, including a biography of Pope John Paul II, a volume on Catholic social doctrine and a study of the conservative Catholic organization, Opus Dei. He is Librarian of Heythrop College, University of London.

Acknowledgements

The editors would like to thank the University of Wales, Aberystwyth, and in particular the Department of International Politics for financial support in bringing the project to fruition, and are especially grateful to the secretaries in the department: Louise Barham (to September 1998), Ardwyna Davies and Vicki Jones for their unstinting and excellent work in the preparation of the manuscript. Also, thanks to John Esposito's administrative officer, Patricia Gordon, for essential work in linking both sides of the Atlantic, and to the University of Wales Press for showing considerable understanding about the difficulties inherent in a multifaceted project of this nature.

Introduction

JOHN L. ESPOSITO AND MICHAEL WATSON

This book results from a collaboration, both inter-institutional and inter-disciplinary. It has brought together scholars from Britain and the USA, with the initiative coming from the University of Wales (UK) and the Center for Muslim–Christian Understanding, Georgetown University (USA), others having been drawn in from Bath University (UK), London Guildhall University and Heythrop College, London University (UK). James Piscatori, at the Oxford Centre for Islamic Studies, was one of the principal initiators at the University of Wales (his previous post). There was general agreement on the importance and interest of investigating religion's role and voice in respect of the question of global order. The latter has become an increasingly prominent aspect of international relations since the collapse of the Soviet Union and the 'bipolar world' of the cold war. This momentous event has been joined by the phenomenon of globalization which has come rapidly to the fore in the past decade as a concern of economists, political scientists and sociologists. As a shaper of events and developments globally, its importance for global order is undeniable.

But where is religion in all this? Certainly it is often ignored (globalization is seen overwhelmingly as an economic and technological matter). Yet religion, too, has recently emerged into political and social consciousness internationally, if only or mainly as a result of the resurgence of a militant Islam and in particular its challenge to modern (Western) values and power. However, the notion of a religious resurgence or renewal goes wider than this and what it involves invites exploration, specifically as to its place and part in the global order of post-Communism and globalization (including the associated question marks raised against the *modern* world as such, now almost exclusively seen in terms of market capitalism and liberal democracy).

Such, broadly, is the book's agenda. It is not intended as a study of the meaning of global order or, much less (it hardly needs saying), of religion. But some clarification of the title's terms is called for, even if their use is in a straightforward, conventional sense (as commonly or broadly 'read'). Thus 'religion' is taken to denote the major faiths considered as 'world religions', namely having today a world-wide presence and open to any human beings; they share a belief in a reality distinct from that of 'commonsense' or scientific empiricism, yet present in the latter's development, normative as well as material. Religion in this respect deals essentially with matters of the spirit and the spiritual dimension of life, which involves a leading concern with good and evil and other ethical questions. There is both a generic focus on such religion and specifically, of individual world faiths, on Christianity, Buddhism and more especially Islam – the latter justified by its prominence in terms of religious resurgence, at least as perceived by public and élite opinion in many countries (not least Western ones).

The role and significance of religion for global order is deciphered in terms of its ideas and its 'ideology', that is, its set of values, norms and beliefs relevant to contemporary politics and society (wherever and whatever), as well as the activities and interventions of religious leaders and authorities, institutions, organizations and movements. The 'global order' envisaged in this analysis is simply a new designation for the perennial concern with political and social order but now extended to the global level, that is, pertaining to the globe as a whole. 'World-wide' might be considered a synonym and often it can suffice, but ultimately world has a narrower connotation, referring to the human dimension of life on earth (and indeed often applied to an aspect of this, for example, the political or Western world). This restrictiveness applies even more to 'international' which refers only to the 'world' of states – whether the concern is international economics or, as is usually emphasized, the political aspect of international affairs.

'Global' signifies that, while we are certainly interested in states as important institutions and actors in respect of 'order', this is insufficient given the range of forces now at work and the contemporary reach of events and developments; the latter can affect not just humanity but life and indeed nature, as a whole. It is 'order' on this grander scale that is now at issue; but, quite evidently, world and international order remain subsets and essential ingredients of global order. As regards 'order' itself, as a concept it cannot avoid a certain ambiguity. It can be a generic idea referring to some form or pattern exhibiting continuity with evolutionary change – in fact, in historical terms, possessing a considerable and evident stability. For us it has a more specific and substantive sense: a concrete state of affairs which is *dominant*, or rapidly becoming so, in space (the globe) and time (contemporary) in respect of human activity and the surrounding beliefs, values and ideas; this may not be equally true of all the major sectors of human activity and it is clearly less true of contemporary governmental politics than of economics, finance, business and technological development.

Beyond this, the 'order' we are concerned with is not just that which *is*, namely the actually dominant one (the *status quo* globally). It is also one which is being sought – that is, a normative order, which can act additionally as a basis for critique of the actual order. Here religion may come more into its own, rather than as a 'really existing' alternative order in serious contention with the *status quo*; though the possibility of that cannot be ruled out a priori, principally in the case of Islam (hence also, partly, our particular attention to it). The general question arises whether religion stands, in major respects, in a contradictory position *vis-à-vis* the dominant global order or coexists comfortably not to say supportively with it. The *status quo* may, indeed, be challenged as not a 'true' order from a normative perspective, including one that sees it in fact as disruptive of order in and of society around the globe (promoting excessive change affecting cultures, social and indeed political relation-ships, and *pari passu* failing to ensure sufficient continuity and stability for a valid 'order' to exist). Religion may well have something to say in this respect.

However, we start from the premiss that there is today a global order (of sorts), one truly global. As such it is 'new', dating from the 1989–91 period, with the end of the ideologically bipolar world. Prior to then there was the 'old' order of the world divided in two politically and economically and of the military confrontation of the 'superpowers' (the USA and USSR), so it was not global in the full sense. This old world order was still essentially an international order based on the pre-eminence of states (though in the West and Third World this had already been eroding for some fifteen years prior to 1989, notably with the reassertion of market ideas). It was an order resting largely on a balance of power between the leading states, which had become, with the cold war, structured around a balance between the two ideologically opposed superpowers. The 'new' global order is based mainly on the dominance of a form of economics and finance – market capitalism – allied to modern liberal ideas and values (including, to a greater or lesser degree, a commitment to liberal democratic institutions and processes of government). At the same time, the idea and practice of 'civil society' as an area of human institutions and activity distinct from both state and market has come much more to the fore world-wide. What religion's relationship with this change is, and especially with the new order, is a major interest: religion's own situation has changed and its role has grown in significance.

In the post-cold war world, some have come to see religion as a main threat to the new order, as a source globally of division and disruption, thereby enhancing any centrifugal tendencies; this view has become especially prevalent in the secular West and is expressed not least by politicians and media commentators. More specifically, the threat is understood as one to Western interests and values (mainly by Islam). Outside the West, religion's more active role is more appreciated by reforming and popular forces – if not always by rulers. These perspectives clearly require examination and explanation. Beyond this, the religious response to the global phenomenon, and what religious ideas and values can and do contribute to the debate, are also important concerns; this is especially true given the decline of political ideology as a source of competing, alternative world-views. So the relationship of religion to the question of global order emerges as a diverse and complex one in the realm of thought and ideas as well as that of practice, on which we cannot hope to be exhaustively comprehensive but nevertheless can seek to throw significant light.

The book is organized in three basic parts. In Part I (Chapters 1–5), general themes, issues and tendencies of the 'global order–religion' relation are explored. In Chapter 1 the editors set forth the contemporary context in which basic issues and questions are to be considered. The process of unrelenting change central to modernity is increasingly cast in 'global' terms. The modern world has seen the collapse of one of its principal pillars: Communism as the 'really existing' comprehensive alternative to market capitalism and liberal democracy. In general there has been a relative decline of state power and a corresponding increase in that of economic forces (notably corporate capitalism). Religion and nationalism have also seen a resurgence world-wide. In this situation, where religion fits in relation to the developing critique of the new global order (and of modernity more generally) is a key question. Those lines of the critique and challenge which have a particular resonance with religion are drawn out and religion's role in the context of (civil) society as a basic 'building block' of contemporary order, along with government and economic institutions, is highlighted.

In Chapter 2 Scott Thomas sets out the meaning and source of religious resurgence in the critiques of liberalism and the failings of modernization and secularization (processes central to Enlightenment liberalism). Postmodernism, in part at least, reflects these failings, and is more open to spirituality. Religious resurgence poses difficult dilemmas for liberalism, in particular, how to respond to it. The liberal system on which international and global order are now predominantly based is subject to challenges 'from above' and 'from below' – its weaknesses manifested increasingly at both levels: the growing ineffectiveness of the state in the system's 'Centre' (the North) and the growing assertion of the system's 'Periphery' – in which religion including Christianity is involved – against its subordination to the West materially and culturally. The official Western view focuses on economic and security threats and even alternatives are debated within the parameters of liberal discourse. Religion needs to be brought into the reckoning and the dialogue, on a global basis, in public deliberations; but this goes against a central presupposition of liberalism with its fundamental doctrine of public–private dualism.

In Chapter 3 James Piscatori examines the phenomenon of transnationalism, which is not new but in recent decades has surged, despite being largely downgraded by state advocates and international relations specialists. Transnationalism, in devaluing boundaries, challenges the shibboleth of state sovereignty. Even where transnational linkages are recognized, religion is generally not seen as contributing very much to them. Yet traditionally it has, of course, reached across states and nations and today it is more active in that respect than ever before. While contemporary transnationalism is dominated by Western economic and other actors and interests, the Periphery (in relation to these) could be said to be increasingly 'talking back' through a transnationalism in which religion plays a leading role. This is particularly true of Christianity world-wide and most notably of Islam. While Islam's transnational reach has financial and logistical support from Islamic states, this is by no means the origin of it nor is it thereby reduced simply to an instrument of state power politics (in so far as it is viewed as such, the effect can be ambiguous for states, as likely to enhance as subordinate the transnational movement). New communities are created which are significantly 'deterritorialized' and likely to challenge the 'local' established authorities in the name of the wider tradition, faith and legitimacy; yet in time they also become receptive to local cultural characteristics to some extent. So there can be a two-way flow which can help integrate the local and transnational and in so doing contribute to changing both, notably towards greater recognition and respect for differences.

For Michael Walsh, in Chapter 4, Catholicism is a global force, but John Paul II has developed the global reach of his office as no pope before him. The papacy's political and diplomatic role is based, historically, on the territorial sovereignty it has exercised in Italy; yet it rests ultimately on its spiritual authority, certainly for the one billion-plus Catholics world-wide. The pope has the Holy See as his government, based in the Vatican City State, and which is officially represented in other states and international bodies by diplomatic officials (nuncios); under John Paul II the number has greatly increased. The basic concern is to safeguard the mission of the Roman Catholic Church and the Holy See, especially in unwelcoming states. Indirect influence in global affairs is also sought through the work of Catholic 'experts' (scientists, economists, etc.), notably sponsored by the Pontifical Commission for Justice and Peace. Its mission has increasingly been laid down, especially since the 1960s and under John Paul II, in the development of a globally oriented Catholic social doctrine.

A contemporary case in which the papacy's intervention is well displayed is the Middle East: after drawing closer to Israel, the pope provoked its displeasure by support for Palestinian rights, especially after the Israeli annexation of Jerusalem (the papacy's is a strong voice for Jerusalem's international status). None the less, Israel's signing of the peace accord with the Palestine Liberation Organization led to the establishment, for the first time, of formal diplomatic relations between Israel and the Vatican. This reflects the top priority given to the pursuit of peace, recently shown also in support for the Northern Ireland Agreement and for a similar process between Spain and Basque separatists. A particular concern is to develop harmony in Christian–Muslim relations (a certain convergence in social doctrine having a part in this), hence the attention to the Middle East, which sometimes provokes US unease. Europe is another priority focus, with strong support in particular for its unification (the Vatican has joined the Eurozone), but extended to the Urals. Such a European community is called on to recognize its roots in its common Christian heritage, in the necessary pursuit of reconciliation and solidarity for a peaceful Europe. However, the papacy's ambitions are ultimately global, as an ethical guide not to say mediator in international relations, notably through its development of a 'pedagogy of peace' and of world-wide links of solidarity. Yet today the optimism engendered by the collapse of Communism seems to be evaporating (and attention may also turn more, on John Paul II's death, to internal Church problems).

Starting from the so-called 'threat vacuum' identified after the end of the cold war, John Esposito in Chapter 5 explores in depth the tendency to see Islam filling this vacuum, with its corollary of the West and the Islamic world being on a collision course destructive of global order. Islam's resurgence has seen it emerge as a global force, characterized by political and social activism, including playing a role in some nationalist struggles; but also with new élites based in the professions. The pressure is often for political and social reform, with demands for 'Muslim' states to democratize, so that Islamists (the 'radicals') have emerged as leading the opposition to authoritarian and conservative regimes in the Muslim world – causing Western states to fear for 'old friends' from cold war days who are essentially pro-Western, pro-secular and/or pro-capitalist (though hardly politically pro-liberal).

These pressures have meant, even without regime changes, that such states have become more independent and less predictable. Order and stability in this case is equated with the *status quo*, rationalized as acceptable because Islam is understood as inherently 'undemocratic' – while in fact there are specific historical reasons for any such legacy. Islam does have to face various human rights issues, but the debate goes on within it and there is a process of change including religious reinterpretation. Blocking of political participation and dialogue could, however, endanger this process. Islam, even its 'radicals' or 'fundamentalists', should not be stereotyped – it is far from monolithic. Nevertheless, Islamic resurgence does represent a challenge, crucially to achieve a closer alignment of government and Islamic culture, including the belief in social justice; but also, for the West, to desist from seeking to prop up regimes with tenuous legitimacy in the face of popular contestation (regimes which play for the West's support on its fear of 'fundamentalism'). What is clear is that the failure of secular socialism and nationalism has left political and social order in the Muslim world largely dependent on repression – or accommodation with popular Islamism (and the latter can hardly be gainsaid ultimately).

Part II examines the momentous change, from the 'old' order to the 'new' global one, in three major geopolitical 'cases' which highlight religion's place and importance in this change. First, in Chapter 6, Paul Badham elucidates the crucial break that occurred in Eastern Europe in the late 1980s which effectively caused the collapse of the Communist bloc. Despite the Communist system's policy towards religion of 'cultural strangulation', religion's role was highly important if not decisive in the change, specifically in the trail-blazing case of Poland. In this a transnational element was also crucial, in the part played by the Vatican and Pope John Paul II. Religion represented a counter-culture and alternative social space to the official ideology and channels, leading in 1980 to the creation of the Solidarity movement expressing Catholic social ethics. There was a significant convergence between national and religious identity, but at least as important was the failure of a Communist identity based on a secular ideology to implant itself in the hearts and minds of most people in opposition to the cultural heritage based around Christianity.

This heritage was a vital resource in sustaining resistance in Eastern Europe and, with Church encouragement, in helping keep the revolution a 'velvet' one; given this, and the popular, deep-seated character of the movement, the Communist hierarchy were deterred from using military force. Church representatives from the pope to local level, were able to act as channels and mediators, often enhanced by previous ecumenical experience. With the revolution came renewal in Christian education, music and art, and social and political activity – a reminder that religion is not simply worship and prayer. Post-1989 has provided a 'window of opportunity' for religion's role in society, but whether it leads to a dominant faith or plurality of faiths – or ultimately, after all, to an amorphous, consumerist materialism – remains unresolved (even if the latter has gained ground).

Change in the Middle East, as Simon Murden recounts (Chapter 7), has seen religion even more prominent, its resurgence and major entry onto the socio-political stage necessarily going hand in hand in Islam. Two centuries of Western hegemony and accompanying modernization had been laid over Islamic culture and belief, except for a small Westernized élite. Through them secularism, socialism and nationalism made inroads, but by the late 1960s this modernization was in crisis through its social and cultural dysfunctions and insufficiently rooted legitimacy. Traditional forms of community and civility were being destroyed. The official response was slow, and then focused on economic reforms. Outside government a rapidly growing recourse to Islamic values and teachings occurred. Islamic organizations stepped in to provide welfare, education and health care – and the vehicle for opposition to government.

The Islamic revival from the 1970s became unprecedently widespread across the Middle East and was generated in an urban setting amongst technical, professional as well as clerical strata. The key issue was what Islam could do for Muslims in the modern world – rescue them from decline, purify society, combat external forces of corruption. For radicals (or fundamentalists) the triumphant moment was the Iranian Revolution, unifying political and religious authority to enforce the *sharia* law as the law of the land, to pursue social justice and roll back Western economic and cultural influence. Despite this success which energized militants everywhere, there was no general revolutionary wave; states responded to the threat by a variable mixture of re-Islamicization, reform and coercion. By the 1990s the militant movement had begun to emphasize local social struggles. The aim was re-Islamicization 'from below', focusing on the requirement for personal and social behaviour to be 'authentic', in line with tradition. Violence is not eschewed when local leadership is at stake and, if necessary, for the community's 'purification'. This action is supported by the development of transnational networks and is difficult for states to control, resulting in a condition of endemic instability within the social body. This remains cast within the overarching context of militant Islam as the opposition to the prevailing, globally affected order in the Middle East – and of the widespread belief in a fundamental civilizational struggle with the West (strongly reflected in the Palestine–Israel conflict).

In Chapter 8, Jeff Haynes analyses a similar religious upsurge in the Third World generally in the 1970s and after, with its challenge to the officially received ideas of modernization and secularization. This is often located outside, if not divergent from, established religious hierarchies and focuses on community activity, in which religion is not a purely personal or 'private' affair. As such it is an integral facet of an 'identity crisis', which is primarily a response to social and cultural components or accompaniments of modernization, and in particular the adoption of Western ideas, values and practices (not least of the nation-state itself). These are contested and the Western-based global order is brought into question. Proponents of the major modern political world-views – realist, liberal and Marxist – have been perplexed by this crisis, and a leading interpretation to emerge is of a 'civilizational clash' (with a pessimistic if not inevitabilist flavour).

Religion is seen as politically important in the Third World and especially in its conflicts, in respect of ethnicity, reinforcing this, and of fundamentalism. Yet it is equally significant in terms of syncretistic movements drawing on indigenous roots and of communitarian movements (based on liberationist ideas and associated notably with base Christian communities). Political culture has thus emerged, thanks largely to religion, as a crucial variable in Third World societies' development: beliefs and values that people hold dear mobilizing them against reigning Western orthodoxies about economic, social and political development. Urbanization, education, social mobility, economic and scientific rationality have not diminished the social and political possibilities of religion – and not just fundamentalism. Not all aspects of modernization are wholly rejected, only that which is synonymous with secularization. Religion remains relevant, socially and politically, as much in a public collective as a personal, private way, and 'loss of faith' is rather *vis-à-vis* secular government (of whatever political ideology). Political religion in the Third World can hardly be seen as a serious threat to the current liberal capitalist dominated global order. Yet it can still provide a rational alternative to Western-style modernization, especially with its concomitant secularization, for many people in the Third World.

The chapters in Part III focus on explaining the failings of the contemporary order, whether in terms of the damage it is doing to people and nature generally or its inability to be truly global, both inclusive and pluralistic (at the level of thought as well as practice). Beyond this, visions are expressed of what is called for in different respects, including certain practical projects, for global order to be made whole, with mutual respect and justice for people and creation in all its diversity. Each chapter approaches critiques and visions from a specific perspective, dealing with an important dimension of the problematic: economic and social development, the specifically theological (exemplified by Judaism) and the ecological. In the visions, deep spiritual resources are drawn on for the holistic goal of order to be achieved.

In Chapter 9 Sulak Sivaraksa, from a Buddhist position, develops both an ecumenical diagnosis and alternative. Global North–South inequality and the military economy continue to grow, under the driving force of 'techno-capitalism'. The ultimate value pursued is the control of life: the looming consumerist monoculture leads on inexorably to the commodification of life. For modern, Western(ized) people priority is given to worship of money, to consuming more and to better 'high' technology – increasingly at the expense of human and ecological relations, and space for spiritual life. But an alternative way of living is already known from sacred texts. The most important freedom is an 'inner' one of consciousness, open especially to the inter-connectedness of life. The strategic challenge is to link up alternative movements and develop their dialogue, but in particular in the Third World where available religious resources are greater (suffering in the West from partly self-inflicted diminution). The Spirit in Education Movement represents such an undertaking: of Asian inspiration and emphasizing education of heart and soul no less than of intellect and will – notably including continuity with cultural traditions as well as ecological sensibility – it is nonetheless globally and ecumenically oriented.

Dan Cohn-Sherbok in Chapter 10 considers the importance of inter-faith relations for global order as a significantly theological task (the ground of faith needing to be prepared for institutional dialogue). Yet theology oriented to such dialogue has not yet been sufficiently developed, as exemplified by the case of Judaism treated here. Thought has evolved from a traditional 'exclusivism' to a modern 'inclusivism', in which other faiths are no longer necessarily false if they contradict one's own – their integrity is recognized; but our revelation remains the definitive one. The need is to move from this Judaeo-centric (or Christo-centric, etc.) view to a 'theocentric' one, with faiths as different responses to the same divinity and whose paths intersect on the ascent to the Infinite. None have been doctrinally static since their origins. Today in the global world, there is realization of the very long-run reality of the world religions: the 'triumph' of one, by its followers' efforts, is not on the (remote) horizon. Each stands as an authentic religious expression – recognition of which calls for genuine opening to each other. Theologians now work, unavoidably, in a transreligious global context. This prompts increasing mutual encounter, including in each other's spiritual activity, as well as in the praxis of social and political concern. Diversity in religious expression remains the norm: the aim – and need – for theology's new awakening, is to enhance reciprocal understanding and identify what is common to religion in the emergent global consciousness, with clear repercussions for religion's response to the global order phenomenon.

The final chapter, by Jack Haught, challengingly and stimulatingly widens our horizon to the cosmic context of global order. Consideration of the crucial part to be accorded nature in the achievement of an enduring global order is placed in the context of the universe; this is to be seen as a cosmos, possessing meaning and value as an ordered whole, which is reflected in the earth's eco-system. Modernity has led to a loss of such a holistic understanding (as existed previously, for example, in the 'Great Chain of Being'). Matters of meaning and value have been expunged from nature, which has been reduced to simple mechanism. Can this materialistic determinism, in its 'cosmic pessimism', provide an ethical basis for an environmental protection policy? Some scientific 'pessimists' have argued for one on fundamentally anthropocentric grounds, of purely human need and potential – which can equally justify continued exploitation/ manipulation of nature – while a number, notably in defending biodiversity, have stressed the preciousness of life more generally; but even this 'preciousness' depends finally on what man (*sic*) in his achievements, has brought to life. A dualistic view of nature as serving or subordinate to humanity and without an intrinsic value, will eventually prove ecologically unsatisfactory. Instead, nature's worth needs to be seen in its inherent beauty, referring to an objective aspect of the universe, namely the 'ordering of novelty' or 'harmony of diversity' or 'unifying of complexity' these point to a dynamic balance in beauty, too much 'order' leading to a banal even 'dead' homogeneity and too much 'novelty' to a breakdown of coherence, even to chaos.

This vision is best captured by process theology. Cosmos is not a static condition and creation is an ongoing, open process, in which human creativity can be in partnership with God in enhancing its aesthetic intensity, or can disturb the balance between order and novelty/diversity. This goes to the heart of religion: without the spiritual insight, of the divine source and inspiration of the cosmic process, humanity can only too readily be seen as 'in charge' and unconstrained in its immediate material, 'worldly' inclinations and (hubristic) ambitions; beauty is then demoted as a significant or practical consideration. Ecological degradation is the outcome of this tendency's ascendancy in world politics and economics. Humanity's capabilities require it to assume its responsibilites in sustaining the cosmic process, recognizing that it is not just for humans (it can exist, already has, without them) or valueless apart from them. Global order can no longer ignore its long-run ecological, cosmic basis and to take this successfully on board more than techno-scientific and economic rationality is called for: spiritual values emerge once again as an integral element in finding the answer – and dialogue with religion as a *sine qua non* of this.

I

Themes, Issues and Tendencies

1

Overview: the significance of religion for global order

JOHN L. ESPOSITO AND MICHAEL WATSON

In the modern world, as the second (Christian) millennium ends, unprecedented economic and social change is the order of the day and expressed increasingly strongly in 'global' terms. In all this is religion being left behind and marginalized by modern progress, as secularist ideas would have it? Is it now a somewhat quaint, purely private and personal affair? This view is apparently widespread in Western academia, not least in the social sciences. In particular, with very few exceptions, 'standard texts' in politics and international relations wholly or very largely ignore religion.[1] This goes too for studies dealing with global questions, including transnational forces and normative concerns in which religion might be thought to have a moderately significant presence or relevance.[2] Perhaps a main reason for this – other than, God forbid, simple prejudice! – is the preoccupation with those institutions, structures and persons ('agents') perceived as powerful in the contemporary modern world ('modern' being equated with 'secular' and ruling out religion for consideration in most instances as having little worldly influence). We hope in this book to help rectify to some extent this ignorance and, more specifically, the lacuna in the relatively new studies of the global dimension of human existence.

Religion and global change

Religion is indeed substantially involved in contemporary politics around the world,[3] if not always directly yet in ways that have an important bearing on politics at all levels. The world-wide resurgence of religion, in the late twentieth century, has affected personal and political life. Its importance and impact in politics is witnessed in South Africa's anti-apartheid movement, Muslim politics, liberation theology in the Third World, Jewish fundamentalism in Israel, Hindu fundamentalism in India, conflicts in Bosnia, Kosovo and Lebanon. This book will bring out the significance of this in a number of major instances and respects. More specifically and crucially it is concerned with religion's place in and following the momentous events and developments of the past two decades, which surely signal the move into a new era (most notably symbolized by the proliferation of the prefix 'post-'[4]). In this change 'the global' has rapidly emerged as a central feature, both as regards the repercussions of certain developments or as the nature and 'site' of others. In all this, religion has renewed its challenge to some of the major aspects – political, social and cultural – of the modern world. It needs to be said that 'challenge' does not necessarily mean 'rejection' or threat. But it has to be recognized that modernity has often been hostile to religion, supremely of course in its Marxist or Communist variant. Communism's liberal democratic-cum-capitalist opponent, if not atheist, has generally pursued a secularist course even while proclaiming 'neutrality', in reality tending to lean towards marginalizing religion as a purely private matter of 'saving souls'. Modernity, basically, has often represented so much confidence in man's powers, theoretical and applied, that any reference to the transcendent or spiritual was felt to be redundant.

Particularly noteworthy today is the modern world's identification with things Western. Its character is, indeed, overwhelmingly derived from Western culture and more especially from its roots in the European Enlightenment and the first scientific and industrial revolutions. This is a question in the first place of beliefs, ideas and values, but also, of course, in their practical outworking in terms of society. This involves the absolute sovereignty of the nation-state, the dominance of economics, of a mechanistic conception of the universe and nature and of the ever greater and faster exploitation of 'resources', non-human in particular but also human. Materialism has become the reigning paradigm of rationality and the underlying political and social ideology, largely shared by left and right (the latter the 'popular' version of the former's élite, intellectual status). This modern world in the West's image is now having to face the emergent global phenomenon ('globalization') to which it has itself been leading under the impulsion of its capitalist market component, closely allied with 'mainstream' technological development (for example, non-renewable energy, rather than renewable). In this global context, other forces are reacting and renewing themselves and some are able to feel substantially at home. Most notably amongst these are the major world religions, with their universal missions and transnational character (Hinduism less so in these respects).

Whereas religion can be readily linked to the global dimension, nationalism, especially of the ethnic variety, is the renewed force generally regarded as the one challenging, not to say threatening, the progressive development of a stable and beneficial (for all) global order. A great many of the conflicts in the post-cold war world have been ethnic or tribal, with a greater or lesser religious element: Bosnia, Kosovo, Chechnya, Rwanda, Somalia, Sri Lanka, Sudan. Religion, often in its fundamentalist guise, has been seen as an adjunct to the forces of nationalism and ethnicity.[5] Even where religion may be viewed itself as the primary motivation, in some of the cases which are classed as 'fundamentalism', this still puts it, almost inevitably, in the 'threat' category (such as the Islamic Salvation Front in Algeria or Gush Emunim and Hamas in Israel/Palestine, see pp. 154–8, 161–2, 178 below). But the questions to be asked are: is it truly a threat and, if so, 'how much' of a threat? In fact, such an understanding (of 'threat') is by no means comprehensive in terms of what religion's contribution is or could be, and its significance. This is brought home by a cursory look at the main events that heralded the change from the 'old' world order. Amongst these pride of place is undoubtedly held by the downfall of Communism as a political-cum-economic system and, effectively, the only 'real' alternative to capitalist liberal democracy (hence the rather justifiable claim, it seemed, of 'the End of History'). In this, religion's role both ideologically and practically can scarcely be gainsaid, as is explored in a later chapter; but, perhaps more significantly, there has been the renewal of religion's place in society in the ex-Communist bloc, itself closely linked to the new importance of 'civil society' as a major dimension of public or collective life. The state was truly 'rolled back' by citizen activism associated substantially with churches and other religiously based or backed groups (peace and human rights, environmental, trade union and professional/intellectual). For religion in other places, civil society has also become a 'mission' arena of choice, including in the West where it promotes the breaking down of the classic liberal secular private/public division. It involves competing with or replacing state organizations and provision in respect of social action and activities (welfare for the young and old, some health care, housing, education, aid and development non-governmental organizations).

A second event of world-wide significance is the Islamic resurgence, with its major political and social elements, and signalled and symbolized above all by Iran's Islamic Revolution. Really more a movement or process, its dynamic character is by no means entirely politically and socially 'reactionary' (as it is often viewed from a Western perspective). The impact of political Islam can be witnessed from Egypt and Sudan to Malaysia and Indonesia. Some at least of its critique of Western modernization is pertinent – including for the West – finding an echo with that of the Communitarians (see Chapter 2). Basic issues of social justice are forcibly expressed: oppression and political authoritarianism, maldistribution of wealth and marginalization (of both believers and the poor). Christianity, too, though less spectacularly, has increasingly added its critical voice, globally and regionally. This may also be seen as a 'disturbance' of the emergent global order, not least religion failing to stick to its modern secular 'script'.[6] Notable instances of this, attacking the systemic nature of world poverty and racism, may be traced back to the 1960s when the World Council of Churches saw the balance of its membership tilt towards the developing regions of the world and the Roman Catholic Church had its *aggiornamento* in the Second Vatican Council; in particular this opened the way for the progress of liberation theology in Latin America (and subsequently in Africa and Asia), representing a substantial about-turn in respect of the Church's traditional association with the wealthy ruling élite and role in the region. In the Philippines, the Catholic Church and other Christian bodies played an important part in the overthrow of the authoritarian regime of President Marcos,[7] who for a long time had received the at least tacit support of Western governments and business; likewise, in the case of the Nicaraguan revolution which saw the end of the Somoza dictatorship.[8] Recently the papacy, too, has raised its voice in respect of many of the same social justice issues as political Islam, issues present in the (post-Communist) development of modern society globally.

Religion and the state at the beginning of the twenty-first century

What we see in the above are events of momentous significance for politics and society world-wide. They have tilted things away decisively from the dominance of the state *vis-à-vis* society (also since re-Islamization remains primarily societal rather than statist, even if the Islamic state remains an ultimate goal), and perhaps even more away from the modern wholly secular state. Compared to just twenty years ago the modern state, backed essentially by one, or in liberal democracies two, major political ideologies ('left' and 'right') has been significantly weakened. Religious resurgence has played its part in this, but also benefits importantly from it. In the long rivalry between religion and the modern state, the latter seemed to have emerged very largely victorious; but the 'death of God' and the triumph of the secular state had clearly been announced prematurely. Of course, in the 'weakened state' scenario other forces have been at work, above all economic and financial ones, even if significantly abetted by developments in communication and information technology. These are usually seen as the prime if not sole cause of the faltering of the world order which rests fundamentally on the pre-eminence of the nation-state system that emerged from the seventeenth-century 'Westphalian Settlement'.[9] This asserted the absolute sovereignty of the state over its own territory and its inviolable right to independence from outside interference or control (primarily of other states, but also of any international or transnational bodies, such as notably at the time of the Roman Catholic Church). Later, after the French Revolution, the sovereign state took on a 'national' dimension, to do with the Revolution's preaching of popular sovereignty; so the nation-state gradually became the arena of (liberal) democratization – some would argue squeezing out or radically transforming other forms, such as that of industrial or economic democracy.[10]

Military power was basically the way the state preserved its 'hard shell'. Today military power, border police or customs are no guarantee of the impermeability of a state's borders. The liberal, capitalist economy *has* to be open to trade, capital movements and information flows; currency exchange rates can scarcely be controlled. Thus with the development of huge transnational (or 'global') business corporations and of global markets, in particular financial, the weakness of states in matters of economic and social policy choice within their own boundaries – notably its narrowing – has become increasingly evident. States are also largely powerless to prevent individually the cross-border spread of major environmental problems or of foreign cultural influences through satellite television and, increasingly, the internet (World Wide Web especially); in fact, these increasingly impact societies and individual national citizens – in 'developed' states already an influential and constantly growing proportion of them. This development may lead to greater cosmopolitanism in society in more and more countries (the basis for what David Held calls 'cosmopolitan democracy',[11] as a response to corporate globalization) – though leaving a 'periphery' of marginalized 'locals' without the means or desire to become cosmopolitan – *or* to the transnational spread of more powerful cultures and in particular the emergence of one with a substantial dominance over others; today this is undoubtedly associated with the world-wide ascendancy of a commercial and consumerist mass culture (see, for example, George Ritzer's work[12]) as the contemporary expression of market capitalism. In the face of this situation, religion has at times been a recourse for politicians as one of relatively few forces available to shore up the state by its contribution to national identity, rooted historically, and resistance to the globalizing forces. Religion has also been appropriated by opposition movements to delegitimate the established state regime and mobilize popular support against it. This is most likely to occur in non-Western countries, where the transnational globalizing forces are identified as 'Western' or more specifically 'American' and in which religion is a major factor in such awareness (Muslim and Hindu countries, in particular, but also Eastern Orthodox Christian ones).

Religious institutions and leaders may be suspicious of the motivations of politicians turning to religion to strengthen national identity and/or bolster the state (or overthrow it). Certainly in the West there has been a pronounced distancing from nationalism in the past half century, notably by the Vatican and the World Council of Churches (and most of its associated regional bodies, such as the Conference of European Churches). However, religion can take the initiative in finding common cause with the state, or responding favourably to its overtures, in opposition to foreign influences and especially those emanating from contemporary globalization (including international bodies facilitating it, notably the International Monetary Fund and the World Bank). In this respect, what needs to be stressed is that such a 'partnership' between religion and politics is not with 'the state' in the modern secular sense; it very largely depends on the state itself defending if not promoting the religion and its associated culture, and allowing it full scope in the public arena, including politically. Even then there may well remain a tension between state and religion, at least at an ideological level, since the religions we are concerned with are world religions with a universal mission, in terms of the values and beliefs subscribed to (at the least, these have universal validity) and a diaspora of religious communities.

Ultimately, the state that has emerged on the world scene in the past century is not a reliable partner for religion, tending to be a strong rival for allegiance – and a zealous one if its suspicions are prompted – the more so since it has its own professional personnel with distinct ambitions and at least some different values (this goes in particular with the development, gradually if not precipitately, of secular interests and, most probably, secular ethos). There is little to suggest that this divergence can be overcome by subordinating the state to religious authorities, for these then inevitably become subject to the needs of the exercise of political power which sooner or later clash with their commitment to their spiritual beliefs and values (whose have been most compromised in instances of theocracy is an interesting historical question!); clearly, to retain power at crucial political junctures usually means sacrificing or compromising religious commitments. In any case, throughout the last few centuries, taking the treaty of Westphalia (1648) as signalling the turning-point, the modern state has followed its own course of development to become the most powerful of society's institutions, a structure performing key societal functions (notably providing security to its inhabitants in an increasingly comprehensive range of forms and ways) and being the centre of policy-making through its legislative sovereignty. Its advance has seen the place and role of religion recede, first and foremost in the West but, as the twentieth century progressed, increasingly in the other regions of the world as well.

But what of the twenty-first century? Does the convincing case, noted above, for the at least relative decline of the state – certainly its lesser or weaker place and role in society's affairs world-wide in the last quarter of a century – mean that religion will be faced with more promising prospects for its societal importance (including politically) than for a long time? This is undoubtedly the case in the Muslim world and (most of) the former Soviet bloc: in these, religion has re-emerged as a powerful social, cultural and political force; and the state has had to take significant note, at least, of religion's needs and claims. But even if the balance between religion and the state has shifted, or is shifting, back in favour of the former (in the main simply restoring, one might say, something of a real balance in the relationship), is religion really that much better placed in relation to society's development as a whole? The answer to this, in which we are particularly interested, certainly varies in respect of religion's contribution, according to the form this takes (including the particular faith, of course) and its normative content (or vision) – as we hope this book brings out. A crucial consideration in evaluating this is the recognition that today, while the modern state is not such a powerful rival for religion as in the recent past, there is another rival which has been growing in strength rather spectacularly in recent decades (and particularly in the last one, following Communism's collapse). In this case, that of market capitalism, there is no direct threat to religion as there has been from the modern state; indeed, the market system is generally portrayed as completely open to religious practice and belief, putting no obstacles in their way – and thus scarcely to be viewed as a rival. The latter may be said to be true, formally at least, in respect of allegiance and of the question of identity and belonging in a collective rather than personal sense (though in the burgeoning world of the large, transnational corporation, with its own symbols and internal culture in more and more instances, this is becoming increasingly open to question).

Religion, society and contemporary capitalism

In considering how religion is placed in the context of a globally ascendant market capitalism, it needs to be remembered that market economics is a product of the Enlightenment no less than the ideas forming the modern state, and that both belong fundamentally to the world of secularism and materialism. Whereas modern statist socialism is clearly at odds with market capitalism, this is not the case with the modern state *per se* – that is, as long as it refrains from interfering with the working of the market economy in ways that (at the 'macro-economic' level) impede profit maximization and (at the 'micro' level) the autonomy of managerial decision-making. Indeed, the liberal state is able to provide an excellent complement to market capitalism (even as this today transcends state boundaries) by taking care of important 'external costs' to business such as property security, legal framework for commercial transactions, education and training, etc. In general terms, social order along with political stability are key requisites for successful business. To these the contribution of religion may be viewed as relevant, by influencing individual behaviour; but in similar vein it is not, according to market (neo-liberal) economics, to interfere in economic and social matters, interference which could only affect business performance for the worse.

It is thus clear that the weakening of the state does not in itself necessarily represent a weakening of secular liberalism. The state, indeed, becomes more fitted to play its role alongside the market economy in the all-encompassing liberal order of society, as this moves from a nation-state basis to a transnational level and is well on its way, in its economic component at least, to a global level. It is market capitalism that now emerges in practice as the principal and powerful bearer of secular liberalism, not in the formal way that the modern state often has been, but essentially in promoting a materialistic ethos at a popular and individual level (setting up consuming and having as life's *raison d'être*); here secularism may be said to be a secondary side effect or even, perhaps, unintended consequence. It is not so surprising that the close relationship in modernity between materialism and secularism philosophically should be replicated in social behaviour, nor that market capitalism, a supreme modern 'invention', is an arrangement whose priorities favour this tendency (it may also be seen as favouring a pagan or idolatrous world-view, such as 'worship of the Golden Calf' or the so-called 'Cargo Cult'[13] – summed up in Christ's strong warning against worshipping Mammon).

The basic point here is that in the post-Communist world of the dominance of market capitalism, religion may not be as 'liberated' in the role it is called on to play as might first appear. It is clear that a critical question for religion's contribution to and place in global order concerns the relationship with global market capitalism. Subsequent chapters point to certain conclusions in this respect. It certainly cannot be assumed that this relationship is, or should be, the obverse of the 'foe' one which was clearly the case with Communism (or any Marxist variant of socialism). It is very doubtful that religion should stick to the 'script' written for it in secular liberalism, political or economic, which is the single heart of modernity; and it needs to recognize that, within this, capitalist economics is the pre-eminent thought system (or non-party political ideology, neo-liberalism) and the market the predominant institution. The relationship is important not just for religion, but also in light of the disappearance of any effective alternative political ideology to neo-liberal economics and its complement in secular liberal statism ('neutral', limited, non-*dirigiste*). The resurgent forces of Islam, while of course rejecting Communism/Marxism, saw that for them other secular ideologies including nationalism and above all liberalism were hardly more acceptable in terms of key religious beliefs and values; of course, in the first place this was largely so because these ideologies were 'Western' and alien. But Christians in the developing world, and some now in the former Communist bloc, have a comparable response: the belief that neo-liberalism is a system of exploitation by rich Western (or capitalist) countries and economic interests.

All this makes it unlikely that religion world-wide is going to be an uncritical partner, let alone ally, of global market capitalism and an international (state) system which helps sustain the global order based on it. Religious institutions and organizations in the West are themselves increasingly subject to transnational pressures from their (more numerous) fellow believers in other parts of the world – manifested notably in the South African sanctions issue – to oppose the asymmetrical structure of economic relations inherent globally in neo-liberalism, as expressed also in international financial and trade organizations. Yet religion in the West does not really have to be told by others of the inadequacy of the secular liberal world-view, and in particular of its free-market economics component. It only has to look in its own backyard in modern history and not least in its contemporary period. Wealth may have been, and continue to be, generated, especially for those living within the bounds of the liberal system's heartlands (and its boundaries may gradually be modified – though the 'lead' countries remain such, even if their rank order changes and one or two new ones, usually smaller, join them). That this is based on the exploitation, through favourable financial and trade 'terms', of the resources and markets of those 'peripheral' to the heartlands, is not, however, the critique envisaged here. What is at issue is its social and cultural effects, not least affecting religion itself. This has been well analysed by some social scientists with no particular religious axe to grind (even if subject to the secular bias of social science generally). In the long run this is very probably the more powerful critique. It is a critique well expressed today in the West by the Communitarian school of thought (see below, pp. 39–44). However, Fred Hirsch's analysis of the late 1970s in *Social Limits to Growth* (recently reissued) has scarcely been bettered,[14] in particular part III, 'The Depleting Moral Legacy'; the 'legacy' here refers essentially to Judaeo-Christian ethics which have provided the normative basis for a common, collective life (society) in Western countries. But these socially orientated and community-building norms – emphasizing relationship, trust, justice, service, sharing and a common human dignity – are weakened by the spread of the individualistic ethos which goes with market capitalism's erection of self-interest as the determining motivation in human affairs; this is especially the case with the classical (*laissez-faire*) or neo-liberal form that has again become predominant with the decline of statist socialism.

Alongside the strong individualistic thrust of neo-liberalism goes the commercialization, commodification and contractualization of more and more areas of human activity and relationships, previously considered outside the money economy or subject to a distinct public or professional ethos of service; thereby the sphere of instrumental reason and calculation is progressively widened (as Hirsch notes, partying for contracts or golfing to forge and tie up business deals). A phenomenon associated with this, in Linder's ironic formulation, is 'the harried leisure class',[15] for which time's commodification ('is money') becomes an ever present reality and the pace of life rises seemingly inexorably. Churches and other religious bodies are not, of course, immune from these tendencies; but in so far as they are less affected than other bodies then they are likely to find themselves increasingly marginalized in their role and influence. However, there is a counterside to this general development, indeed a 'downside' for society, as Hirsch saw clearly. Free-market capitalism in ignoring the role of social ethics and social relations – if necessary rationalized as liberal 'neutrality' – nevertheless has an indubitable effect in weakening these and the social responsibility and social cohesion that goes with them. A certain social disruption has been accepted by market economists as a price to pay for economic growth, but when it becomes increasingly common (so that it may be called endemic) in the new global market system, the 'price' moves to a qualitatively higher level – the threat of not just social 'inconvenience' but of actual disintegration and the effective decline of the community. 'Society' and 'community' become terms largely empty of content (as Mrs Thatcher, when UK Prime Minister, famously proclaimed as the norm) and the market is seen as all sufficient; yet it can hardly be argued convincingly that its chief values include the sort noted above, and in particular trust, mutual relationship and solidarity, which are not mainly dependent on a pecuniary basis. The heritage of cultural 'goods' which are crucial for maintaining a community's integrity and continuity, and in which religion also figures prominently, will similarly not be provided for or only inadequately on the basis simply of pecuniary gain (and especially the free market's short-term profit mechanism). This has been a major factor in the world-wide religious resurgence.

It is in the light of these sorts of considerations and concerns that one of the principal academic proponents of neo-liberalism in the 1970 and 1980s, John Gray, became one of its sternest critics in the 1990s.[16] His is a significant revision precisely because his analysis has come to take in a wider perspective than neo-liberalism's attribution of overwhelming importance to economics and the market, by pointing to the consequential effects of doing this on the non-economic areas of life – social, cultural and, not least for him, the natural environment. These effects become that much more deleterious when the market's area of free movement of goods, services, investment and monies becomes global, since the territorially defined basis of cultural diversity and identity, of social cohesion and of biodiversity as a crucial element in eco-system maintenance,[17] is progressively undermined. Paradoxically, Ernest Gellner recognized these tendencies affecting cultures and community in his concept of 'social entropy', which would seem to capture their negative quality;[18] but in fact he welcomed it as a central (and centralizing) as well as universalizing force in the development of the economic and political forces of liberal modernization (which seems to have become an end and good in itself – as the sole expression of reason[19] – no matter where it might lead). Johnston and Sampson in *Religion: The Missing Dimension of Statecraft* examine, in a section on 'materialistic determinism', the disruptive consequences of market forces for 'residential stability' and the knock-on effects for the integrity of family, social and community relations: ' "economic man" is fully alienated man, ready to abandon friends, neighbours, and perhaps his (extended) family for incremental material rewards'.[20]

Religion and responses to neo-liberal globalism

In these circumstances, the conservation of cultural identity and diversity, of community values (for social cohesion) and of the natural environment become a top priority (as John Gray's recent analysis exemplifies). At stake here are important elements in the notion of civilization, in which religion figures largely[21] and which in Western civilization specifically means the Judaeo-Christian tradition (of course, Christianity now figures significantly outside 'the West', and perhaps more so in Africa, parts of Asia, South America, the former Soviet bloc). However, as is to be expected, the contemporary dominance globally of neo-liberal economics and the free market is not without challenge, philosophically and ideologically, as this book shows. The main problem is how an alternative, even in the sense of one retaining broadly liberal elements, is to be forged into a practical programme and make its way in the world. Political revolution is itself a distinctively modern concept and phenomenon, and most probably one of the things that is being left behind in postmodernity, given the large-scale disillusion it has produced: the rationalistic idea that one dominant order could and should be replaced wholesale by another, ready-made, has raised and dashed more expectations, often in cruel fashion, than any act conceived by humans in modern times (from 1789–91 France to Pol Pot, via 1917 Russia, Fascism and Maoism, to name the main Promethean acts). A much more likely recourse, certainly in the West where it has already been evident, is to the *national* expression of self-interest, even if opposed by neo-liberal free-market economists and supporters as encouraging protectionism. This should probably be given some careful consideration, but only in a moderate form. The great danger, here, as we touched on earlier and as later chapters refer to, is that of arousing a more virulent nationalism – danger of either of two opposing outcomes for religion: creating a powerful secular rival for allegiance; or of sucking religion into the virulence and strongly encouraging a militantly politicized type of religiosity or religious nationalism as in India (the BJP), Sri Lanka, the Muslim world, Kosovo, Bosnia and Israel. The second outcome is primarily associated with the Third World, but in certain respects the so-called New Christian Right in the USA can be said to come into this category (given its militant fundamentalist, authoritarian patriarchal and nationalist elements).

Besides the danger of awakening an aggressive and xenophobic nationalism, recourse to national self-interest as a defence against globalization relies for success in practice on a reassertion of the modern nation-state – which would mean from a religious perspective, the danger sooner or later of strengthening a 'state secularism based on anthropocentricity or even anthropolatry'[22] (hostile to the space for the divine and sacred in society). Such beliefs, in humankind's superior powers, remain today a powerful source of the forces degrading the environment. Another alternative advanced to curb global economic forces, while remaining broadly within secular liberalism, is focused on the concept of 'citizenship' or more specifically democratic citizenship. The aim is to transpose citizenship to a 'higher' territorial level than the nation-state and indeed to the global level. In itself this appears a noble aim, but it has to be said that the concept is a rather narrow political (indeed Western) one and is anyway in practice in difficulties at whatever territorial level one cares to consider around most of the world (not least in competition with 'consumer sovereignty'). A crucial and basic problem, as Klausen and Tilly point out, is that, 'In a liberal order, there is, inevitably perhaps, a mismatch among the reach of political, social and economic systems.'[23] They are in fact talking primarily about Europe, but it applies even more in terms of global order; and it is the reach of the political system component that is the most limited, because of the 'blockage' the nation-state represents. Whereas political sectarianism, and social and cultural/religious forms associated with it, threaten global order, **any** global order, at least the 'new citizenship' seeks to take global order out of the predominant grasp of economic forces. But how? While its connotation can and has been widened theoretically, seemingly giving it more purchase on events and developments, to have practical effect this needs to occur in terms of social and cultural attitudes much more widely. Where are the forces in society supporting and promoting it, including most importantly transnationally? Citizenship movements as such are rather thin on the ground; and political parties by and large remain tied to the state.

It is altogether unlikely that 'citizenship', especially world-wide, can be the answer in its own right, but only as part of a broader development of social, cultural and then subsequently political forces – particularly those already with a significant transnational reach such as religious ones. Democratization may here be a more useful concept, in particular as a broader one. In the aftermath of the fall of the Soviet Union, it has become a common slogan and clarion call, and supported world-wide by many diverse movements and organizations, not least religious ones – even though these are often blunted, if not suppressed (at least temporarily), by authoritarian states. History from Ancient Greece to today shows that democracy, as an irrepressible and progressively realized idea, can take a number of forms while retaining a basic authenticity (of course, it can also be used as a sham façade, as modern totalitarian systems have demonstrated). Democratization is a process that can be successfully adapted, as is true of many ideas and institutions that have been appropriated from one civilization to another.

Reshaping global order: civil society and ecumenism

However, in whatever guise democratization emerges, and wherever, it cannot be separated in practice from the importance of civil society, which more specifically refers to the role of intermediate structures distinct on the one hand from central or local state (or para-state) organization and on the other from economic and financial organizations focused on profit-making. This is where, if nowhere else, religion is to be found in terms of institutions, organizations, associations, groups and movements. Participation in political organisations whose *raison d'être* was and is in state politics may be at a low ebb, especially in the West, but activism is burgeoning in civil society ones, some falling within the post-materialist aspect of postmodernism.[24] A range of social, cultural and indeed political causes are supported and pursued (in no particular order): women's, Green and conservation, social welfare, peace, human rights, development, fair trade, ethical investment and banking, alternative technology, the 'new consumer' movement, minority languages and culture, heritage (and yet others). These quite often have overlaps or at least interconnect, but some would argue – in rather modernist style – for the need for greater co-ordination. However, the aim is often not to impact political decision-making directly or at least solely, but also to work on and through society in a diverse way to change economic and social behaviour and to pressurize economic agents directly. Leading instances of this activity are the campaign to change significantly, or otherwise halt, the Multilateral Agreement on Investment (aimed at 'freeing' global multinational corporation investment), which was to have been concluded in April 1998 but became subject to further extended negotiations, and the Jubilee 2000 campaign to cancel Third World debt, which is a religious-based one into which some secular groups have been drawn.

Religion is often involved in these civil society activities, in its own right or simply as a substantial source of participants, and it can act to varying degrees, according to the place and subject(s) of concern, as an umbrella where a plurality of groups and approaches exists (as long of course as proselytizing is eschewed). Often it is not religious authorities and formal institutions *per se* which are the protagonists – though they may be (as in Jubilee

2000) – but what may be called para-religious bodies of clergy and especially rank-and-file believers. Apart from the faith of their members – generally, reflected in the names of the groups - these are not readily distinguishable in their activities from any similar, formally secular groups and organizations. Compared to the political and economic systems which are dominant, including in their rivalry, in modernity, civil society is certainly the space in which religion can breathe more easily and through which it can best contribute to the development of a different order. Islam in its resurgence and renewal is finding this to a growing extent, as is Christianity world-wide. Islamic organizations provide educational (schools and universities), medical (clinics and hopitals) and social welfare (legal aid, child care, housing) services; they also operate newspapers, publishing houses and TV stations, and have played leadership roles in professional associations of physicians, lawyers and journalists. Of course, a crucial thing for the civil society movement to have a significant impact on the question of global order is its transnational reach. Increasingly transnational networks are being forged and developed. In particular, this applies to non-governmental organisations (NGOs) operating at least partly under the wing of the UN, most notably in the 1990s at the series of world conferences it has organized on the environment and development ('Earth Summit'), social development, population and women's position. Religious institutions and bodies are prominent in this context, including amongst those with recognized international status as UN participants. But some of the more dynamic and 'globalizing' or transnational NGOs are not (yet?) in this category. They may effectively have consultative status in some world region institutions of governance, such as the EU, or formally so, as in the Organization for Security and Cooperation in Europe (such as the Helsinki Citizens Assemblies); in both, the religious 'presence' is significant.[25]

Where religion can have an advantage is in its transnational character and reach, which in terms of effective structure and process has come more to the fore in recent decades. It often has a framework in which cross-communication and dialogue can occur and, on occasion, a largely common position adopted. The 'advantage' may be said to be for itself in seeking global influence, but it is also in strengthening the growing movement challenging the neo-liberal global order from what is finally a different but still global perspective. This emphasizes the order of the human and (all-encompassing) natural worlds as one of 'unity-in-diversity'. The challenge is to maintain tension or balance between the two, neither relapsing into the sectarian fragmentation and probably violent conflict of nationalism and fundamentalism nor progressively assimilating the 'harmonizing' norms and values of the neo-liberal global economy to which politics, society, culture and religion are increasingly subjected (as largely 'dependent variables').

Within religion there has been, chiefly since the Second World War, an important movement towards 'unity-in-diversity', known as ecumenism. While mainly a Christian affair to begin with, inter-faith relations have gradually come to occupy a more prominent place.[26] In this movement, while syncretism is eschewed, the principal different religious 'families' come together in dialogue, originally to seek common theological and doctrinal ground for some structural unity; however, in recent times they have been at least as much concerned with working together in practical projects and campaigning in respect of many of the issues and causes noted above. The laity or ordinary believers have become much more involved in such activity. It also often has specifically global or transnational dimensions – as witnessed by the consultations and agreement of the Vatican and many Islamic leaders at the UN Cairo population conference as well as the UN women's conference in Beijing.

Unity-in-diversity in this practical way is a certain wisdom that has come out of the ecumenical movement. In this formula, religion has to be a major aspect of global diversity, including in its close connection with the cultures of the major world regions. But ecumenism shows a way of reducing barriers, including of misunderstanding and mistrust, and creating the occasion for a constantly and practically renewed degree of unity, in particular in response to the world's problems and possibilities. Its influence is to promote understanding, acceptance of pluralism, and to help overcome, or at least dilute, those boundaries that divide people the most: political (national and ethnic/racial), social (status and class), economic (rich and poor, employed and unemployed), and of course religious ones as such. This is undertaken by working at a number of levels, from local to global, within the movement. The major religions, and notably Christianity, Islam and Buddhism, are of course global and universalizing as well as spatially rooted; but in particular they all have non-economic values and norms to sustain. Inter-faith and inter-church relations are thus of considerable significance for global order and specifically in the sense of one that, in sustaining the values of justice, peace and ecological integrity, is less single-dimensioned than the current order in its basic tendency. We believe that this is the message that emerges, in the main, from the succeeding chapters. A principal opposition, and alternative principles, to the existing global order reside in religion[27] – with much, in reality, being shared in these respects, even when largely regionally manifested.

Notes

[1] Religion has begun to make an increasing appearance in textbooks covering political ideologies, but largely in the guise of 'fundamentalism' – and as such generally treated as something of an aberration in the 'modern world': see, for example, R. C. Macridis, *Contemporary Political Ideologies* (NewYork, HarperCollins, 5th edn., 1992); I. Adams, *Political Ideology Today* (Manchester, Manchester University Press, 1993).

[2] A typical recent (and in most respects excellent) book is D. Dewitt, D. Haglund and J. Kirton, *Building a New Global Order* (Oxford, Oxford University Press, 1993). See also M. Hersman and A. Marshall, *After the Nation State* (London, HarperCollins, 1994), and J. Piscatori's chap. 3 below, which indicate the lack of consideration of religion in recent global/transnational studies.

[3] This is convincingly demonstrated in G. Moyser (ed.), *Politics and Religion in the ModernWorld* (London, Routledge, 1991).

[4] The best known are postmodern, post-Communist, post-industrial, postmaterial, post-ideology, post-Enlightenment, post-nation-state, post-secular . . . and post-Christian (though not post- other world religions – notwithstanding that they have fewer adherents than Christianity).

[5] See notably M. Juergensmeyer, *The New Cold War* (Berkeley, University of California Press, 1993). Also, Walker Connor, *Ethno-nationalism* (Princeton, NJ, Princeton University Press, 1994).

[6] Namely, concentrating on private, personal salvation; see, for example, E. Norman, *Christianity and the World Order* (Oxford, Oxford University Press, 1979).

[7] An impressive illustration of a non-Catholic position in the struggle for change (from first-hand experience) is M. Maggay, *Transforming Society* (Oxford, Regnum Lynx, 1994).

[8] See C. Jerez, *The Church and the Nicaraguan Revolution* (London, Catholic Institute of International Relations, 1984); and D. Haslam, *Faith in Struggle* (London, Epworth Press, 1987).

[9] For an excellent account of this, see J. A. Hall, *International Orders* (Cambridge, Polity Press, 1996); also L. H. Miller, *Global Order* (Boulder, CO, Westview Press, 3rd edn., 1994).

[10] See R. Dahl, *After the Revolution* (New Haven, CT, Yale University Press, 1970) and *Preface to Economic Democracy* (Berkeley, University of California Press, 1985); also P. Hirst, *Associative Democracy* (Cambridge, Polity Press, 1993).

[11] D. Held, 'Democracy: from city states to a cosmopolitan order?', *Political Studies*, 40, special issue (1992), 10–39; and with D. Archibugi, *Cosmopolitan Democracy: Agenda for a New World Order* (Cambridge, Polity Press, 1995).

[12] G. Ritzer, *McDonaldization of Society* (One Thousand Oaks, CA, Pine Forge Press, rev. edn., 1995).

[13] See P. L. Berger, *Pyramids of Sacrifice* (London, Faber & Faber, 1976).

[14] F. Hirsch, *Social Limits to Growth* (London, Routledge, 1977, reissued 1996). For a 1980s discussion of Hirsch's analysis, see K. Kumar and A. Ellis, *Dilemmas of Liberal Democracies* (London, Tavistock Press, 1983).

[15] S. B. Linder, *The Harried Leisure Class* (New York, Columbia University Press, 1970).

[16] J. Gray, *Beyond the New Right* (London, Routledge, 1993) and *Enlightenment's Wake* (London, Routledge, 1995).

[17] See E. O. Wilson, *The Diversity of Life* (Cambridge, MA, Harvard University Press, 1992).

[18] E. Gellner, *Nations and Nationalism* (Oxford, Blackwell, 1983). For a discussion of social entropy in the context of minority nationalism, see the conclusion in M. M. Watson (ed.) *Contemporary Minority Nationalism* (London, Routledge, 1990).

[19] E. Gellner, *Postmodernism, Reason and Religion* (London, Routledge, 1992).

[20] D. Johnston and C. Sampson, *Religion: The Missing Dimension of Statecraft* (Oxford, Oxford University Press, 1994).

[21] S. Huntington, 'Clash of civilisations', *Foreign Affairs*, 72, No. 3, (1993), 22–49.

[22] T. Mitri in A. Hulbert (ed.), *Islam, Europe and Modernity* (Brussels, European Ecumenical Association for Church and Society, 1996).

[23] J. Klausen and L. Tilly, *European Integration in Social and Historical Perspective* (Lanham, MD, Rowman & Littlefield, 1997), 11.

[24] R. Inglehart – see his numerous works (with others), beginning with *The Silent Revolution* (Princeton, Princeton University Press, 1977), rep. 1993 (New York, Irvington Press) and in particular his chapters in J. R. Gibbins, *Contemporary Political Culture* (London, Sage, 1989).

[25] Examples of the religious presence in the European Union are the special EU programme 'Giving Europe a Soul' (which is an inter-faith collaboration with the EU Commission) and the regular meetings between EU officials and parliamentarians and the representative Church bodies: notably the European Ecumenical Commission for Church and Society, the Catholic European Study and Information Centre, the European Contact Group for Church and Industry, the Churches' Committee for Migrant Workers, the Commission of the Episcopates of the EC.

[26] For a significant demonstration of this, see the recent work of Hans Kung on a global ethic, including *A Global Ethic for Global Politics and Economics* and as ed., *Yes to a Global Ethic* (both London, SCM Press, 1997 and 1996 respectively).

[27] R. H. Roberts, 'Globalised religion? The parliament of the world's religions (Chicago 1993) in theoretical perspective', *Journal of Contemporary Religion*, 10, No. 2 (1995).

2

Religious resurgence, postmodernism and world politics

SCOTT THOMAS

> Modernism has already played itself out in principle. Accordingly, societies that have been built on modernism are destined to collapse. Indeed, the total failure of Marxism – a side current of modernist society . . . and the dramatic breakup of the Soviet Union are only precursors to the collapse of Western liberalism, the main current of modernity. Far from being the alternative to failed Marxism, and the reigning ideology 'at the end of history', liberalism will be the next domino to fall.[1]

The global resurgence of religion is a response to the widespread crisis in secular materialism in both the Western industrialized countries and in the Third World. In developed countries the crisis in secular materialism is evident in the failure of liberalism, in the way secular liberalism has – unwittingly – contributed to the social and political crisis that now confronts the secular, liberal, democratic state.[2] This social crisis is apparent in the intransigence of urban poverty, the decay of public infrastructure, the growing brutality of criminal violence, and in the widespread feeling that problems can no longer be solved, controlled or even adequately addressed. The political crisis is apparent in the deepening fragmentation of the political culture and the flagging confidence in government, politicians and, to some extent, in the political process itself.[3] This social and political crisis has led to a resurgence of institutional religion and includes Christian fundamentalism, Evangelicalism, Pentecostalism and Orthodox Judaism, and the rise in broader conceptions of spirituality, such as the new religious movements and 'new age' religions.

In the Third World the crisis of secular materialism is evident in the failure of the modernizing, secular state to provide a legitimate basis for political participation and a basic level of economic welfare for its citizens. This has led to the resurgence of religion, nationalism and a proliferation of ethno-national and religious conflicts. The crisis in the secular state has led 'authenticity' to rival 'development' as the primary way to understand the political aspirations of the Third World. The search for authentic identity, meaning and economic development indicates a new direction in the politics of developing countries: an attempt to 'indigenize' modernity rather than to modernize or to modernize tradition.

Amidst this crisis of the secular liberal state in the West and the secular modernizing state in the Third World it may be time to re-evaluate what has been lost as well as what has been gained by the separation of religion from domestic and international politics. The main political project of liberal internationalism, the search for a cosmopolitan ethic rooted in the Enlightenment rationalism of the West, can no longer be sustained in the multicultural, postmodern, post-secular world that has been developing since the end of the cold war. If a belief in democracy and in universal human rights is to be maintained in this global, multicultural, international society then another basis for universal moral values will have to be found than the Enlightenment rationalism of the West and, contrary to the expectations of secular liberalism, one source may very well be the social ethics of the main world religions.

Religion and the crisis of the liberal state

Over the last two hundred years many political thinkers and political movements have criticized the defects of liberalism, whether they were seen to be its individualism, atomism, alienation, or market-orientation.[4] The most recent critique comes from the 'Communitarians', a broadly based group of scholars who have dominated academic debate since the 1980s,[5] and have influenced the Clinton administration in the United States and the Blair government in Britain in the 1990s.[6] Although the critique of liberalism presented here draws on many of their ideas, it suggests that Communitarianism does not go far enough. It has underestimated the extent to which liberal ideas and practices were first embedded in the moral foundations of religion – Christian theism – and it does not acknowledge the extent to which globalization has altered conceptions of the self more radically than the Communitarianism's critique of the ontology of liberalism. In addition, the Communitarian critique of the liberal theory of the state still accepts secular liberal premisses about the privatization of religion and political secularization without recognizing the detrimental effect political practices based on them have had on the kind of values brought into the public square.

One of the most central Communitarian criticisms of liberalism is its ontology, its theory of the self, and the detrimental effect the working out of this theory has had on society. According to this critique, liberalism celebrates the myth of the autonomous, rational individual, free from religion, tradition and community. In so far as this theory is embodied in our institutions and practices,[7] it has contributed to the deterioration of society and the erosion of the civic culture, the broad base of values and beliefs about government, politicians and the political process that support civil society and democratic institutions.

Communitarian critics point out that liberalism's presupposition of social 'atomism', rooted in the Enlightenment, is based on an overly individualistic conception of human nature and of the human condition.[8] Michael Sandel calls this conception the 'unencumbered self'. In reality what we are as ourselves is constituted by various attachments based on religion, family and community; these are so basic to our nature that we tend to forget under liberalism that they are part of us and make us who we are.[9]

Communitarian critics argue we ignore or set these attachments aside at great cost to our personal well-being and to society. The personal cost of setting these attachments aside is that they leave us alone, isolated from the traditions and communities where we find deep meaning and substance to our moral beliefs and to our lives. The social cost of setting these attachments aside is that their absence produces a society fragmented by an individualism that draws no connection between a society's past and present, that promotes personal ambition at the cost of personal relationships and the neglect of institutions of civil society, including the family, and, most importantly, it separates the individual from the larger collective enterprise called 'society'. Consequently, there is a declining sense of belonging, citizenship and obligation to the larger national community.[10] Our societies are fragmented, divided into 'lifestyle enclaves' formed by groups of individuals that share the same values, aspirations, consumption habits and leisure activities without any common set of values or larger commitment to the societies to which they belong.[11]

Many liberals contend this argument is based on an inaccurate reading of the liberal tradition. Locke, Hume and Kant, for example, never denied the social construction of individuals (they did not believe in 'atomism') or that man has a social nature, nor did they deny that social virtues are required for the proper functioning of liberal polities.[12] Therefore, the liberal tradition contains within itself the resources necessary to handle the political and social problems that confront the modern liberal state.[13]

However, both liberals and their Communitarian critics fail to recognize the extent to which early modern liberalism was embedded in the moral foundation of Christian theism.[14] Kant's rational ethic was rooted in a conception of human nature derived from Lutheran pietism, and Tocqueville went so far as to call religion the first of America's political institutions because he saw that religion provided the moral foundation for the country's political institutions. It did not do so directly, because of the separation of church and state, but indirectly by supporting those mores and values that constrain individualism and promoting bonds of social obligation and solidarity that make democracy possible.[15] For all its difficulties and foibles, Christianity, or the Judaeo-Christian tradition, along with the civic republic tradition of ancient Rome, formed the common moral discourse within which political debates were conducted in early modern America, and which provided the foundation for civil society in Western liberal states.[16]

Liberals have underestimated the extent to which liberal ideas and institutions were embedded in this common discourse, a discourse that may not be silent but is being challenged, and has been for some time, by competing secular discourses,[17] and now in our plural, global international society it is being challenged by non-Western voices and discourses.[18] Liberal theory as well as the practice of liberal polities are faced not only with the familiar challenge of secularism, but increasingly with the less familiar challenge of cultural and religious pluralism. Although this challenge is most often articulated in the debate over 'multiculturalism' in the United States,[19] it is really a global issue: how can liberal democracy be constructed in polities embedded in non-Western cultural and religious traditions rather than the Enlightenment rationalism of the West?

The Communitarian critique of the ontology of liberalism does not go far enough because it needs to consider the way that globalization – the rapid technological changes that have altered the worlds of finance, trade, travel, communications and information – has altered conceptions of the self. The 'unencumbered self' of modern liberalism has been reinforced by what I call the 'suspended self' of globalization, transnationalism and cyberspace. The radical individualization and commodification of life created by globalization – the global cornucopia of ideas, values, religions and spiritualities, and consumer goods – that make possible the malleability of personal beliefs, identities and lifestyle choices in the postmodern world, have no purpose beyond personal pleasure, self-actualization and self-gratification. Nothing is at stake beyond the manipulable sense of well-being and the management of individual experience and the environment to provide it.[20] Cyberspace and transnationalism devalue physical reality – place, identity and community – by making possible virtual identities and transnational lifestyle enclaves that blur reality and allow people to evade personal responsibility.[21] Thus, the self in liberal states is more 'unencumbered' and 'suspended' from communities of identity and meaning than Communitarians acknowledge – with even more detrimental consequences for the civic culture necessary for liberal democracy.

What makes the development of postmodern, transnational lifestyle enclaves detrimental for democracy and civil society is the way they differ from the sectarian Protestantism of the religious revivals of the nineteenth century. Sectarian Protestantism was a source of both individualism and community,[22] while lifestyle enclaves, based on an individualistic search for personal identity and self-actualization, have no larger connection to community or society, and at their most extreme opt out of society, sometimes with dangerous, anti-democratic intentions.

The new religious movements that emphasize personal fulfilment in ways that transcend the materialism of post-industrial society have been combined with the devolution of power in the information age, in which there is a greater dispersion of lethal knowledge about weapons beyond the control of states, to form what is increasingly called 'post-materialist' terrorism. The most spectacular example was the Aum Supreme Truth sect's sarin gas attack in the Tokyo subway, but the American militia movement, some (but not all) animal rights groups, and so-called 'deep ecology' movements such as Earth First, are a part of this new form of terrorism. It represents a shift away from more 'rational' forms of terrorism, practised by liberation movements, rebels and separatist groups, who have political objectives, toward an 'irrational' world of individuals, religious cults and social movements committed to 'post-materialist' causes.[23]

The Communitarian critique of the liberal state does not go far enough. It has not recognized that the Enlightenment rationalism which supported political secularization, the separation of church and state in the interests of religious toleration, also separated the individual from the traditions and communities that help form and sustain the moral values and the sense of belonging and civic obligation necessary for any reasonable conception of society and for a civic understanding of how politics should take place.

Communitarians point out that the liberal theory of the state has been based on a search for a secular, rational basis for moral action which is independent of any religious values or any conception of the good life. It is concerned with finding appropriate procedural rules or principles for political action that secure for the individual the greatest possible freedom (individual rights) to pursue the good life – so long as it does not infringe on the liberty of others in society to do the same. Rational, autonomous individuals come together to determine procedural rules to govern their common life in societies in which the state maintains moral neutrality, and its constitution and laws regulate the play between individuals' competing values and goals without promoting any values and goals of its own.[24]

Jonathan Sachs, the Chief Rabbi of the United Hebrew Congregations of the British Commonwealth, argued in his Reith Lectures in 1990 that the historic task of liberalism in promoting individual liberty and separating religion from the state weakened the moral fabric on which the liberal state rests. Historically, religious communities have been the natural environment for the formation of moral values but we have underestimated the religious faith necessary to sustain them.[25] Harvey Cox, the liberal Protestant theologian at Harvard University who was the herald of 'the secular city' thirty years ago,[26] now acknowledges, '[p]rogressives have begun to realise that to purge the public square of religion is to cut the roots of the values that nourish our fondest causes'.[27] Liberalism's search for procedural rules has been one attempt to find a secular foundation on which moral values could be preserved but this has eluded us because the common moral discourse (the Judaeo-Christian and the civic republican traditions) in which these rules could be embedded has been eroded by alternative, narcissistic values and competing discourses.

Many Communitarians want what they claim are the moral virtues of communities without acknowledging the way religious traditions and communities nurture and promote the moral values they believe society lacks.[28] The only role they seem to see religion playing in society is a negative one, such as the attempt by the Christian fundamentalists to impose their moral values on American society and by Islamic fundamentalists to impose their views on Muslim states.[29] Charles Taylor criticizes the atomistic ontology of liberalism for its vision of a society constituted by individuals and for individuals, that ignores the principles of belonging and obligation necessary to sustain any viable conception of society. But where does the sense of belonging and obligation come from, how is it nurtured, encouraged and supported? He hopes for a revival of the civic republican tradition of ancient Rome that was one of the sources of civic life in early modern America.[30] But how will it re-emerge in societies where the 'unencumbered self' of atomistic liberalism is reinforced by the 'suspended self' of globalization, transnationalism and cyberspace?

In the past it has been religious traditions that have nurtured, encouraged and supported the sense of belonging and obligation in society which Taylor wants to revive. 'Religion', the Victorian preacher, Edward Irving, said more baldly than I would want to say, 'is the very name of obligation, and liberalism [or what we now may call 'neo-liberalism'] is the very name for the want of obligation.'[31] The academic debate over 'social capital' and 'social virtues' as a corrective to atomistic liberalism has become so important because of the absence in society of a sense of belonging and obligation. What we have failed to recognize until now is that the civic culture necessary for a functioning democracy and a thriving civil society are only indirectly influenced by a country's political institutions; they are most effectively based on commonly shared norms and ethical values, but these norms and values were often embedded in communities of meaning, identity and religious tradition that have now fragmented, declined or even disappeared.[32]

Liberalism says these religious resources are not permissible in the public square because mixing religion and politics leads to intolerance and is undemocratic (towards those who do not share the dominant religion's values).[33] Unfortunately, the moral neutrality of the liberal state, the assumption on which political secularization is based, is a myth. Liberalism's support for political secularization in a laudable attempt to promote religious tolerance has opened the public square for other, more illiberal and intolerant ideas. Liberalism's ontology and its attempt to limit religion to the private sphere has led to what Richard John Neuhaus has called the 'naked public square', a conception of society as a secular, value-free arena in which all meanings and choices are essentially private.[34] For the state not to actively promote certain values, such as racial or religious tolerance, is to leave the public square open to the domination of other values, including the forces of the free market:

> Despite the valiant efforts by John Rawls and other liberal theorists to privilege values like equality and tolerance, the effect of their campaign for an empiricist metaphysics and a neutral public realm left them with little ability to mobilise popular campaigns for equality. So, the freeing of public space from values and spirituality left the world impoverished and more easily dominated by market forces.[35]

In addition the liberal state, in the absence of a consensus in society on basic values and the lack of a sense of obligation, is pulled every which way by the competing interests, values and pressure groups that make up the pluralism of democratic societies. This is why the search for 'a new public philosophy', a defining purpose or a concept of the common good that can impose some direction on democratic pluralism, has become important for the liberal project.[36]

In the United States the left may need to re-evaluate its opposition to mixing religion and politics because this has only made it easier for the right to monopolize religion in pursuit of its political agenda. Harvey Cox, writing in one of the country's leading left-wing magazines, states 'To rule out religious imagery [in political debate] is to ignore a discourse that at its best can speak powerfully against greed, ennui and coldness of heart.'[37] Liberals, following Marx, forget that religion not only consoles, it challenges and confronts as well. This may not be as necessary in Britain, where the Christian Socialist Movement has been an important force in the Labour Party or on the continent where the tradition of Catholic social thought has helped to limit the more extreme social consequences of free-market capitalism.

At a more practical level, no matter how the debate in liberal theory may proceed, it is difficult to mobilize society for political action on the bases of abstract liberal theory. Michael Walzer has pointed out that effective social criticism is derived from and resonates with the habits and traditions of actual people living in specific times, places and communities.[38]

So far this chapter has argued that Western, liberal societies, to the extent that their institutions and practices are informed by a narrow individualism and atomistic conception of society, have reached the social and political limits of this conception of public life. But the idea that religion should be brought back into politics and that religious traditions and communities can help restore the civic values – such as mutuality, belonging, obligation and tolerance – on which a genuinely liberal and democratic polity rests, contradicts one of the most basic assumptions of both liberalism and modernity, that political modernization and political development includes as one of its most basic processes the secularization of politics. However, these liberal assumptions about religion and politics, associated as they are with modernity, may no longer hold true in a society that is becoming post-secular as well as postmodern.

Postmodernism and the resurgence of religion

The social and political crisis of the liberal state is occurring at the same time as there is a growing awareness of the limits to secularization, the disenchantment of the world.[39] There is growing disillusionment with a world reduced to that which can be perceived and controlled through science, technology and bureaucratic rationality. In so far as postmodernism shows a greater sensitivity to the human limits to the disenchantment of the world – limits which modernization theory denies – postmodernists share a basic insight with those theologians, cultural critics and artists who recognize the limits of this disenchantment.[40] This is why postmodernism is concerned with religion, spirituality and the sacred, even though this dimension is often overlooked.[41]

Secularization theory links the decline in religion to the process of modernization, and so it includes powerful assumptions and images of what we believe modernity is all about. This is why secularization could more properly be called a 'myth' than a theory. Its social function is mythic, for it provides an emotionally coherent picture of a modern world in which religion and spirituality are explained away as responses to some kind of deprivation, whether it be psychological, social or political.[42]

The narrow, institutional definition of religion many sociologists use to gauge the degree of 'secularization' in society (such as church attendance and membership) is not sufficient, because the social structure of religion (the way belief and observance are expressed) has changed as a result of modernization and globalization. Religion in the West has been 'restructured' more than it has declined.[43] The institutional definition of religion corresponds to Ernst Troeltsch's famous 'church' and 'sect' types of religious community, but it is his third type, mysticism, religious individualism or what could be called 'spirituality', which best describes the way religion is expressed in the postmodern West. It is about the realm of symbol, feeling and meaning, and how the individual relates to the world,[44] and is expressed in forms of faith and belief more diverse, more broadly conceived than mainline denominations and narrow fundamentalisms. It includes a widespread return to mythology, new religious movements, New Age spirituality and Native American religions.[45] This was one of the most important – although under-reported – news stories of the last decade.[46]

The desacralization of the natural world is an important part of modernity and an indicator of secularization.[47] Thus the widespread resacralization or re-enchantment of nature expressed within the growing concern for the environment, is one more indication that we are now living in a post-secular, postmodern world. The impersonal, rational, mechanical conception of the universe that provided the paradigm of modern science, and to a large extent still informs the view of 'science' held by social scientists, is being replaced by a naturalistic view of the world. For the first time since the fragmentation of the medieval world-view, the distinction between science and the humanities is breaking down, a distinction that was one of the defining characteristics of modernity. This may very well be one of the most significant intellectual changes of our time,[48] and has led some philosophers to call for the 're-enchantment of science' in a postmodern world.[49]

Thus, in contrast to the secularization myth of modernity there has been a persistence of faith and a growing re-enchantment of the world. Religion and spirituality rather than becoming marginal and vestigial in the West are moving to the centre of our cultural preoccupations because of the social and political crisis in the secular, liberal state, disillusionment with a world based on science, technology and bureaucratic rationality, the recognition of the limits to humankind's ability to manipulate nature, and intellectual changes in science and the humanities.

These changes help explain the rise in new forms of politics in which concerns about the self, identity and meaning are becoming as important – and may be more important in some instances – than material, or 'economistic' issues like wage rates. Any politics that fails to recognize the deep multiplicity of human nature is doomed to failure. Postmodern politics is bringing religion back into politics in new ways. The resurgence of religion and diverse forms of spirituality in Western post-industrial societies is part of the broader shift towards a 'post-materialist' politics, often expressed by the new social movements, including religious ones,[50] and a new 'politics of meaning' that has tried to link religious and spiritual concerns with social and economic ones.[51]

The crisis of the secular state in the Third World

In the Third World the crisis of secular materialism is evident in the way modernization theory and Marxism have contributed to the failure of the modernizing, secular state. This has led to the resurgence of religion, nationalism and a proliferation of religious and ethno-national conflicts since the end of the cold war.

In many developing countries secular nationalism and Marxism have failed to produce economic development and more political participation, and the neo-liberal prescription of free markets and open economies has seemingly produced greater domestic inequality than development. Ernest Gellner has argued that since the period of colonial occupation and the impact of the West, the developing countries have been confronted with a dilemma: should they emulate the West in order to gain equality in power (spurning their own culture), or should they affirm their own cultural and religious traditions – but remain materially weak?[52] In many countries this dilemma of identity and development was resolved in the first years after independence by emulating the West. The first generation of Third World élites that came to power beginning in the late 1940s – Nehru's India, Nasser's Egypt, Sukarno's Indonesia (and going back to the 1920s, Atatürk's Turkey) – espoused a similar 'modernizing mythology' inherited from the West. The modernizing mythology included democracy, secularism, democratic socialism and non-alignment in foreign policy. These élites believed strong 'developmental states' could promote political stability and economic development, and this would be undermined if religion, ethnicity or caste, often associated with regional identity, dominated politics.[53]

The failure of this modernizing mythology to produce development, and the failure of the modernizing, secular state is made evident by 'political decay',[54] the decline of politics into authoritarianism, patrimonialism and corruption since the late 1960s, and by 'political collapse', the disintegration of some states, particularly in Africa since the late 1980s.[55] Dissatisfaction with the project of the post-colonial secular state and the conflict between religious nationalism and secular nationalism was one of the most important developments in Third World politics in the 1990s.[56]

The resurgence of religion is part of the search for authentic identity, political representation and more equitable development in the Third World. Because of this situation 'authenticity' has begun to rival development as the key to understanding the political aspirations of the non-Western world.[57] It has often been accompanied by demands for democracy or greater political participation, which was also one of the most important developments of the late twentieth century.[58] A new 'revolt of the masses' is taking place. States that allow greater participation are having to respond to more popular, less élitist, less secular perspectives on politics, which means political élites have to be more responsive to the religious concerns of ordinary people. This is particularly true in the Muslim world where the resurgence of Islam and its ability to resist secularization reflects its role as an important source of national identity.[59] The retreat from the 'modernizing mythology' that animated the domestic politics of developing countries since independence has influenced their foreign policies as well, and this issue will be examined next.

The global resurgence of religion and the liberal dilemma

The liberal West is wary of any analysis that suggests religion should be brought back into politics. When the public square *has* been filled with religion it has often been oppressive, something Jews know only too well. It is the spectre of this oppression that animates the conflict between Orthodox Serbs, Catholic Croats and Bosnian Muslims in the former Yugoslavia. The fact that the resurgence of religion in Central Europe, Central Asia and Russia has been accompanied by anti-Semitism, racism and xenophobic nationalism only reinforces the liberal unease about mixing religion and politics.

It is for this reason that the West has responded to the global resurgence of religion in the Third World in a number of ways. Liberal academics have tried to undermine the misperceptions many academic analysts, political commentators and policy-makers have about other religions, particularly Islam.[60] Islamic studies in the West have not yet reached the dimensions of cold war sovietology, but in contrast to the old cold war warriors, Western Islamic scholars maintain close contact with their counterparts in the Islamic world.[61] Even though official US policy, as President Clinton indicated in his speech to the Jordanian parliament, denies that the global resurgence of Islam conflicts with Western interests and democratic principles, it has been difficult for this perspective to influence foreign policy because of deeply ingrained perspectives on the non-Western world among the policy-making élite.[62] As a result, the US has adopted a less imaginative approach. It has opposed religious groups that threaten the stability of states important to Western interests, and it has tried to isolate 'rogue states' and regimes committed to state terrorism. This has only fuelled the Islamic opposition in countries like Algeria and Egypt, and brought together Islamic countries that are usually at odds with each other, as the December 1997 meeting of the Organization of the Islamic Conference in Tehran and the almost universal Arab opposition to American and British attempts to bomb Iraq for obstructing UN weapons inspectors indicate.[63]

The West has responded to the global resurgence of religion mainly by waiting – until modernization has done its work, notably the expected 'disenchantment' of the developing world. Western governments have accepted they will triumph through stealth; all they need to do is stay the course and not lose faith in Western values. According to this view globalization is creating a world civilization based on instant information, economic inter-dependence and individual freedom, and there has been a short-term reactionary response expressed in the upsurge of interest in religious, cultural and ethnic values and identities. But the powerful momentum of Western science, technology, democracy and free markets will be impossible to resist. There is no separate, religious way to promote economic development. Democracy and human freedom are linked to capitalism, and this has proved to be *the* only formula for economic prosperity.[64] Although there will be conflicts along the way, the best policy for Western security is to help the Third World modernize and become more like us.[65] The West will win in the end because of the universalism of Western culture, for in V. S. Naipaul's words, Western culture is the universal civilization.[66]

This perspective of global modernization does not provide an adequate explanation of how the resurgence of religion will influence contemporary global international society, in which the interplay of religion, ethnicity and nationalism pose some of the greatest threats to international order. In order to understand why, we have to understand how these new threats may undermine international society. Ferdinand Tönnies distinguished between a *gemeinschaft* understanding of society as something traditional and organic, involving bonds of common sentiment, experience and identity, and a *gesellschaft* understanding of society as a contractual relationship that is modern, functional and constructed. Adopting this distinction, Barry Buzan argues modern international society developed according to a functional, contractual *gesellschaft* understanding of society because it was a rational long-term response to the existence of an increasingly dense and interactive international system. Even if states do not share a common culture, the regularity and intensity of their interactions will force them to develop a degree of accommodation with each other by working out common rules to avoid unwanted conflicts. Thus, according to Buzan, international society can evolve functionally from the logic of anarchy – an international system without any overarching authority – without any pre-existing cultural bonds, or common religious or moral understandings between states.[67]

As Buzan acknowledges, what is missing from this functional, *gesellschaft* understanding of international society is the notion of a shared identity, which is central to any meaningful concept of society. He asks, 'How does shared identity come about in a *gesellschaft* society in which the units [i.e. states] start out with different cultures?'[68] The answer is provided by the 'neo-realist' theory of international relations. Kenneth Waltz argues that anarchy generates like units, that the density and scope of the interaction between states makes them more alike and it is easier for them to accept each other.[69] The classic example, most interestingly, is Japan's reshaping of itself into a modern, Western-style state in the nineteenth century.[70]

What does this understanding of international society mean for international order, given the global resurgence of religion? The liberal response to the resurgence of religion is based on faith and hope. It is based on a secular faith that modernization and economic development will diminish the appeal of religious revival (that is, cycles of religious revival occur in the peripheral sections of any modernizing society), and it is based on a political hope that neo-realist theory about the way the international system creates homogeneous states is right. In the end, the world will come to resemble the liberal vision: the disenchantment of the developing world will take place, globalization, modernization, democracy and capitalism will produce a global culture that will generate tolerance and mutual respect, and modern like-minded states in the international system will diminish the likelihood of war and provide the basis for international order.[71]

The coming postmodern, post-secular international order will not be kind to this vision of modernity and democratic liberalism. The first part of this chapter explained why a conception of modernity that marginalizes the role of religion in society and politics cannot account for the persistence of religion in a postmodern world, nor can it help us anticipate the way religion will influence world politics in the future. This part of the chapter explains that the modernizing, neo-realist prediction about the homogenizing influence of the international system will not come about because it is based on the hegemony of Western culture in international society and this is coming to an end.

The global resurgence of religion challenges the modern, secular construction of the Westphalian state system from above and from below. It challenges it from above by questioning the Western cultural univeralism (implicit in globalization) on which the international system is based, and it challenges the Westphalian system from below by undermining the modern, secular construction of the states themselves, the main components of the international order.

The challenge to the modern international system from above

Although the decline in the hegemony of Western culture and political power that created modern international society has been evident for some time, it is really only in the post-cold war world that states from non-Western religions, cultures and civilizations have been able to challenge the hegemony of Western values and practices that are embodied in the institutions of international society:

These projects [from Tokyo to Kuala Lumpur, Beijing to Cairo] of reaffirming indigenous non-Occidental cultural traditions, in economic and political forms . . . have vastly different causes, contents and prospects. What they have in common is a repudiation of the West's claim to universal authority for its institutions and values that is bound to transform political life in the coming century and to force on Western societies a deep change in their understanding of themselves.[72]

Huntington has argued that economic modernization and the processes of globalization separate people from their local identities, and weaken their allegiance to the nation-state. Religion fills this gap by providing an alternative basis for identity and commitment that transcends state boundaries and unites civilizations. As a result, states from different cultures promote their values in the international system and struggle to control international organizations.[73] From this perspective the UN Conference on Human Rights in Vienna in 1993 and the UN Conference on Population in Cairo in 1994 represent the first battle grounds of the post-cold war 'clash of civilizations'.[74]

Another manifestation of this challenge comes from the states of the Pacific Rim, and from Japan, which according to neo-realist theory is the country that is supposed to be the classic example of the way the international system reproduces homogeneous modern states. Yet the 'Japanese model' of economic development, Japanese trade practices and the organization of its capital market have increasingly challenged the Western, Anglo-Saxon conceptions of economic liberalism that have dominated international economic institutions since Bretton Woods.

Into the next century Japan will increasingly challenge the hegemony of Western ideas that support the existing construction of the Westphalian international order. Some of Japan's 'new nationalists', such as Takeshi Umehara, the director-general of the International Research Centre for Japanese Studies in Kyoto quoted at the beginning of this chapter, argue that Japan offers the Third World a better model of development than the West *because it modernized without losing its soul.* Ancient Japanese philosophy offers an alternative organizing principle for society to the atomism of Western liberalism.[75] The validity of Umehara's thesis is not as important as the fact that it is indicative of Japan's growing ideological and political confidence, a confidence built on its economic and technological success – just as the West's ideological hegemony in the modern world was built on its economic and technological (and consequently, its military) success.

The challenge from below

The global resurgence of religion challenges the Westphalian construction of international society from below by undermining the cohesiveness of states and their convergence on a common Western model. The neo-realist prediction about the homogenizing effects of modernization within the anarchical international system is based on the hegemony of Western culture in international society. According to this view, the modernizing mythology non-Western states have imported from the West is true, and the secular, liberal construction of states will continue to hold them together. But the first part of this chapter argued that the crisis in secular materialism that is undermining the liberal state in the West and the modernizing state in the Third World is associated with the resurgence of religion reflected in broader conceptions of spirituality and 'post-materialist' political concerns about meaning, identity and authenticity.

For the first time since the beginning of the modern world there is a growing, non-Western heritage of ideas that is challenging the Western hegemony of ideas that constructed the institutions of international society. This challenge is put into perspective when we realize that in historical terms the last 500 years of Western dominance is a short interlude in the last thousand years of Asian dominance.[76] The revolt against the West, leading to decolonization in the 1960s and the subsequent North–South dialogue, did not challenge the Western hegemony of ideas in the international system. The demands for political power and economic justice were conducted within a Western political discourse. But this is now changing. The predictions of modernization and neo-realist theory about the homogeneity of states breaks down when states are no longer weak and are capable of challenging the ideological basis of the international order. This is why '[t]he defining project of our age is finding terms of peaceful co-existence with diverse cultures'.[77]

What is to be done?

The first part of this chapter argued that the West has lost a universal moral discourse within which to work out agreed principles of morality or procedural rules for liberalism because conceptions of rationality upon which values and principles are constructed are embodied in particular traditions and communities. This has made the need for a liberal accommodation with religious and cultural pluralism greater than ever before. Liberals underestimated the importance of religious traditions and communities to sustain the institutions of domestic society, and they have underestimated the importance of religion, culture and the moral traditions of communities in which the institutions of international society are embedded.

Global international society is becoming a genuinely multicultural international society for the first time. At the same time both the hegemony of Western discourse on what constitutes modernity (is there a 'non-Western modernity' that is different from 'Western modernity'?) and the Western practices of international society derived from the Westphalian settlement are being challenged in the Third World, particularly by Islam and by the states in the Pacific Rim. Western liberal states perceive this to be an economic threat and security problem because they have no alternative vision of how states might interact, apart from neoliberalism in economics and liberal pluralism in politics.

Liberal pluralism, in so far as it is based on moral scepticism and relativism, constructs a world of competing states with no common cultural or ethical discourse other than that of the Enlightenment rationalism of the West, within which to arrive at common principles and procedural rules to regulate or govern the relations between states and other global actors. This is why the search for a global 'cosmopolitan ethic' and for mechanisms of 'global governance' is conducted from within the discourse of Enlightenment rationalism – secular, rational liberals have no other way to proceed.[78] The alternative is too ghastly to contemplate for the likely outcome, if the universality of the Enlightenment rationalism of the West is denied, is the 'clash of civilizations' Huntington has predicted – unless his solution, a balance of power between civilizations, is also accepted as the basis of global order.[79]

Theorists of international relations who disagree with the construction of the international political dilemma of liberal pluralism described in this chapter, as it was explained earlier, can only do so by asserting their faith in Enlightenment rationalism and hope that the predictions of neo-realist theory and modernization theory about the homogeneity of modernizing states and the disenchantment of the world comes true in the end. But a world order cannot be grounded on faith and hope, so what alternative to liberal pluralism is there for order in a global, multicultural international society?

We may need to step out from underneath the shadow of the Westphalian settlement to recognize the constructive role religion can play in international society. Enlightenment rationalism may not be a sufficient basis for a cosmopolitan morality in a multicultural world. This is not because there are no universal moral values. Many Western conceptions of human rights are rooted in what Michael Walzer has called a 'thin morality' common to all cultures and civilizations.[80] The problem is that Western values supporting human rights, international humanitarian law and the other institutions of international society have been articulated and defended by academics, the United Nations, human rights NGOs (such as Amnesty International and Human Rights Watch) and Western aid agencies using a Western intellectual discourse. The decline in Western political and ideological hegemony, the global resurgence of political religion and the rise of the Pacific Rim accompanying the global spread of democracy means this is no longer an adequate basis for order in a global, multicultural international society.

A new basis of world order will have to be worked out, but how is this going to happen? It may very well be the case that the main world religions can provide resources for the 'thin morality' common to all people. This entails not only a theoretical task of identifying such a thin morality among different cultures and religions but a practical task of bringing religious perspectives into foreign policy and international development policy. The work of the International Committee of the Red Cross is one example of how this can be done. The laws of war, for example, can be formulated in ways that are consistent with the social ethics of other religious and cultural traditions.[81]

Another way is through the more active use of cultural diplomacy. Although most foreign-policy élites recognize that technology and democracy have changed the nature of diplomacy in a number of ways, this has not altered their approach to religion and politics. It is widely recognized that traditional, inter-state diplomacy, in which the internal character of governments was irrelevant, has given way to a more pluralistic form of diplomacy. The West feels the powerful impact of religion in other countries because the growing saliency of religion in policy-making is taking place at the same time as the spread of telecommunications, information technology and the democratization of politics. Public diplomacy, people-to-people contacts, subnational groups and transnational actors all have an increasingly active role in the diplomacy between states so that human rights, the appropriate values for social policy and ethical concerns more generally have become some of the main issues in diplomacy.

There is a religious and cultural dimension to all of these issues, but the West has not adopted a more pluralistic approach to diplomacy on these issues because the liberal legacy against mixing religion and politics has made Western governments profoundly uneasy about how to handle them. This will have to change, and the conference on 'World Faiths and Development' hosted at Lambeth Palace, London, in February 1998 by the World Bank and the archbishop of Canterbury is one indication that the Western approach to religion is changing.[82] Western governments need to engage foreign governments, religious leaders and their organizations in foreign countries on their own terrain. They will have to engage them in a religious discourse on policy matters of common interest, such as on strategies for economic development that are sensitive to religious concerns, human rights, abortion and women's rights, and even on principles of foreign intervention in places such as Bosnia.[83] Just as labour attachés have been for some time assigned to embassies to deal with local trade unions, in countries where religion is becoming a particularly salient aspect of policy-making, cultural attachés could monitor religious developments and maintain a dialogue with religious leaders and organizations on politics and matters of social policy.

The main world religions are interpretative communities. They may have fixed texts and fixed doctrines but not fixed interpretations of these texts and doctrines. There is a conscious creative and reflexive side to religion. As interpretative communities, religions interpret their traditions in terms of the present and the present in terms of the religious tradition. There is, in other words, a dialogue between past and present that enhances self-understanding among a religion's adherents, and social understanding among the religious community. They are in dialogue with their adherents and with society on the contemporary significance of the religious tradition in developing countries, and they are working out the contemporary significance of their traditions and values for modern social life. The dialogue, and sometimes the clash, has not been between civilizations as much as it has been within them. The outcome of this dialogue is vital for Western interests and the best way the West can influence it is through a cultural diplomacy that takes the values and concerns of other religions and cultural traditions seriously.

This perspective on cultural diplomacy can be applied most readily in the areas of foreign assistance, environmental policy and the ethics of micro-enterprise and business. Western foreign aid can support Islamic and Christian NGOs working on development tasks and humanitarian assistance in conflict situations.[84] Such aid can help articulate and formulate a social space where common humanitarian principles can be put into action. In the short run, this can provide meaningful assistance, and in the long run it can reinforce understanding and tolerance, values that are an important part of a democratic political culture.

The environment is another area where religious leaders and groups in developing countries can benefit from Western foreign aid policy. There is a growing recognition that what development takes place should be in harmony with the environment, and a country's religious and cultural traditions are important for this understanding. How, for example, Thailand's industrialization policy can be consistent with Buddhist principles of environmental management is an issue of concern to religious leaders and groups in Thailand, aid agencies and a government that is increasingly sensitive to public support for its policies.

The privatization of state enterprises and the encouragement of micro-enterprises are a key part of economic liberalization, and this is another area where the West, through cultural diplomacy and foreign aid, can support development in the Third World. It is increasingly being recognized that the market economy is grounded in social life. This cannot be understood apart from the larger questions about how these societies organize themselves, and religion is central to this understanding.[85] This was the perspective behind the first Beijing International Business Ethics Conference held in October 1996. The recognition that an effective market economy operates within a moral community, whether that community is informed by Christian, Islamic or Confucian values, in the West or in the Third World, opens up another area where policy can support development in ways that are sensitive to the religious and cultural traditions of different societies.[86] These are only possibilities, but they suggest a new approach to engage with global order in areas of culture, diplomacy and development in the multicultural world society that is emerging after the end of the cold war.

Notes

[1] Takeshi Umehara, 'Ancient Japan shows postmodernism the way', *New Perspectives Quarterly*, 9, No. 2 (Spring 1992), 10–13.

[2] By referring to 'secular liberalism' I recognize there is a tradition of Christian political thought that relates Christianity to liberalism. R. Bruce Douglass and David Hollenbach (eds.), *Catholicism and Liberalism: Contributions to American Public Philosophy* (Cambridge, Cambridge University Press, 1994). James W. Skillen and Rockne M. McCarthy (eds.), *Political Order and the Plural Structure of Society* (Atlanta, GA, Emory University Studies in Law and Religion, 1995).

[3] Jean Bethke Elshtain, *The Trial of Democracy* (New York, Basic Books, 1995).

[4] Raymond Plant, *Modern Political Theory* (Oxford, Basil Blackwell, 1991), 74–137, 320–79.

[5] Shlomo Avineri and Avner de-Shalit (eds.), *Communitarianism and Individualism* (Oxford, Oxford University Press, 1992).

[6] 'Father of Tony Blair's big idea', *Observer* (24 July 1994); Bruce Frohnen, *The New Communitarians and the Crisis of Liberalism* (Lawrence, KS, University of Kansas Press, 1996).

[7] Francis Fukuyama contends that only over the past few generations has the United States become as individualistic as the liberal theory which Americans say they believe in said they were; prior to this time, as Alexis de Tocqueville documented, American society showed

greater levels of trust and associational life. Francis Fukuyama, *Trust: The Social Virtues and the Creation of Prosperity* (London, Penguin, 1996), 10.

[8] Charles Taylor, 'Atomism', in Avineri and de-Shalit (eds.), *Communitarianism*, 29–50.

[9] Michael Sandel, 'The procedural republic and the unencumbered self', in Avineri and de-Shalit (eds.), *Communitarianism*, 12–29; Michael Sandel, *Liberalism and the Limits of Justice* (Cambridge, Cambridge University Press, 1982); and Charles Taylor, *Sources of the Self* (Cambridge, Cambridge University Press, 1989).

[10] Charles Taylor, 'Cross-purposes: the liberal-communitiarian debate', in Nancy L. Rosenblum (ed.), *Liberalism and the Moral Life* (Cambridge, MA, Harvard University Press, 1989), 159–82.

[11] Robert Bellah, Richard Madsen, William M. Sullivan, Ann Swindler and Steven M. Tipton, *Habits of the Heart: Individualism and Commitment in American Life* (Berkeley, University of California Press, 1985), 72.

[12] Stephen Holmes, 'The permanent structure of antiliberal thought', in Rosenblum, *Liberalism and Moral Life*, 227–53; Stephen Holmes, *The Anatomy of Antiliberalism* (Cambridge, MA, Harvard University Press, 1994).

[13] Rosenblum (ed.) *Liberalism and Moral Life*.

[14] Graham Maddox, *Religion and the Rise of Democracy* (London, Routledge, 1995); Nicholas Wolterstorff, *John Locke and the Ethics of Belief* (Cambridge, Cambridge University Press, 1996).

[15] Robert Bellah et al., *Habits of the Heart*, 223.

[16] Robert Wuthnow, *Christianity in the 21st Century* (Oxford, Oxford University Press, 1993).

[17] Owen Chadwick, *The Secularization of the European Mind* (Cambridge, Cambridge University Press, 1975).

[18] Peter Berger, *The Heretical Imperative* (New York, Doubleday, 1980), chap. 6, 'Between Jerusalem and Benares'.

[19] Nathan Glazer, *We Are All Multiculturalists Now* (Cambridge, MA, Harvard University Press, 1997); Will Kymlicka, *Multicultural Citizenship: A Liberal Theory of Minority Rights* (Oxford, Oxford University Press, 1995); Will Kymlicka (ed.), *The Rights of Minority Cultures* (Oxford, Oxford University Press, 1997).

[20] Philip Rieff, *The Triumph of the Therapeutic* (1966); Christopher Lasch, 'Philip Rieff and the religion of culture', in C. Lasch, *The Revolt of the Elites and the Betrayal of Democracy* (New York, W. W. Norton, 1995), 213–29.

[21] Mark Slouka, *War of the Worlds: Cyberspace and the High-Tech Assault on Reality* (London, Abacus, 1996); Jeff Zaleski, *The Soul of Cyberspace*

(San Francisco, Harpers, 1997); Douglas Groothuis, *The Soul in Cyberspace* (Chicago, Baker House Books); John Gray, 'Cyberspace offers a hollow freedom', *Guardian Weekly* (16 April 1995), 12.

22 Fukuyama, *Trust*, 283–94.

23 Martin Wollacott, 'The dangerous whiff of random terror', *Guardian Weekly* (26 March 1995), 14; 'Third wave terrorism', *New Perspectives Quarterly*, 12, No. 3 (Summer 1995), 2–13.

24 See the articles by Nozick, Kymlicka, Rawls and Dworkin in Avineri and de-Shalit (eds.), *Communitarianism*.

25 Jonathan Sachs, *The Persistence of Faith: Religion, Morality and Society in a Secular Age* (London, Weidenfeld & Nicolson, 1991).

26 Harvey Cox, *The Secular City: Secularization and Urbanization in Theological Perspective* (London, SCM Press, 1965); Daniel Callahan (ed.), *The Secular City Debate* (New York, Macmillan, 1965).

27 Harvey Cox, 'The transcendent dimension', *The Nation* (1 January 1996), 21–3.

28 Daniel Bell, 'Together again?', *Times Literary Supplement* (25 November 1994), 5–6.

29 Amitai Etzioni, 'On communitarianism and its inclusive agenda', *Tikkun*, 8, No. 5 (September/October 1993), 49–51.

30 Bellah, et al., *Habits of the Heart*, 27–35.

31 Chadwick, *Secularization*, 22.

32 Robert Putnam, *Making Democracy Work* (Princeton, NJ, Princeton University Press, 1993); Fukuyama, *Trust*.

33 'The God squad: religion and politics are best kept apart', *The Economist* (26 October 1996), 20–1.

34 Richard John Neuhaus, *The Naked Public Square: Religion and Democracy in America* (Grand Rapids, MI, Eerdmans, 1986).

35 Michael Lerner, *Jewish Renewal: A Path to Healing and Transformation* (New York, A. Grosset/Putnam, 1994), 167.

36 Michael Sandel, 'America's search for a new public philosophy', *The Atlantic Monthly* (March 1996), 57–74.

37 Cox, 'Transcendent dimension', 23.

38 Michael Walzer, *Spheres of Justice* (New York, Basic Books, 1983).

39 Marcel Gauchet, *The Disenchantment of the World: A Political History of Religion*, trans. Oscar Burge (Princeton, Princeton University Press, 1997); Thomas Moore, *The Re-Enchantment of Everyday Life* (New York, HarperCollins, 1996).

40 Malcolm Bradbury, 'What was post-modernism? The arts in and after the cold war', *International Affairs*, 71, No. 4 (October 1995), 763–74.

41 Philippa Berry and Andrew Wernick (eds.), *Shadow of the Spirit: Postmodernism and Religion* (London, Routledge, 1993).

42 Robert N. Bellah, 'Between religion and social science', in Robert N.

Bellah (ed.), *Beyond Belief: Essays on Religion in a Post-Traditionalist World* (Berkeley, University of California Press, 1970, 2nd edn., 1991), 237–59.

[43] Robert Wuthnow, *The Restructuring of American Religion* (Princeton, NJ, Princeton University Press, 1988), chap. 1; Robert Wuthnow, 'Understanding religion and politics', *Daedalus*, 120, No. 3 (Summer 1991), 1–20.

[44] Ernst Troeltsch, *The Social Teachings of the Christian Churches* (1911), trans. Olive Wyon (London, George Allen, 1931), vol. 1, 328–82; vol. 2, conclusion.

[45] Gerald Parsons (ed.), *The Growth of Religious Diversity: Britain from 1945*, vol. 1, *Traditions* (London, Routledge, 1993); vol. 2, *Controversies* (London, Routledge, 1994).

[46] This is the view of *The Utne Reader*, a leading digest of the best of the alternative or left-wing press in the US, in a review of the 1980s. '10 events that shook the world', *Utne Reader*, 62 (March/April 1994), 58–71; John Naisbitt and Patricia Aburdene, *Megatrends 2000: Ten New Directions for the 1990s* (New York, Avon Books, 1990), chap. 9 ('Religious revival of the third millennium').

[47] Mircea Eliade, *The Sacred and the Profane* (New York, Harper Torchbacks, 1961).

[48] Brian Appleyard, *Understanding the Present: Science and the Soul of Modern Man* (London, Picador, 1993); Rupert Sheldrake, *The Rebirth of Nature: The Greening of Science and God* (New York, Bantam Books, 1991); Patrick Glynn, *God the Evidence: The Reconciliation of Faith and Reason in a Postsecular World* (Washington, DC, Institute for Communitarian Policy Studies, George Washington University, 1997).

[49] David Ray Griffin, *The Re-enchantment of Science: Postmodern Proposals* (New York, State University of New York Press, 1988).

[50] Peter Beyer, *Religion and Globalization* (London, Sage, 1994).

[51] Michael Lerner, *The Politics of Meaning: Restoring Hope and Possibility in an Age of Cynicism* (New York, Addison-Wesley, 1996).

[52] Ernest Gellner, *Postmodernism, Reason and Religion* (London, Routledge, 1992).

[53] James Mayall, 'International society and international theory', in Michael Donelan (ed.), *The Reason of States* (London, George Allen & Unwin, 1978), 133–6.

[54] Samuel P. Huntington, *Political Order and Changing Societies* (Cambridge, MA, Harvard University Press, 1968).

[55] I. W. Zartman, *Collapsed States: The Disintegration and Restoration of Legitimate Authority* (Boulder, CO, Lynne Rienner, 1995).

[56] Mark Juergensmeyer, *The New Cold War: Religious Nationalism Confronts the Secular State* (Berkeley, Los Angeles, and London, University

of California Press, 1993); Jeff Haynes, *Religion in Third World Politics* (London, Open University Press, 1994); David Westerlund (ed.), *Questioning the Secular State: The Worldwide Resurgence of Religion in Politics* (London, I. B. Tauris, 1996).

[57] Robert Lee, *Overcoming Tradition and Modernity: The Search for Islamic Authenticity* (Boulder, CO, Westview Press, 1997).

[58] Samuel P. Huntington, 'Religion and the third wave', *National Interest*, 31 (Summer 1991), 29–42; *The Third Wave: Democratization in the Late Twentieth Century* (Oklahoma City, Oklahoma University Press, 1991).

[59] Gellner, *Postmodernism*.

[60] Fred Halliday, *Islam and the Myth of Confrontation* (London, I. B. Tauris, 1996); John Esposito, *The Islamic Threat* (Oxford, Oxford University Press, 1992).

[61] Richard Gott, 'Reason blinks in the light of faith: how a largely secular West can deal with an increasingly religious world order', *Guardian* (20 April 1996), 31.

[62] 'America and Islam: a wobbly hand of friendship', *The Economist* (26 August 1995), 43–4.

[63] 'Islam's political football', *The Economist* (13 December 1998), 63–4; 'Mid-East jigsaw changes shape', *Financial Times* (28 February/1 March 1998).

[64] Robert L. Bartley, 'The case for optimism; the West should believe in itself', *Foreign Affairs*, 72, No. 4 (1993), 15–18; Jeane J. Kirkpatrick, 'The modernising imperative: tradition and change', *Foreign Affairs*, 72, No. 4 (1993), 22–4.

[65] Graham Fuller, 'The next ideology', *Foreign Policy*, 98 (Spring 1995), 145–58.

[66] V. S. Naipaul, 'Our universal civilization', *The New York Review of Books* (31 January 1991), 22–5.

[67] Barry Buzan, 'From international system to international society: realism and regime theory meet the English school', *International Organization*, 47, No. 3 (Summer 1993), 327–52.

[68] Ibid., 335.

[69] Kenneth Waltz, *Theory of International Politics* (Reading, MA, Addison-Wesley, 1979).

[70] Hedley Bull and Adam Watson (eds.), *Expansion of International Society* (Oxford, Oxford University Press, 1984), chap. 12.

[71] Michael Doyle, 'Kant, liberal legacies and foreign affairs', parts I and II, *Philosophy and Public Affairs*, 12, No. 3 (1983), 205–35; 12, No. 4 (1984), 323–53.

[72] John Gray, 'Cold sun rises at the end of the cold war', *Guardian* (20 January 1995).

[73] Samuel P. Huntington, 'The clash of civilizations', *Foreign Affairs*, 72, No. 3 (Summer, 1993), 22–49.

74 'The soul of the new world order', special issue, *New Perspectives Quarterly*, 10, No. 3 (Summer 1993).

75 'The new nationalists', *The Economist* (14 January 1995), 19–21.

76 Felipe Fernandez-Armesto, *Millennium: A History of the Last Thousand Years* (New York, Scribner, 1995).

77 Gray, 'Cold sun rises'.

78 David Held, *Democracy and the Global Order* (Cambridge, Polity Press, 1995).

79 Huntington, *Clash of Civilizations*.

80 Michael Walzer, *Thick and Thin: Moral Arguments at Home and Abroad* (Notre Dame, IN, University of Notre Dame Press, 1994), 1–11.

81 M. K. Ereksoussi, 'The Koran and the humanitarian conventions', *International Review of the Red Cross* (Geneva, May 1969); Yadh Ben Ashoor, 'Islam and international humanitarian law', *International Review of the Red Cross* (Geneva, March–April 1980); L. R. Penna, 'Written and customary provisions relating to the conduct of hostilities and treatment of victims of armed conflicts in ancient India', *International Review of the Red Cross* (Geneva, July–August 1989); Yolande Diallo, *African Traditions and Humanitarian Law: Similarities and Differences* (Geneva, ICRC pamphlet, n.d.); Yolande Diallo, *African Traditions and Humanitarian Law* (Geneva, ICRC pamphlet, 1978); Mutoy Mubiala, 'African states and the promotion of humanitarian principles', *International Review of the Red Cross* (Geneva, March–April 1989).

82 Press statement by Dr George Carey, archbishop of Canterbury and Mr James Wolfensohn, president of the World Bank, 'World faiths and development – dialogue', 18 February 1998.

83 Noam J. Zohar, 'Boycott, crime, and sin: ethical and Talmudic responses to injustice abroad', and Sohail H. Hashmi, 'Is there an Islamic ethic of humanitarian intervention?', *Ethics and International Affairs*, 7 (1993), 39–73.

84 Nazmul Ahsan Kalimullah and Caroline Barbara Frazer, 'Islamic non-governmental organizations in Bangladesh with reference to three case studies', *The Islamic Quarterly*, 34, No. 2 (1990), 71–92.

85 Fukuyama, *Trust*; Lawrence E. Harrison, *Who Prospers: How Cultural Values Shape Economic and Political Success* (New York, Basic Books, 1992).

86 Shirley Roels, 'Letter from China', *Books and Culture: A Christian Perspective*, 3, No. 2 (March/April 1997), 5.

3

Religious transnationalism and global order, with particular consideration of Islam

JAMES PISCATORI

Transnationalism has long been a feature of the international landscape, even if it was not clearly recognized as such in earlier periods – or, indeed, by observers today who often appear to regard it as a condition of the second half of the twentieth century. In the nineteenth century, French Catholic and American Protestant missionaries opened colleges in the Levant, British and German military officers advised the high commands in China, Egypt and the Ottoman empire, and, generally, Europeans and North Americans became routinely involved in 'civilizing' the life of nations far distant from their own.

The historical roots of transnationalism go much deeper, in fact, and, at least in the case of the Christian and Muslim worlds, one could argue that trans-local networks and activities developed from the medieval era and probably earlier. In both Europe and west Asia, traders, scholars and pilgrims regularly crossed locally defined borders and created networks defined by broader loyalties, and, in the Islamic world, the self-perception of a broad community of the faithful (*umma*) was well entrenched certainly by its late medieval period.[1] With regard to the emerging European order, from the seventeenth century when national states were in the process of solidifying, parallel developments ensured that national frontiers were neither uncontested nor impermeable. Scientific and technological advances, industrialization and urbanization, which transformed semi-feudal localized societies into hierarchically and centrally organized nation-states, could not themselves be contained within the borders of any one state. The demands of economic specialization and trade also created new patterns of interaction and networks of actors. Moreover, by the end of the nineteenth century, cosmopolitan-tinged ideologies such as imperialism, pan-Slavism, international socialism, Christian evangelicalism and liberal capitalism had further complicated the interstate order. That such ideologies served mainly to aggrandize the power of individual nation-states did not detract from the fact that, even as the mythology of nationalism was being vigorously promoted and 'the nationalist pail' was presented as 'half-full or better', it was in reality 'half-empty and leaking'.[2]

Conceptualizing transnationalism

Despite the coexistence of local and transnational forces over the centuries, as the disciplines of political science and international relations became established in the twentieth century, the unambiguous model of a territorially demarcated, power-driven state system asserted itself. The complexity of the political world notwithstanding, a naturally conservative bias emerged among those who had committed themselves to the study of the principal centres of power in the modern world. As schools of thought, realism and idealism may have largely differed in the relative emphasis that each placed on moral considerations in the formulation and implementation of national interests, but the obvious common presupposition was that nation-states were the decisive components of international affairs.

In the early 1970s, however, the theoretical literature of international relations became increasingly absorbed with the tensions within the system and the failures of state-driven models of politics. The world was now seen as increasingly dominated by forces and organizations that ranged beyond national boundaries;[3] economies, societies and politics were viewed as irrevocably interdependent;[4] and a more complex model of world politics was proffered to replace the antiquated idea of 'international politics'.[5] Marxian analysts preferred to speak of 'world systems' such as capitalism, which develop according to their own rhythm, operate in terms of their internal rules and steadily expand their geographic reach.[6]

In the late 1970s, it appeared to a small number of observers that the realms of social, political, economic and cultural interaction had become so extensive and encompassing, and the role of the nation-state so relatively irrelevant to the process of creating and managing them, that politics would better be understood as global. By the late 1980s, an increasing number of scholars had turned to the framework of 'globalization'[7] to shed light on the politics of humankind, which was seen as progressively shaped by concerns like the environment, international capital, human rights and inequalities of wealth that defied territorial boundaries. From the mid-1990s some scholars have preferred 'globality' to globalization out of concern that the latter concept implies a process of development guided by set laws and with a defined end, whereas the former is a new stage of universal organization lacking, however, any organizing agent or determined meaning. Transnationalism remains a useful analytical device, but increasingly the territoriality on which it is based becomes less relevant.[8]

Individuals associated with the World Order Models Project (WOMP) have urged a new 'human governance' that would seek to counter the economic and political hegemony of the developed North, globalization from above, with 'transnational democracy',[9] a kind of globalization from below. Economists have been particularly active in charting the effects and especially the benefits of a world market that has become intimately interconnected. They have regarded the new forms of interaction as so important that natural resources, location and the capacity to engage in mass production have been transcended as paramount ingredients of economic success; talent, mobility and innovation, all purportedly subject to governmental influence and encouragement, are today far more useful and relevant. The political implication is both far-reaching and optimistic: 'countries can choose, through their policies, to be rich – or to be poor'.[10] Anthropologists and sociologists have been less sanguine and have noted that cultural autonomy may be endangered by globalizing trends. Humanity, it has been argued, is being increasingly drawn into a popular culture that is defined by American–European consumer lifestyles and propagated by potent telecommunications networks. In 1990, one writer commented with regard to the Filipino attraction to American popular culture: 'an entire nation seems to have learned to mimic Kenny Rogers and the Lennon sisters, like a vast Asian Motown chorus'.[11]

The impact of such revolutionary developments has been unclear. As early as the 1940s, the argument had emerged that patterns of 'functionalist' co-operation between state and non-state actors on matters of 'low politics', such as health, transportation and communication, would eventually 'spill over' into the 'high politics' of war and peace and encourage the emergence of a peaceful system.[12] Although Inis Claude and others in the late 1950s and 1960s persuasively demonstrated the inability of functionalism to effect a radical change in the interstate order,[13] the optimistic strand of thinking acquired new vigour in the 1970s with WOMP.

One writer argued, for example, that the processes of transnational interaction and 'functional interpenetration' would lead to 'denationalization', symmetrical interdependence and the diffusion of power. Hence, 'the over-all political, if not military or economic, relations among the big powers [would] increasingly become interdependent, taking the form of competition and cooperation rather than confrontation'. In time, the developing world culture would lead to a new emphasis on equality and the erosion of 'not only specific forms of authority such as the nation-state but authority in general'.[14] The teleological bias of this and other transnational theories was thus manifest; as Kenneth Thompson has remarked, for 'enlightened liberals' transnationalism came to replace world government as both the virtual panacea for current difficulties and the culmination of historical processes.[15]

In the eyes of other observers, however, although they too argued on the basis of end-product, the prospects of transnationalism were more tentative and the implications for the territorial state less dire. Samuel Huntington argued that, far from necessarily eroding the sovereignty of the nation-state, transnational organizations may actually work to the advantage of the state, particularly the weak state, by connecting it to greater networks and thus enhancing its powers. What conflict there is between the two kinds of institution is 'complementary rather than duplicative':

It is conflict not between likes but between unlikes, each of which has its own primary set of functions to perform. It is, consequently, conflict which, like labour-management conflict, involves the structuring of relations and the distribution of benefits to entities which need each other even as they conflict with each other.[16]

In the second edition of their book on transnationalism, Robert Keohane and Joseph Nye reaffirmed their belief that the nation-state was not obsolete nor patterns of interdependence symmetrical. 'Interdependence would not necessarily lead to cooperation', nor would 'its consequences . . . be benign'.[17]

Fred Halliday usefully reminds us that much of this debate over transnationalism versus the state involves each side talking past each other because of two differing notions of the state. Much of the debate centres on whether the territorial-national state will give way to forces that cut across territories and conventional sovereignties. But there is also a second, Weberian and Marxist, concept of the state that envisions it as the panoply of administrative institutions of a society. To ask whether transnationalism undermines the state is, in his view, to concentrate only on the first conceptualization and to risk missing the various ways in which transnational forces affect the development of the state itself – that is, the processes of change within the set of coercive and administrative structures and the relationship between these and the society they govern.[18]

Seyom Brown, capturing the sense of uncertainty that permeates much of the conceptualizing of the phenomenon, thought that transnationalism could move in contradictory directions. On the one hand, it was possible that 'such an interpenetration of societies could delay or dissuade resort to war-provoking actions by providing an alternative arena for conflict – namely, a rich web of interaction for bargaining, registering grievances, and threatening sanctions *before* total nation-to-nation hostility develops'. On the other hand, the new transnational regimes would not automatically possess the kind of legitimacy that national structures possess, and 'if opposed they might need to resort to coercion'. 'Widespread discontent among disadvantaged groups would increase the prospects of active conflict, including physical combat, among would-be authorities, and contracts and other inter-group commitments would lack stability.'[19]

Political economists have generally viewed the rapid and uneven expansion of international trade and transnational capital as confirming the hegemony of the developed Northern states, especially the United States. The Southern states of the Third World are inevitably victims, economically dependent and politically subject to neo-imperialism.[20] Samir Amin has argued that the only solution can be 'delinking' (*'deconnexion'*) by which the countries of the South seek to develop a kind of 'autocentric development'. The Third World state needs to embark on a socialist future by first disengaging from hegemonic transnational capitalism. Amin's solution is thus the exact opposite of the common presupposition that only through integration with the world system will one's long-term prosperity be realized: 'It is a matter of subjecting the mutual relations between the various nations and regions of the whole of the planet to the varying imperatives of their own internal development and not the reverse.'[21]

Others, pointing to a more salutary transnational impact, have approvingly noted the strengthening of local government machineries as a result of the income generated by external investments. Centralized 'rentier', oil-producing states of the Middle East are a clear example.[22] Peter B. Evans argues, however, that the relationship between the transnational economy and the states of the 'periphery' has not been as clearly one-sided as either school of thought contends. Third World states have unquestionably been dependent, but they have not simply been the passive loser, nor have their societies been the uncomplicated beneficiary, of the interdependence game. Rather, the more developed of these states have been able to create strong state bureaucracies that often mediate between local and transnational capital. For this reason, the advantage possessed by host countries of multinational enterprise, the developed countries of the North, may not automatically be crushing. As the mining of copper in Chile illustrates, their position may become more disadvantageous with regard to the international market, since transnational organizations may in practice prefer to deal with local strong bureaucracies in order to exploit resources more profitably. 'Transnational capital continues to deal with the state on the basis of a contradictory relationship that contains bases for conflict as well as common interests.'[23] One must add, of course, that the improved state bureaucracies that emerge from transnational interactions often become the fearsome instruments of a repressive state.

Among political economists, Susan Strange has responded to what appear to be the new analytical priorities of international relations, globalization and interdependence. Looking at where authority lies in the world economy, she argues that a number of fundamental changes are occurring that belie the simplicity of a transnational versus state perspective: the gap between strong and weak states is growing, particularly in regard to their abilities to control their own economies; power has shifted in considerable part to non-state actors ranging from multinational firms to organized crime and to communications industries; governments often exercise their power through non-state actors such as international organizations, as when managing foreign debt; and areas of uncertainty, such as co-ordination of exchange rates, have emerged over which no one exercises real power, to the extent that a vacuum exists at the 'heart' of international political economy. In short, power is increasingly diffused, and while the state has clearly not disappeared, it may be said that, relative to the position it was formerly thought to hold, it is in 'retreat'.[24]

Among those who are mainly concerned with cultural matters, the impact that transnationalism is having also remains a matter of contention. Ernest Gellner argued that, in light of the powerful trends towards homogenization by which nations wish to create industrial societies and people across the world seek to imitate European–American culture, 'genuine cultural pluralism ceases to be viable'.[25] Others have worried that, first, 'Coca-colonization' and, now, 'McDonaldization'[26] have become less savoury aspects of the everyday life of the global order.

Yet Ulf Hannerz finds the argument that transnationalism is a tool of the hegemonic West to be overstated. We are now living in a 'global ecumene', which makes nonsense out of the simple model of centre dominating periphery. Transnationalism 'ignores, subverts, and devalues rather than celebrates national boundaries', but the effect is not necessarily felt in one direction only. When we are talking about culture, in fact, 'the peripherals talk back', as when Westerners flock to Indian mystics, dance to reggae music and read the magical realist novels of Latin American authors. Moreover, to assume that the overbearing centre destroys authentic local traditions in the pursuit of multinational profits is to apply stereotyped standards of authenticity and cultural purity; these may be caricatures of societies that are constantly changing and exist in an intimately interconnected world.[27]

Religion as a transnational force

The theoretical literature on transnationalism has devoted some, though minimal, attention to religious phenomena. The Vatican and the World Council of Churches have been favourite – and obvious – examples of the non-state transnational institution. But, for the most part, religion has been understudied in analyses of transnationalism. This is all the more apparent when, as the above discussion indicates, transnational linkages and penetration have been studied from a number of perspectives in order to assess their impact on questions of political and economic security. The institutional bias of much of the transnational literature may in part explain the dearth of references to forces which are more diffuse and less organized and which often take the form of social movements and shifting constellations of special interest groups, such as those dedicated to human rights concerns. But it is also likely that religious forces and movements have been regarded as remote from the central questions that affect states and other significant actors in world politics.

The explanation for this relative neglect lies in two assumptions embedded in the social sciences. One presupposition, especially evident in theories of modernization and political development, is that the future of the integrated nation-state lies in secular participatory politics. There have been several variations on this theme, but the common Western – specifically, American – ethnocentric bias is obvious.[28] The suspicion that nation-building would be ill-served by obscurantist beliefs and priestly tyrants has lingered, even if often implicitly conveyed. Churches and piety are properly private matters, and politics must be separated from religion in order to avoid dogmatism and encourage tolerance. National leaders must remain somehow neutral and removed from religious entanglements. As with ethnicity, religion has thus been relegated to the category of a problem that must not be allowed to intrude on the search for national unity and political stability.[29]

The other, related, assumption of the social sciences is what Albert Bergesen has called 'neo-utilitarian'. He is mainly referring to the individualist assumption behind world systems and international relations theories that leads both to underemphasize the social dimension of politics and to regard the system as the willed product of prior existing units. But one may extrapolate from his argument that much of the social sciences have also adopted a preference for the 'conscious rational actor'.[30] Religion and rationality are sometimes thought to be complementary, but essentially different, modes of experience; often they are viewed as uncompromisingly antagonistic to each other. According to one writer, 'rationalism [and] fundamentalism constitute two states of mind irreducible to one another, incapable of integration'.[31] Whether the liberal theories of the Enlightenment or Marxist interpretations of history, rationally defined interests are assumed to be the guiding light of individuals and societies. Modernity, which is reasonable and progressive, is pitted against tradition, the repository of primordial affinities such as kinship, ethnicity and religion.

Modernization theory has been particularly egregious in both dichotomizing modernity and tradition, and conflating the former with secularism and the latter with religion. As even the most fleeting invocation of the Iranian Revolution suggests, this is counter-empirical as well as theoretically arguable. Rather than political stability, revolution, led by the discontented middle classes, was the consequence of the Shah's enthusiastic modernization programme. And, contrary to what often passes as conventional wisdom, the 'tradition' of the ayatollahs proved to be flexible and susceptible to reinvention, in the process allowing the creation of a modern government and policies. But, as Robert Wuthnow argues, the secular bias of modernization theory is also found in other key theories of the social sciences. World-system theory gives analytical privilege to material conditions, and critical theory, while acknowledging that religion may contribute to protest movements, worries that in its fundamentalist guise at least it runs against the rationality that must lie at the heart of civilization.[32]

It is useful to be reminded that, if the social sciences have presented a distorted picture by assuming that secularization is, or ought to be, the norm, much the same thing could be said of its seeming obverse – that modernity is simply equivalent to resurgent religion. Since the largely unexpected events of the

Iranian Revolution in the late 1970s, it has become a commonplace to argue that the conditions of the late twentieth century have produced a 'return' or 'revival' of religious belief, often in the highly charged form of fundamentalism. However, reduced church attendance, open questioning of doctrines on birth control and abortion, declining enrolment of the clergy and the weakening political position of the religious establishment across Western Europe stand in partial contradiction of the resurgence argument. Yet it is also clear that *this* pattern does not always hold in Eastern Europe and other parts of the world, that even in Western Europe religious beliefs do not wane or disappear entirely on the individual level and that a relative diminution in the institutional place of religion does not mean social and political powerlessness.[33] Both the secularization and resurgence theses are, therefore, a less accurate depiction of reality than is sometimes presumed, but there remains undoubted common sense in recognizing the phenomenon that Gilles Kepel provocatively calls 'the revenge of God'.[34]

Religious factors, and specifically transnational religious ones, may be seen as important to political and security concerns for several reasons. First, religion can directly affect the internal politics of states and thus qualify state power, as conventionally understood. North American Evangelical Protestant movements, for example, made such inroads into Guatemala that the Catholic Church there nearly disappeared as an institution in the early 1980s; and tacit, though unstable, alliances were at times formed with politicians who essentially destroyed the kind of competitive politics that liberation theology activists had hoped to encourage.[35] In the case of China, religions have always been regarded with suspicion, the more so when they are connected externally. Buddhist monks were imported in the first century from India and Central Asia in order to bolster the rule of local kingdoms, but by the ninth century, when they were no longer essential for regime security, the state acted against their interests and affirmed its supremacy over religion. The Muslim and pseudo-Christian rebellions that confronted the Qing dynasty in the second half of the nineteenth century convinced it that transnational religions were especially dangerous, and yet, much like the Ottomans at roughly the same time, it was impelled in the unequal treaties to accept concessions to superior Western power.

As resented as these were, there was also a begrudging under-standing that international acceptability to some extent depended on allowing well-connected religions to operate in China. The People's Republic of China has combined both attitudes: religion is subject to strict bureaucratic controls, but transnational religi-ous linkages are seen as enhancing China's international position. Indeed, the only religions that the state formally recognizes are precisely those with clear connections abroad: Buddhism, Catholicism, Protestantism, Islam and Taoism.[36]

Because of its symbolic power, religion has increasingly become the language of politics in many societies. Governments and opposition groups are often in direct competition for control of this symbolic discourse, thereby creating a 'politics of language'[37] in which the stakes are high: who speaks authoritat-ively for what is proposed as the definitive religious tradition? As in the cases of Guatemala and China, this competition may take on a sharp edge when the capabilities of groups within the society are enhanced by connection with a variety of external networks. In Algeria of the late 1980s and early 1990s, the Front Islamique du Salut (FIS) became a vital competitor of the Front de Liberation National-influenced government in deciding who would be the arbiter of Algerian Islam, and its position was undoubtedly strengthened by financial support from patrons such as Saudi Arabia[38] and the mobilizing experiences of Algerian *mujahidin* who had served in Afghanistan and now were no longer content to put up with what was regarded as un-Islamic govern-ment at home.[39] One writer, Rachid Boudjedra, has pointed to yet another transnational connection: the (largely secondary school) teachers from Egypt, unable to find work there, who became employed in Algerian schools. Presumably influenced by the ideas of the Egyptian Muslim Brotherhood or its radical offshoots, they were thought to have introduced similarly Islamist ideas to Algerian youth.[40]

Second, transnational religious concerns help to create new political constituencies and new communities, which become in effect actors competitive with the state or other hegemonic institutions. In Latin America, Catholic liberation theologians have deliberately set out to mobilize the poor into new grass-roots movements that seek a radical reform of the political *status quo*. In Guatemala, Catholic clerical reformers from outside have helped

to instil political consciousness among the quiescent Ixil peas-
antry and, aided by the work of a number of the North
American-supported local Evangelical churches, profound
political changes have been set in motion:

> New forms of association have set up new channels of
> communication, including a new consciousness of 'rights' vis-a-vis
> larger political structures. A new class of 'promoters' in bilingual
> education, development projects, and cultural revitalization have
> made visible progress in advancing themselves, and sometimes their
> communities . . . [Ixils] do not appeal to laws or government, nor do
> they even look to transformations at that level. Instead, they construct
> new rituals of equality in religious services and build new personae as
> literate entrepreneurs and administrators who can hold their own with
> previously superordinate non-Indians. By changing the cultural and
> political landscape, they change the terms in which struggle is
> understood and engaged.[41]

As the development of Sufi brotherhoods in Islam testifies over
the centuries, the encouragement of alternative forms of
community and engagement is scarcely limited to the Christian
world. In Singapore in 1936, a new English-language journal,
Genuine Islam, appeared, which transmitted the Sufi ideas
favoured by its patrons, and, foreshadowing current publications
like the *Journal of the World Muslim League*, it regularly reported
on Muslim concerns in Egypt, Palestine and even Germany.[42] In
so doing, it fostered a sense of affiliation that not only surpassed
the immediate political community but also, through awareness
of events and conditions elsewhere in the Muslim world,
positively identified with a world-wide spiritual enterprise. The
Niassene Tijaniyya, centred on Kaolack in Senegal, has a network
of lodges (*zawiyas*) across the African Sahel and now in America,
which provide a meeting place as well as accommodation and
spiritual comfort for adherents from many countries and
backgrounds. Moreover, celebrations of the birthday of the
Prophet Muhammad and of the founder of the order, Shaykh
Ibrahim Niasse, and the pilgrimage (*ziyara*) to Kaolack offer
adepts throughout the world the occasion to meet and to
consolidate a sense of identity that does not overlap with that of
their own states or that of Senegal. The sense of identification is
enhanced by the social welfare which the African state is unable

to provide but which is offered by the Sufi order. The result is the creation of 'a sacred space that transcends the nation-state'.[43]

Since the 1970s especially, religious forces and movements have become so self-consciously organized and extensive that they cannot be contained within national borders and have thus come to be a decisive factor in the arena of world politics. As Arjun Appadurai has noted, 'primordia . . . have become globalized'.[44] Where once one's identity was rooted to territory, ethnicity and religious fundamentalism have become 'deterritorialized' to the point where adherents, such as Sikh or Muslim activists, identify with each other as much as, if not more than, they do with fellow citizens of their national homeland. Migration in search of work or political freedom, socialization through the defining literature and practices of the new movement, and immersion into the global culture contribute to this reorientation and reorganization of religious identification – and, by extension, of world politics. Marxists would see the crises of late world-wide capitalism as the main reason for anomie and the turn to unorthodox politics such as the green and fundamentalist movements, but most analysts would agree that these movements and concerns are transnational and 'trans-class':

> The petty bourgeois employee of IBM in Germany, in Senegal and in Indonesia cannot develop a common class consciousness. In Senegal or in Indonesia he might perhaps fill this vacuum by a wretched juxtaposition: being at one and the same time alienated in the firm and its technology but a religious fundamentalist. But the same might be true for the factory worker, the unemployed in the shanty-town, the peasant-labourer-employee, etc.[45]

Because such religiously based identities and communities have acquired coherence some national governments, with one eye on their domestic publics and the other on rival states, seek to serve as patrons of the new movements. In effect, they hope to cultivate new constituencies by which to enhance their own influence. The rivalry among Saudi Arabia, Iran and Pakistan is illustrative of this,[46] and helps to explain one aspect of what may be termed the 'macro-politics of conversion'[47] and missionary work in Islam. Access to and control of means of communications – Qur'an and other book publishing, television and radio programming – are crucial to this plan. The Saudis, for example, have not only distributed millions of copies of the Qur'an in various languages, but also regularly reach out to various groups throughout the world through their ownership of periodicals such as *al-Majalla* and *al-Watan* and such newspapers as *al-Sharq al-Awsat* and *al-Hayat*, published principally in London but also in Saudi Arabia, Egypt and Morocco in the Middle East and New York, Frankfurt and Marseilles in the West. Although legal ownership of these may be in private hands, links with the royal family are substantial: the family of Prince Salman (the governor of Riyadh and brother of the king) in the case of Saudi Research and Marketing controlling *al-Sharq al-Awsat* and *al-Majalla*; Prince Khalid bin Sultan (the Saudi commander during the Gulf War of 1991) in the case of the influential and widely read *al-Hayat*. To these the Saudis (in the person of Shaykh Walid al-Ibrahim, who is connected by marriage to the king) have added ownership of a regional competitor to Cable Network News (CNN), the Middle East Broadcasting Centre, broadcasting in Arabic from London, and the United Press International, the long-established American news service.[48]

Third, transnational organizations and movements contribute to self-awareness of one's traditions and subtly change the way in which individuals and groups approach both the traditions and those invested with authority in their society. This process of standardization, or what may be called 'objectification',[49] has been advanced by modern education, which stresses literacy and routinization of learning, and by the mass media such as radio, television, cassettes and videos, which disseminate ideas broadly and reiterate them. Formal theological tracts may be expensive and difficult to penetrate, but pamphlets and cassettes are either free or inexpensive and they are written in a popular, accessible style. The net effect is not unlike catechismal education.

An example of how ideas are transmitted is a lengthy newspaper article in the Moroccan newspaper, *al-Ishtiraki*, which summarized an account in the Egyptian magazine, *Ruz al-Yusuf*, reporting on a number of cassettes by a variety of religious 'extremists'. Although the tone of the article was disapproving, it could not have failed to introduce readers to ideas with which they may not have been acquainted first-hand.[50] This general process is relevant to the explanation of how a greater number of Muslims, previously unfamiliar with the doctrinal bases of their beliefs, have come to accept that 'Islam' generally, or, for example, 'Wahhabi Islam' – a term used outside Saudi Arabia to refer to a conservative, puritanical practice that is thought to be practised in the kingdom – consists of standards of conduct and judgement that can be applied to themselves as well as to others.[51]

Objectification is thus crucial to self-examination, but it also leads one, perhaps inevitably, to judge whether others measure up to the perceived requirements of the faith – and, more importantly, whether traditional religious officials deserve to possess what Ousmane Kane calls a 'monopoly of the management of the sacred'.[52] In Muslim societies, increased access to religious and other education, and familiarity with currents of thought prevalent elsewhere in the Muslim world, have led to the emergence of new *intellectuels et militants* out of the ranks of engineers, soldiers and secondary school teachers.[53] These are often as hostile to the traditional scholars (*ulama*) as they are to the secular governing élites. In Latin America, improvements in literacy and the ready availability of religious and other texts have contributed to the success of 'base ecclesial communities' (CEBs), formations parallel to and uncomfortably coexisting with the formal Catholic Church; and they have arguably led to the weakening of priestly authority.[54] Direct access to the 'text', written or broadcast, is not only a measure of personal growth, but also a political act.

The process of standardization may also exacerbate interstate tensions in a way unanticipated by a secularized discipline of international relations. There is no doubt that the relationship between revolutionary Iran and Saudi Arabia has mainly been governed by conflicting geo-strategic and, at times, economic interests. But the difficulties between the countries were, at least until the late 1980s, heightened by the repeated questioning and publicly formulated objections to the other's religious credentials – particularly, Khomeini's denunciation of Wahhabism as a deviation from true Islam in his sermons, speeches and final will and testament,[55] which, crucially, were reported and repeated in the official media. To cite another example, the Omani government became so committed to its defence of the orthodoxy of Ibadism, the sect of Islam practised there, that its relationship with the Saudi government deteriorated when a leading Saudi religious official made critical comments about the supposed heterodoxy of Ibadi doctrine.[56]

The impact of global communications

As is clear, networks of interdependence are increasingly incorporating individuals and societies across the globe. A significant part of this involves widening communication webs that alter perceptions of ourselves as well as others. It is a world of instant and universal awareness, where the 'local' difficulty – owing largely to such mega-corporations as CNN or the BBC and the Internet – is known intimately and almost as it happens, magnifying its import and plugging far-flung individuals into the currents of world politics and culture.

The information revolution has had three obvious effects: (a) it has collapsed distances, subverting and altering notions of home and exile; (b) it has seemingly sped up time, marking awareness of the far distant as well as nearby events in terms of minutes and seconds, not hours or days as even in the recent past; and (c) it has stimulated a reimagining of the communities to which individuals feel an attachment.[57]

While everyone can agree something profound is occurring, there is less consensus on whether this is salutary. One debate centres on equality. Some have seen a great leveller in the broad dissemination of information and images, and acknowledge that a rough, though not consistent, equality has at times emerged. Anthony Giddens began his 1999 Reith Lectures by citing the example of Central African villagers viewing a video of *Basic Instinct* when it had not yet opened in cinemas in London.[58] Moreover, the communications revolution may be empowering. The broad availability of the information superhighway and of such technologies as the computer, modem and facsimile machine, the reduction in economies of scale and the lowering of entry barriers to markets around the world mean – though each for different reasons – that the previously voiceless group or weak state may now challenge established injustices and power and join universal debates.[59] The position of non-state actors may thus be improved, but the old hierarchies of international relations may also be challenged as small states through the information revolution acquire more non-coercive 'soft power'.[60]

Others, such as Zygmunt Bauman, foresee only the increase of polarities and the creation of new class divisions. As information swirls effortlessly around the globe and as cognitive as well as physical mobility increases for a small segment of the world's population, there is a 'progressive breakdown in communication between the increasingly global and extraterritorial élites and the ever more "localized" rest'.[61] Communication is globalized, but it becomes increasingly disconnected from the 'human condition' that it is meant to describe and explain. In this scenario, the marginal are further marginalized and the only ones empowered are those who control the levers of information and entertainment – pre-eminently, of course, the news, music and cinematic industries of the West, especially the United States.

Another debate concerns the extent to which social and political solidarity has been enhanced. Optimists find in the new technologies the opportunity to bring far-away tragedies closer to home, in the process bridging narrow differences and building transnational coalitions. This may be particularly pertinent at times of environmental disaster or when conflict takes on Bosnia- or Rwanda-like dimensions of human tragedy. Pessimists, however, regard the communications revolution as pernicious and intimately tied to what Manuel Castells calls the 'informational economy'.[62] This enables existing power centres to advance their supposed liberal brand of market capitalism and to dull sensibilities with the spread of a universal culture of entertainment and consumerism. Rather than creating new forms of community, the information revolution is ultimately atomizing: it 'creates a kind of social liberal bond entirely made up of networks, separating humanity into individuals isolated from each other in a hyper-technological universe'.[63]

The globalization of communications and universalization of information are not incompatible with past trends in Islamic civilization. Marshal Lyautey, the first Resident General in Morocco (1912–25), was aware of the powerful communications network of Muslim societies and accordingly referred to Islam as that 'great sounding board'. The writings of one *alim* (or religious scholar) were known to other *ulama* (pl. of *alim*) throughout the lands of Islam; the words of the *khutba*, or sermon, resonated in the immediate congregations and often beyond. Islamic tradition has always valued in every activity the possibilities for learning and the acquisition of knowledge, and the vast collection of scholars, pilgrims, merchants and mystics who have travelled the world over the centuries – on *hajj*, *ziyara* (minor pilgrimage) or *rihla* (travel for the sake of knowledge) – have brought one part of the *umma* into contact with others, stimulating a powerful sense of both the richness of diversity and the strength of transnational pulls.

In contemporary society, Muslims like everyone else are both the controllers and the victims of the high-tech information revolution. As already noted, the proliferation of newspapers, journals, satellite broadcasting, fax machines, CD Roms, mobile telephones, home pages and web sites has provided Muslims with an understanding of the problems and achievements of their fellow believers across the world – making, for example, the plight of Muslims in Kosovo or the southern Philippines a matter of broad and urgent concern. It has raised *umma*-consciousness, and thereby given a push to trans-state communal identification.

As we would expect on the basis of the general theoretical ambivalence, the impact on the state itself in the Muslim world is equivocal. On the one hand, these technologies have given Muslim governments the ability to control access to, or to shape and censor, new ideas and trends. The Saudis, for example, have sought – not always successfully – to limit access to the Internet by restricting users and routing online connections to CompuServe Inc. in the United States via a local service, al-Wasit.[64] The Iranian government also tried to limit what it deemed the corrosive effects of international communication. Although this ban has subsequently not been enforced, in December 1994, the Majlis (National Assembly) prohibited the importation and use of satellite dishes.[65]

Robert O. Keohane and Joseph S. Nye point to a radically different way in which state power, while increasingly challenged by non-governmental actors, may actually increase: governments may certify their legitimacy by the free and open attitude towards information, thus endowing themselves with a kind of persuasive authority.[66] This approach works best in democracies, but various regimes in the Muslim world appear implicitly to accept that they must allow access to more and more informational sources. Middle Eastern societies, especially those in the Arab Gulf, are increasingly penetrated by digital technology, the Internet and mobile telephones, and structural changes have been introduced in the economy whereby state communication monopolies are contested by private sector competition.[67] In addition, businesses of all sorts increasingly require access to the Internet through such web sites as arab.net in order to survive in the informational economy.[68]

On the other hand, governments are rendered more vulnerable in the new information age. Their oppositions are increasingly able to penetrate the fortress of the national security or *mukhabarat* (intelligence service) state, reaching over, as it were, established borders and hierarchies. States no longer have information monopolies; civil society, aware and articulate, is capable of striking back.[69] Many of the main Islamist groups today, such as Hizbullah in Lebanon, Hamas in Palestine and even the Taliban in Afghanistan, have their own web sites and are thus able to spread their message, if not universally, then at least to computer-literate student, professional and intellectual élites.[70] One Saudi dissident notes the inherent advantages to be found in the elusive high technology and extra-territoriality of the Internet: 'The Saudi government can't undermine this. With the Internet, I can attack them from anywhere in the world. They aren't nervous. They are scared to death.'[71] The image of the backward-looking 'fundamentalist' – anachronistic and raging against the evils of modernity – is faulty for a number of reasons, but especially if it included the sense of technological ineptitude or wariness.

Governments – and societies – are also left exposed, perhaps, by the existence of a transnational class that owes its allegiance to its corporate masters. These 'symbolic analysts', as Robert Reich calls them,[72] endorse the values of privatization and the market economy and convey the cultural assumptions of an alluring, entertaining, successful West. If the French fear such an invasion, in part for commercial reasons, one can imagine the resentments in the Muslim world at what seem, to many, to be waves of materialistic, pornographic Westernization. But like the French again, Muslims may also object to the obvious unequal power relations between cultural brokers and consumers. Ali Mohammadi points out that, even though states like Iran may have easily acquired technological hardware, their cultural dependency is assured by the need to import software and the hope of gaining access to, or indeed control, satellite communications which are in the hands of corporate giants.[73]

That modern information technologies inevitably bring Muslims closer into contact with Western ideas and values is not in doubt. Contrary to the received wisdom on the subject, however, it does not necessarily follow that Islam will either cede ground to them or go to war against them. In the 1950s, Daniel Lerner said the choice for the future was stark: 'Mecca or mechanisation'.[74] In the 1980s, Regis Debray spoke of Muslims having to choose between 'the local ayatollah and Coca-Cola'.[75] From the early 1990s, Samuel Huntington has juxtaposed a modern West with a tribalistic, recalcitrant Rest which prominently includes Islam,[76] and Benjamin Barber has pitted 'Jihad' against 'McWorld'. To Barber, the forces of infotainment may well prove decisive: 'Over the long run, would you bet on Serbian nationalism or Paramount Pictures? Sheikh Omar Abdul Rahman or Shaquille O'Neal? Islam or Disneyland?'[77]

The force of this argument is obvious, but it may be premissed on a view of culture and religion as less pliant than they in fact are. The antagonism between consumerism and religion is one thing, but it may be misleading if one were to conclude from such a dichotomization that religions are unyielding and resistant to ideological evolution. Homogeneity is not the only consequence of the information revolution; nor are reactionary fundamentalisms or virulent subnationalisms the only, or even dominant, response. 'Virtual Islam' may seem to float in the ether and 'cyberMuslims' may sign on and off, but they are also helping to clarify, even reinterpret, Islamic teachings in the light of modern conditions and exigencies.

The terms of Muslim debate have, for example, subtly but inescapably shifted so that now a great many Muslims argue that Islam and democracy are compatible. Muslims who do not share this view find democracy an alien system at variance with a normative order based on divine, not popular, sovereignty and a complete, revealed law which makes a legislative body superfluous. But for an increasing number of Muslim intellectuals in societies as diverse as Egypt, Iran, Turkey and Indonesia, the debate is over how Islam is, or can be, democratic, not over whether it incorporates the values of pluralism, tolerance and civic participation.[78] The Muslim minorities of Europe, North

America and Australia, daily living with the demands of a participatory society, are especially important to this process of intellectual change. And the process is no doubt abetted by the close connections between societies of origin and Muslims in the West, the availability of relatively cheap publications, the wide reporting of the ideas of such influential thinkers as Abdolkarim Soroush[79] or Muhammad Shahrur[80] among others, and the ability to download recent speeches or writings from the Internet.

This creative process involved with the politics of identity cannot be divorced from the fragmentation of authority in the Muslim world discussed earlier. In a sense, this demonopolization has been going on for a long time and was first associated with the spread of literacy – and not only in Islam, as the Reformation, particularly in Germany, demonstrates. But now that more and more Muslims possess computer skills, now that the sacred texts have been digitized and are easily available on CDs, what does this do to the authority of the traditional *alim* who has excelled at what is no longer efficient – memorizing the texts and orally instructing the faithful?[81] New kinds of interpreters emerge, therefore, claiming a right to *ijtihad* (independent judgement) and possessing scriptural literacy.

Jon Anderson reminds us that the experience of diaspora is often critical to this fundamental challenge. Thousands of Muslims have been trained abroad and have acquired 'intellectual technologies' that encourage alternative ways of thinking and subversive viewpoints on the nature of Muslim society at the end of the twentieth century. Even – some might say, especially – scientists and engineers have found in their education a new-found confidence to question traditional religious authority. Once they return home, they bring not only their doubts and questions with them, but also the belief that access to modern communications is their right. They often advance and exchange their ideas via electronic mail, mailing lists and bulletin boards. Over time it is possible that they will become new 'creoles', who, like those Benedict Anderson identified in *Imagined Communities* as the progenitors of nationalism, will help to redefine the structure and leadership of normative community.[82]

These 'Young Islamic Turks' vie with each other and the *ulama* to pronounce on what Islam is and is not, but the traditional religious authorities are also able to use the technology to

preserve and defend their power and to advance their understandings of Islam. As Castells reminds us, it is characteristic of
the information age that, even as social relations are being
fundamentally transformed, old élites hope to use the 'power of
technology' to reaffirm the 'technology of power' and renew their
position of status and influence.[83] Some authorities, such as
Muhammad Mutawalli Sha'rawi in Egypt, Ramadan al-Buti in
Syria and Haj Hadi Awang in Malaysia have been particularly
successful, increasing their influence immensely via popular
television broadcasts and cassette recordings of their speeches.

While the end result is unpredictable, the communications
revolution may well encourage, even compel, an opening up of
debate within Muslim societies. The Internet's cacophony of
voices – one late 1998 review noted that there were 463,470 items
listed under the heading 'Islam' and 317,240 under the heading
'Muslim'[84] – suggests that ideas of all kinds are freely circulating.
In the process, a kind of structural, portentous pluralism appears
to be emerging. Multiple voices, facilitated and enhanced by the
new technologies, may be disharmonious and not necessarily lead,
finally or in an easy way, to the normative triumph of pluralism,
but the *de facto* diversity that they represent is not irrelevant to the
development of civil society in the Muslim world.[85]

Technology, to be sure, can be harnessed for morally
instructive purposes. An online *fatwa* service in the United States,
for example, allows individuals to request religious guidance on
issues ranging from dating to electoral responsibilities. Moreover,
the resources of the Internet provide an especially effective tool
for the 'call to Islam' (*da'wa*), the imperative to spread the faith
but also, in the present age, to see to it that nominal Muslims
become more devoted practitioners of Islam. Abd al-Qadir Tash,
referring approvingly to a Vatican missionary programme that
uses the Internet, has argued that Muslims must follow a similar
path: 'One could imagine the millions of people, in every corner
of the world, who have access to missionary information. All they
have to do is to press a few computer keys.'[86]

Yet cyberspace also seems remote, uncaring, dehumanizing –
the very antithesis of Islamic community. The ethic of responsibility in particular seems to be under attack in Muslim as well as
non-Muslim intellectual circles. J. G. A. Pocock lucidly pinpoints
one key problem:

> When a world of persons, actions, and things becomes a world of persons, actions, and linguistic or electronic constructs that have no authors, it clearly becomes easier for the things – grown much more powerful because they are no longer real – to multiply and take charge, controlling, and determining persons and actions that no longer control, determine, or even produce them.[87]

The virtual may seem to take on a life of its own and displace the real, and when the genealogy of information, as it were, is obscured or subverted, it becomes difficult to find who is accountable and should be judged. Moreover, given that electronic neighbourhoods and, to some extent, transnational professional networks are created in cyberspace, participants can evade any real responsibility for them, closing them down with the simple click of a mouse, disengaging without the courage of conviction.

The impact of information overload, of being bombarded with more than we want or perhaps need to know, may be seen by Muslims as morally perilous as well. As Munawar Ahmad Anees reminds us, information is not equivalent to knowledge and may, in any event, be colonized – that is, pretending to be a universal truth but encoded with the cultural biases of the West.[88] As some thus argue, the need to sort out what all the data mean and to discern what value these have for nurturing the soul of Muslim society becomes urgent.

Conclusion

So entrenched has the nation-state been in our political imagination that much of the discussion of transnationalism and now globalization has focused on its survival or demise. It is, in a way, a backhanded compliment to that towering institution that has been accepted as the core of international order since the mid-seventeenth century. It is not simply accidental that religion has seemed present but invisible, for it was the Peace of Westphalia (1648) which, in endorsing territorially based sovereignties, also presumed to move diplomacy to the safer ground of secular relationships. The religious dimension was never entirely missing, of course, and churches, missionaries and religious ideologies often played a complicating role. But it is clear that religious factors have generally been understated in analyses of the international or global order.[89]

The increasing interdependence of the world has brought profound challenges to the primacy of the territorial state, and religious transnational networks of missionaries, mystics and non-governmental actors, as well as diffuse processes of religious change, have contributed to the uncertainty. It is indisputable that the state is not about to disappear; one could even argue that, in a world of multiple actors and decentralized economic power, the state with its command of force and bureaucratic cohesion has had a renewed lease of life. Yet what is also apparent is that alternative communities of affiliation and identity have emerged and lie in uneasy coexistence with the state. These may be smaller (ethnic or subnational) or larger (religious), but they all have in common the articulation of shifting social and political aspirations, if not exactly allegiances. In the specific case of Islam, Sufi brotherhoods and the pan-Islamic *umma* have taken on concrete meanings, owing largely to the enhanced mobility of individuals and capital and the impact of the communications revolution. The state remains firmly rooted, therefore, but other forms of political community are imaginable and, to a certain extent, imagined.

Religion may thus assist in looking beyond the nation-state, but, as Halliday reminded us, there is another, administrative, sense in which the state is understood. Religious elements have helped to mount a challenge to existing authority in this domain as well. The matter of legitimate religious leadership and the form that governance of the community may take are pivotal, and adherents have begun to question old hierarchies and to offer themselves as fresh and alternative authorities who are able both to reinterpret scripture and to provide political guidance. There is little theoretical consensus on whether the information age is bearing egalitarian or inegalitarian fruits, or even whether it will ultimately be constitutive or destructive of trans-local solidarities. But at least on the evidence of contemporary Muslim societies, it is certain that clamorous voices and insistent new claims are being heard and recognized. Although it is premature to suggest that democratization will be the result, it is undeniable that, in substantial part because of religious-based linkages across territorial borders and the nature of religious change in societies, new civic bonds of trust and responsibility are promoted. These in turn are productive of 'social capital' that may, though not necessarily, be translated into more durable structures of civil society.[90]

One does not need to envision cyberspace as the high-tech equivalent of heaven[91] to appreciate that we have been dealing with rather high-flown concepts and what are tantamount to theological controversies in the social sciences. Optimists and pessimists are found on every critical issue: the impact of trans-national forces on equality, communal solidarity and identity, empowerment. There is no lack of defined positions in spite of what Martin Albrow refers to as the indeterminacy and ambiguity of key concepts.[92] It sometimes seems that everything is in flux and all is uncertain, and it may be precisely in such circum-stances of what is often obscurely called postmodernity that religion finds renewed application.

Religious factors, as we have seen, exercise an impact from both the top and bottom. States are challenged by the addition of a range of non-state actors to world politics, such as the Muslim World League or Sufi orders which serve to focus attention on issues of particular Islamic interest like the plight of the world's refugees, the overwhelming majority of whom are Muslim, or which provide alternative networks of support and affiliation. National governments are aware of the potential power of these actors and so at times seek to control them, as have the Saudis with regard to the League, and, at other times, to exploit them and other transnational elements in order to legitimize their own position. Saudi and Iranian support for Islamic movements and institutions around the world may well derive from a sincere commitment to the faith, but it is undeniable that the legitimacy of the guardian of the Holy Places (the Saudi monarchy) and of the vanguard of the Islamic Revolution (the cleric-dominated Iranian regime) is heightened by demonstration of influence and prestige beyond the national borders. As Chinese regimes have understood, transnational religious linkages have helped 'to defend their autonomy and to enhance their power'.[93]

Religious forces are also at work within states and societies. The domestic political equilibrium is often affected by the articulation of new demands and the formation of new political groups and constituencies. In Latin America, for instance, liberation theology has helped to mobilize the poor and underclasses to political activism, and in Muslim societies Islamist groups have confronted regimes with trans-class opposition to what are thought to be un-Islamic and harmful social, political and economic policies. International connections can help to make these challenges from 'below' more formidable; in the case of liberation theology, international Catholic circles have helped to support it, and in the case of Islamist groups links with other Islamist groups abroad, ironically even with state patrons, have provided important assistance. However, regimes may also exploit these external connections to their own advantage and portray their opponents as disloyal agents of outside enemies. In the struggle over political control and the right to speak for religious tradition itself, civil society becomes the field on which national–transnational interactions are played out, and, in the sense of *de facto* pluralism, perhaps their long-term beneficiary.[94]

Transnational religion, in one sense, is ideally suited to the information age. As missionaries have discovered, the new communication technologies facilitate the dissemination of their universalist message. At the same time, the ethical dimensions of religion may provide robust criticism of a communications industry that seems to propagate immoral or amoral values. The impact of these technologies may vary according to class or social position, however. The relatively poor and uneducated have access to often pirated videos and television programming, leaving them open, in the eyes of many religious leaders, to the seduction of a materialistic Western culture – even as they may also be open to broadcast religious propaganda. Yet the politicizing impact of the communications revolution may be most apparent among professional and largely well-to-do individuals who own or have access to computer modems, fax machines or mobile telephones. While it is possible that one destructive effect of exposure to the communications revolution is immorality or secularization, it is striking that for many of these consumers the technology has provided the means both to acquire their new-found devotion and to propagate their faith.

Plainly, contrasting trends are simultaneously at work, and it would be inapt to make definitive pronouncements. The state as an institution is under challenge, and yet it reasserts power;

religion is resurgent, but it contributes to a fragmentation of religious and political authority. To those inclined to see the end of the millennium as characterized by a new world disorder, virulent nationalisms and subnationalisms as well as religious radicalism seem unavoidable. But also conceivable is a more sanguine perspective which recognizes the possibility of sea change. In this vision, both the sense of belonging to a greater enterprise and the need to open up the religious and political order are growing more tangible.

Notes

I would like to acknowledge the intellectual stimulation that I received from the study group on Transnational Religious Regimes of the Committee on International Peace and Security of the US Social Science Research Council. I am grateful to all the participants, and particularly to the group chair, Susanne Hoeber Rudolph, for helping to encourage my thinking on this subject.

[1] Bernard Lewis, *The Political Language of Islam* (Chicago, University of Chicago Press, 1988), 32.

[2] James A. Field, Jr, 'Transnationalism and the new tribe', *International Organization*, 25, No. 3 (Summer 1971), 355.

[3] The most influential work was Joseph S. Nye, Jr. and Robert O. Keohane, *Transnational Relations and World Politics* (Cambridge, MA, Harvard University Press, 1972).

[4] See the important successor volume to *Transnational Relations*: Robert O. Keohane and Joseph S. Nye, *Power and Interdependence* (New York, HarperCollins, 1977).

[5] According to one writer, world politics was increasingly tantamount to 'a polyarchy in which nation-states, subnational groups, and transnational special interests and communities [are] all . . . vying for the support and loyalty of individuals, and conflicts [are] resolved primarily on the basis of ad hoc bargaining in a shifting context of power relationships'. Seyom Brown, *New Forces in World Politics* (Washington, DC, The Brookings Institution, 1974), 186. Karl Kaiser preferred to speak of 'multinational policies': 'Transnational politics: toward a theory of multinational politics', *International Organization*, 25, No. 4 (Autumn 1971), 790–817.

[6] See, for example, Immanuel Wallerstein, *The Modern World System* (New York and London, Academic Press, 1974).

[7] See, for example, Michael Featherstone (ed.), *Global Culture: Nationalism, Globalization and Modernity* (London, Sage, 1990).

[8] Roland Robertson, 'Globalisation or glocalisation', *Journal of International Communication*, 1 (1994), 35; Martin Albrow, *The Global Age* (Cambridge, Polity Press, 1996), 121.

[9] Richard Falk, *On Human Governance: Toward a New Global Politics* (Cambridge, Polity Press, 1995), 2.

[10] This is the view of the World Bank, which argues that '[p]erhaps the greatest feature of today's global economy is that no country is destined to be poor': *Claiming the Future: Choosing Prosperity in the Middle East and North Africa* (Washington, DC, The World Bank, 1995), 1.

[11] Arjun Appadurai, 'Disjuncture and difference in the global cultural economy', *Public Culture*, 2, No. 2 (Spring 1990), 3.

[12] David Mitrany is usually credited with inspiring the functionalist school of thought: *A Working Peace System: An Argument for the Functional Development of International Organization* (London, Royal Institute of International Affairs, 1943).

[13] Inis L. Claude, Jr., *Swords into Plowshares: The Problems and Prospects of International Organization* (New York, Random House, 3rd edn., 1964).

[14] Yoshikazu Sakamoto, 'Toward global identity', in Saul H. Mendlovitz (ed.), *On the Creation of a Just World Order: Preferred Worlds for the 1990s* (New York, The Free Press, 1975), 198–9.

[15] Kenneth W. Thompson, *Ethics, Functionalism, and Power in International Politics: The Crisis in Values* (Baton Rouge, LA, and London, Louisiana State University Press, 1979), 5.

[16] Samuel P. Huntington, 'Transnational organizations in world politics', *World Politics*, 25, No. 3 (April 1973), 366.

[17] R. O. Keohane and J. S. Nye, *Power and Interdependence*, 249. The 2nd edn. of this book was published in 1989.

[18] Fred Halliday, *Rethinking International Relations* (Basingstoke, Macmillan, 1994), 78–82, 106–7.

[19] Brown, *New Forces*, 186–7.

[20] See, for example, Paul Baran, *The Political Economy of Growth* (New York, The Monthly Review Press, 1957).

[21] Samir Amin, *Delinking: Towards a Polycentric World* (London, Zed Books, 1990), xii; see also 66.

[22] See, for example, Fred C. Bergsten, Ted Moran and Tom Horst, *American Multinationals and American Interests* (Washington, DC, The Brookings Institution, 1978).

[23] Peter B. Evans, 'Transnational linkages and the role of the state', in Peter B. Evans, Dietrich Rueschemeyer and Theda Skocpol (eds.), *Bringing the State Back In* (Cambridge, Cambridge University Press, 1988), 216.

[24] Susan Strange, *The Retreat of the State: The Diffusion of Power in the World Economy* (Cambridge, Cambridge University Press, 1995), 14, and, generally, see chaps. 1, 5 and 13.

[25] Ernest Gellner, *Nations and Nationalism* (Ithaca, NY, Cornell University Press, 1983), 55.

[26] See, for example, George Ritzer, *The McDonaldization of Society* (Thousand Oaks, CA, Pine Forge Press, 1993).

[27] Ulf Hannerz, 'Notes on the global ecumene', *Public Culture*, 1, No. 2 (Spring 1989), quotation at p. 70. See also chap. 7 of his *Cultural Complexity: Studies in the Social Organization of Meaning* (New York, Columbia University Press, 1992). Arjun Appadurai makes a useful additional point when he says that for those who ape Western cultural mores, 'the rest of their lives is not in complete synchrony with the referential world' which inspired the imitative practice: 'Disjunction and difference', 3.

[28] To give but two examples: Daniel Lerner, *The Passing of Traditional Society* (Glencoe, IL, The Free Press, 1958); and Manfred Halpern, *The Politics of Social Change in the Middle East and North Africa* (Princeton, NJ, Princeton University Press, 1963).

[29] David Brown, 'Ethnic revival: perspectives on state and society', *Third World Quarterly*, 11, No. 4 (October 1989), 9.

[30] Albert Bergesen, 'Turning world-system theory on its head', in Featherstone, *Global Culture*, 67–81.

[31] Amin, *Delinking*, 184.

[32] Robert Wuthnow, 'Understanding religion and politics', issue on religion and politics, *Daedalus*, 120, No. 3 (Summer 1991), 5–11.

[33] Jeff Haynes, *Religion in Global Politics* (London, Longman, 1998), 214–16.

[34] Gilles Kepel, *La Revanche de Dieu: Chrétiens, Juifs et Musulmans à la reconquête du monde* (Paris, Éditions du Seuil, 1991).

[35] Daniel H. Levine and David Stoll, 'Bridging the gap between empowerment and power in Latin America', in Susanne Hoeber Rudolph and James Piscatori (eds.), *Transnational Religion and Fading States* (Boulder, CO, Westview Press, 1997), 84, 88–9.

[36] Don Baker, 'World religions and national states: competing claims in East Asia', ibid., 144–72.

[37] For an attempt to distinguish between the 'language of politics' and the 'politics of language', see my 'The Rushdie affair: the politics of ambiguity', *International Affairs*, 66, No. 4 (Fall 1990), 769–79.

[38] Prince Sultan, the Saudi Minister of Defence, was reported as confirming Saudi assistance to Algerian Islamists in *al-Sharq al-Awsat* (26 March 1991), but this was vigorously denied by FIS leader Abbasi Madani. See M. Al-Ahnaf, Bernard Botiveau and Franck Fregosi,

L'Algérie par ses Islamistes (Paris, Éditions Karthala, 1991), 35–6. The Saudi opositional group, the Committee Against Corruption in Saudi Arabia (CACSA), believes that the Saudis financed FIS in order to undermine the Algerian socialist government and to disrupt Algerian oil supplies to Europe. See *www.saudhouse.com/fundamen.htm*

39 See, generally, 'Islam: Les Financiers de l'integrisme', *Le Nouvel Observateur* (19–24 July 1990), 4–11; Tim Weiner, 'Blowback from the Afghan battlefield', *New York Times Magazine* (13 March 1994), 52–5; also Barnett R. Rubin, 'Arab Islamists in Afghanistan', in John L. Esposito (ed.), *Political Islam: Revolution, Radicalism, or Reform?* (Boulder, CO, Lynne Rienner, 1997), 179–206.

40 Rachid Boudjedra, *FIS de la haine* (Paris, Éditions Denoël, 1992), 18, 40. His view of these teachers was clearly disapproving: they were 'butcher-instructors', and they had introduced to Algeria the 'green fascism' of radical Islam (green being the colour of Islam).

41 Levine and Stoll, 'Bridging the gap', 89.

42 Petra Weyland, 'International Muslim networks and Islam in Singapore', *Sojourn (Social Issues in Southeast Asia)*, 5, No. 2 (August 1990), 230–1.

43 Ousmane Kane, 'Muslim missionaries and African states' in Rudolph and Piscatori, *Transnational Religion*, 51–5, quotation at p. 59.

44 Appadurai, 'Disjuncture and difference'. He speaks of 'deterritorialization' on p. 11.

45 Amin, *Delinking*, 59; also see p. 52 for 'trans-class'.

46 This rivalry may even extend to periods of great crisis and suffering. The Saudis gave considerable aid, from King Fahd personally and from the Ibrahim bin Abd al-Aziz al-Ibrahim Foundation, for the relief of Bosnian Muslims. One, though perhaps not the primary, reason for this may have been to forestall Iranian inroads into the area. See *The New York Times* (23 August 1992), 16.

47 The term is suggested by David Scott's notion of the 'micropolitics of conversion': 'Conversion and demonism: colonial Christian discourse and religion in Sri Lanka', *Comparative Studies of Society and History*, 34, No. 2 (April 1992), 358.

48 *International Herald Tribune* (30 June 1992), 1, 13; and Jon B. Alterman, *New Media, New Politics? From Satellite Television to the Internet in the Arab World* (Policy paper, 48; Washington, DC, The Washington Institute for Near East Policy, 1998), chaps. 2 and 3.

49 Dale F. Eickelman and James Piscatori, *Muslim Politics* (Princeton, NJ, Princeton University Press, 1996), 37–45.

50 'Shra'it al-tatarruf 'ala al-rasif: jins wa fitna wa tahrid' [Extremist cassettes on the pavement: sex, rebellion and incitement], *al-Ishtiraki* (21 June 1992), 2–3.

[51] See, for example, Robert Launay, 'Pedigrees and paradigms: scholarly credentials among the Dyula of the Northern Ivory Coast', in Dale F. Eickelman and James Piscatori (eds.), *Muslim Travellers: Pilgrimage, Migration and the Religious Imagination* (London, Routledge, 1990), 181–8.

[52] Ousmane Kane, 'Some considerations on Sufi transnationalism in Africa with particular reference to the Niassene Tijaniyya', paper delivered at a workshop of the US Social Science Research Council on Transnational Religious Regimes, Chicago, 24–6 April 1992, 9.

[53] See generally Gilles Kepel and Yann Richard (eds.), *Intellectuels et militants* (Paris, Éditions de Seuil, 1991).

[54] See, for example, Marcelo Azvedo, *Basic Ecclesial Communities in Brazil* (Washington, DC, Georgetown University Press, 1987).

[55] See *Imam Khomeini's Last Will and Testament* (Washington, DC, Embassy of the Democratic and Popular Republic of Algeria, Interests Section of the Islamic Republic of Iran, n.d.). Although no date is given, it is thought that the will was written in its final form in 1983.

[56] Dale F. Eickelman, 'National identity and religious discourse in contemporary Oman', *International Journal of Islamic and Arabic Studies*, 6, No. 1, (1989), 1–20.

[57] For the relationship between distance and accelerated time, see Michael J. Shapiro, 'Sovereignty and exchange in the orders of modernity', *Alternatives*, 16 (1991), 470–1.

[58] Anthony Giddens, 'New world without end', first lecture of the 1999 Reith Lectures, *Observer* (11 April 1999), 31.

[59] See, for example, Falk, *On Human Governance*, 210.

[60] Robert O. Keohane and Joseph S. Nye, Jr., 'Power and interdependence in the information age', *Foreign Affairs*, 77, No. 5 (September/October 1998), 87. Soft power is 'the ability to get desired outcomes because others want what you want. It is the ability to achieve goals through attraction rather than coercion' (p. 86).

[61] Zygmunt Bauman, *Globalization: The Human Consequences* (Cambridge, Polity Press, 1998), 3.

[62] Manuel Castells, *The Information Age: Economy, Society and Culture*, vol. 1, *The Rise of the Network Society* (Oxford, Blackwell, 1996), chap. 2.

[63] Ignacio Ramonet, 'Besoin d'utopie', *Le Monde diplomatique* (May 1998), 9.

[64] 'An intruder in the kingdom', *Business Week* (21 August 1995), 40. One way that Saudis have got around governmental interference is by using expensive long-distance telephone links.

[65] Ali Mohammadi, 'Communication and the globalization process in the developing world' in Ali Mohammadi (ed.), *International*

Communication and Globalization (London, Sage Publications, 1997), 88.

[66] Keohane and Nye, 'Power and interdependence in the information age', 81–94.

[67] 'Region joins the global revolution', *Middle East Economic Digest* (1 March 1996), 5–12.

[68] The American telecommunications firm Sprint has helped companies in Tunisia, Bahrain, Morocco and the United Arab Emirates, among others, to connect to the Internet: Kirk Albrecht, 'The high-tech highway', *Middle East Insight* (March/April 1996), 48.

[69] The phrase, 'civil society strikes back', is Emanuel Sivan's: 'The Islamic resurgence: civil society strikes back', *Journal of Contemporary History*, 25 (1990), 353–64.

[70] Hizbullah's site can be found at: *www.moqawama.org*; Hamas's site can be found at: *www.palestine-info.org/hamas/rightframe.html*; and the Taliban's site can be found at: *www.ummah.net/taliban/*

[71] Cited in Michael Georgy, 'Internet fever sweeps conservative Persian Gulf', *Reuters, Limited* (5 April 1996).

[72] Robert Reich, *The Work of Nations: Preparing Ourselves for 21st Century Capitalism* (London, Simon & Schuster, 1993), 177–80.

[73] Mohammadi, 'Communication', 84. It should be noted, however, that although Oracle, Lotus and especially Microsoft still dominate the market, there are increasing numbers of local software development companies in the Middle East. For example, in 1996, Cairo had more than 200 software firms which employed more than 2,000 programmers. In banks and other businesses, another 2,000 programmers could be found: Albrecht, 'High-tech highway', 47.

[74] Lerner, *Passing of Traditional Society*, 405.

[75] Cited in *The New York Times* (2 January 1994), H1.

[76] Samuel P. Huntington, 'The clash of civilizations?', *Foreign Affairs*, 72, No. 3 (Summer 1993), 39.

[77] Benjamin R. Barber, *Jihad vs. McWorld* (New York, Times Books/Random House, 1995), 83. Barber uses *jihad* as a 'metaphor for anti-Western antiuniversalist struggle' throughout the book (p. 207). Abdul Rahman was found guilty in an American court in 1995 for complicity in the bombing of the World Trade Center in New York in 1993. Shaquille O'Neal is an American basketball star and rap artist.

[78] For a useful overview of various views on democracy, see Gudrun Kramer, 'Islamist notions of democracy', in Joel Beinin and Joe Stork (eds.), *Political Islam: Essays from Middle East Report* (London, I. B. Tauris, 1997), 71–82.

[79] For an excellent review of Soroush's thought, see Valla Vakili, *Debating*

Religion and Politics in Iran: The Political Thought of Abdolkarim Soroush (Occasional Paper Series No. 2 of Studies Department; New York, Council on Foreign Relations, 1996).

80 In various writings, Shahrur has said that if Muslims return to *al-tanzil*, the original text of revelation, they will avoid the misunderstandings which have invested merely human interpretations of an earlier period with sacral status and which have led to religious and social stultification. See especially his *al-Kitab wa'l-Qur'an: Qira'a Mu'asira* (Beirut, Sharikat al-Matbu'at li'l-Tawzi' wa'l-Nashr, 3rd edn., 1993).

81 See Ziauddin Sardar's suggestive article: 'Paper, printing and compact disks: the making and unmaking of Islamic culture', *Media, Culture and Society*, 15 (1993), 43–59.

82 Jon W. Anderson, ' "Cybarites", knowledge workers and new creoles on the information superhighway', *Anthropology Today*, 11, No. 4 (August 1995), 13–15.

83 Castells, *Information Age*, 52.

84 Bahman Baktiari, 'Cybermuslim and the Internet: searching for spiritual harmony in a digital world', paper presented at the International Conference on Muslim Identity in the 21st Century: Challenges of Modernity, London, 31 October–1 November 1998, 1.

85 For the reminder that fragmentation of authority may lead to radicalization rather than accommodation or greater pluralism, see Eickelman and Piscatori, *Muslim Politics*, 131–5.

86 Tash's commentary from *Arab News* was reproduced in *Moneyclips* [Middle East Newsfile Information Service] (25 December 1995).

87 J. G. A. Pocock, 'The ideal of citizenship since classical times', *Queen's Quarterly* (Spring 1992), 55.

88 Munawar Ahmad Anees, 'Epistemology in the robotic culture: the Muslim predicament', in Ziauddin Sardar (ed.), *An Early Crescent: The Future of Knowledge and the Environment in Islam* (London, Mansell, 1989), 92–124.

89 There have been exceptions: Douglas Johnston and Cynthia Sampson (eds.), *Religion, the Missing Dimension of Statecraft* (New York, Oxford University Press, 1994); Peter Beyer, *Religion and Globalization* (London: Sage, 1994); and Rudolph and Piscatori, *Transnational Religion*.

90 See the important analysis of Levine and Stoll, 'Bridging the gap', 73–8. Social capital refers to 'a constellation of orientations, social skills, and cooperative experiences that alter the basic landscape of politics by creating and encouraging the spread of trust as a social value' (p. 65).

91 For Margaret Wertheim's 'analogy between cyberspace and the Christian conception of heaven', see her: 'The pearly gates of

cyberspace' in Nan Elin (ed.), *Architecture of Fear* (New York, Princeton Architectural Press, 1997), cited in Bauman, *Globalization*, 19.

[92] Albrow, *Global Age*, 90–3, for example.

[93] Baker, 'World religions', 145.

[94] It should also be noted that the promotion of *transnational* civil society, or indeed, global civil society, is also possible, but its discussion requires fuller treatment than this chapter allows. For informed analysis on the subject, see M. J. Peterson, 'Transnational activity, international society and world politics', *Millennium: Journal of International Studies*, 21, No. 3 (Winter 1992), 371–88; Ronnie D. Lipschutz, 'Reconstructing world politics: the emergence of global civil society', *Millennium: Journal of International Studies*, 21, No. 3 (Winter 1992), 389–420; and Susanne Hoeber Rudolph, 'Introduction: religion, states, and transnational civil society', in Rudolph and Piscatori, *Transnational Religion*, esp, pp. 9–11.

4

Catholicism and international relations: papal interventionism

MICHAEL WALSH

Christians make up just about a third of the world's population. Of that third, Catholics owing allegiance to the papacy account for well over half. As a proportion of the world's population, the number of Roman Catholics may be declining, but at well over a billion members, Pope John Paul II's Church still makes up just short of 20 per cent of it. It is, therefore, odd to talk of the 'globalization' of Catholicism. It has long been a global phenomenon, though the global effectiveness of the papacy itself is of a much more recent date.

John Paul II, however, has exploited the global pretensions of his office in a way no other pope has attempted, or been able, to do. He has been indefatigable in criss-crossing the world. His visits are always called 'pastoral', and are generally made, in theory at least, to the Roman Catholic hierarchy in a particular country. But that they have had political implications cannot be denied – massive implications at least in the case of the pope's homeland of Poland. There as elsewhere he has preached a doctrine of social justice and of human rights which has made him a hero round the world to many struggling for greater liberty.

When, on 11 January 1999, John Paul II gave the customary papal New Year's address to the diplomatic representatives accredited to the Holy See, there were 169[1] nations represented. Just over twenty years before, at the beginning of 1978 and the last year of the reign of his predecessor, Pope Paul VI,[2] there had been ninety-four nations with diplomatic links with the Holy See, though several of these nations, especially those of the Communist bloc, had left their delegations empty. It is a sign of the current prestige of the papacy that so many nations have wanted to establish, or to restore, diplomatic links.

Most of the recent biographies of Pope John Paul II have been loud in their praise of the global role which he has, apparently, so enthusiastically embraced. But not all Roman Catholics are quite so laudatory.[3] Nor are all Catholics at ease with the role of papal diplomats, which they consider ill-suited to an organization dedicated to spiritual purposes. Papal diplomacy is, however, unlikely to go away: it has a very long history.

Historical background: the foundations of the papacy's role

The first time there is systematic mention of estates 'ruled' by the bishop of Rome is during the reign of Pope Gregory I (590–604). It is to these estates, whose existence entailed the need for a 'temporal', in addition to a spiritual, sovereignty, that papal diplomacy owes its origins. Whatever its spiritual role, from Gregory's time down to 1870 and the fall of Rome to the Italian army during the pontificate of Pius IX, popes had territorial responsibilities and interests, and sometimes, especially during the pontificate of Alexander VI at the end of the fifteenth century, even dynastic ambitions, which necessitated the use of diplomacy.[4]

Much papal diplomacy during the Middle Ages and the Renaissance reflected the need to preserve the territorial integrity of the papal states, and hence papal wealth, and at least to some extent thereby to ensure that relatives of popes benefited from his tenure of office. But papal claims rest ultimately upon the papacy's spiritual authority, and from the Renaissance onwards, with the rise of the nation-states, popes became concerned to placate the European rulers who were only too eager to repatriate, as one might say, ecclesiastical authority from Rome back to their own national bishops whom the rulers could to some considerable degree control.

Papal vicissitudes during the Napoleonic War focused attention on the papal office, and in 1815 Pius VII was invited to send representatives to the Congress of Vienna. This turned out to be a significant date, for it was the last time that the pope was formally represented at an international conference of sovereign states as of right until the 1973 Helsinki conference on security and co-operation in Europe. (It is not surprising, therefore, if the CSCE – now the Organization for Security and Co-operation in Europe – has loomed large in the consciousness of the papal diplomatic service,[5] also with its ongoing scope for a significant role in the field of human rights.) The Congress of Vienna revived the papal states which Napoleon had all but dismembered. Successive popes in the first half of the nineteenth century struggled to stem the rising tide of liberalism and anticlericalism, but in the second quarter of the century the states once again fell apart. Papal diplomacy, therefore, became increasingly preoccupied with what was called 'the Roman Question', the status of Rome itself, while all but a handful of states withdrew their diplomats from the Vatican as it lost its territorial authority, the United States withdrawing its diplomatic links in 1867 and the United Kingdom in 1874.

Papal diplomatic fortunes revived under Benedict XV, who became pope just as the First World War broke out. His 'Peace Points' of 1917 were generally reviled by both sides in the conflict, but none the less made a considerable impact, and particularly upon President Woodrow Wilson who used them as the basis for his own peace proposals.[6] But there were a number of other aspects to papal policy in the aftermath of the war which had considerable repercussions on its diplomatic activity, even though only a handful of Catholic states maintained formal relations with the Vatican. For example, one outcome of the Catholic Church's intense missionary effort during the nineteenth century was the beginnings of an indigenous clergy, and even of an indigenous hierarchy, in some countries still under colonial rule, a policy which was to have important long-term consequences for the dependent territories, and with which the colonial powers themselves were uncomfortable. The number of Catholics subject to the British Crown was certainly one element in the decision to establish unilateral relations with the Vatican at the rank of minister in 1917. There was no reciprocal act on the part of the Vatican until Archbishop William Godfrey was appointed apostolic delegate – which is not quite the same thing as a diplomat, a point to which I shall shortly return – in November 1938.[7]

One reason for the increased diplomatic activity of the Vatican after the First World War was the conviction that the Versailles

Treaty, from which the papacy had been excluded, was unworkable and, particularly over the issue of reparations, unjust. Among the reasons why the Vatican was unhappy with Versailles was the redrawing of national frontiers. It was in the interest of states to have ecclesiastical boundaries that coincided with political ones, but this was something which the Vatican was not always prepared to concede, and which it could attempt to use to bring pressure on a reluctant government to enter a concordat. The Saarland, for example, was not detached from German ecclesiastical jurisdiction, even though it was territorially handed over to France. France might have gained control had its government been prepared to do a deal with the Vatican, but this it steadfastly failed to do. In any case, the Vatican was concerned to protect the fragile Weimar Republic in which the Catholic Centre Party was playing a significant role. Not wishing to seem overly anti-French, however, Benedict XV canonized Joan of Arc – not the first nor the last time when canonization has been an instrument of papal diplomacy.

The impression may have been given so far that the diplomatic activity of the papacy is a continuation of the diplomatic activity of the pope as sovereign of the papal states. Frankly it is difficult to believe that, without the papal states, the papacy would have developed the way that it has, and it would be unrealistic to think that the practice of sending diplomatic representatives does not descend from the territorial basis of papal power. For many centuries the pope, whatever may have been his other claims, was a prince among other princes. That, however, is not the way in which papal diplomats would now wish to defend their role.

The system of papal intervention

Theorists will distinguish two quite different sovereignties in the papacy. One is a temporal sovereignty, once exercised over extensive states in what is now Italy – and, to some degree in France – while the other is a spiritual sovereignty over members of the Roman Catholic Church. The right to send and receive diplomats is one of the marks of sovereignty: only properly constituted, and recognized, states may do so. Yet, as has been seen, when the pope had no formal territorial sovereignty in 1917, even the Protestant United Kingdom thought it appropriate to establish diplomatic links, albeit at less than ambassadorial level. These theoreticians, of whom the late Archbishop Hyginus Cardinale is perhaps the best known in Britain if for no other reason than he was apostolic delegate based in London from 1963 to 1969, will therefore argue that the sovereignty which is being recognized in the exchange of diplomatic relations is not the temporal but the spiritual one. In other words, the juridical entity with which relations are established is not the Vatican City State, of which the pope is temporal sovereign, but with the Holy See, of which the pope is spiritual sovereign. The Holy See is a sovereignty with no particular territorial base, though in practice it is exercised from the Vatican City, established in 1929 by the Lateran pacts. As Cardinale points out, the fact that the pope could, in the person of his secretary of state, sign the Lateran Treaty at all implies that the sovereign kingdom of Italy already recognized the sovereignty of the papacy.[8]

The Holy See, the 'Santa Sede', is the juridical entity to which diplomatic representatives are accredited, rather as, in Britain, they are accredited to the Court of St James. The Holy See is the governing body of the Roman Catholic Church, over which the pope is the monarch: 'The Holy See is to the Church what the government is to the State, with the difference that the monarchical constitution of the Church, being of divine origin, is not subject to change', says Cardinale.[9] That, of course, is the view of a Vatican diplomat, and it does not altogether accord with what the bishops of the Catholic Church might think, especially after the deliberations of the Second Vatican Council, which took place between December 1961 and December 1965. I shall return to that in a moment. For the present I just want to recapitulate the sometimes confusing terminology which is used when speaking of papal diplomacy.

First of all, then, one has to discount the Vatican City State. This entity, which came into being in 1929 and is the smallest independent state in the world (only a third the size of the next smallest, Monaco), exists only to provide a territorial base for the Holy See. The Holy See, the central government of the Roman Catholic Church, is made up of the pope and his 'curia', a word which literally means 'court', but in this instance is used to denote the various offices which constitute this government. It is the Holy See, with the pope at its head, which is the formal agent in sending and receiving diplomatic representation. Just to confuse matters further, however, it is a common practice, even among Catholics, to refer to the Holy See as 'the Vatican'. People will talk about papal diplomacy or Vatican diplomacy, rather than 'the diplomatic policy of the Holy See', though this would be the somewhat heavy-handed, but strictly correct, term to use.

At this point it is not unreasonable to ask what one means specifically by 'the Vatican'. There are, it is perhaps worth noting, a number of books which attempt with varying degrees of success to explain this rather arcane structure.[10] They provide the reader with a good sense of who does what to whom, and why. However, the structure of the papal foreign ministry was altered from the situation described in all but the most recent books by an Apostolic Constitution, *Pastor Bonus*, of 28 June 1988. The pope reorganized his curia so that what had been a separate department of 'The public affairs of the Church' in charge of diplomats was entirely incorporated into the Secretariat of State. This in turn was divided into two, those of 'General Affairs' and of 'Relations with States'. It is this latter department which now has responsibility for the Vatican's diplomatic service as well as for its presence as observers, or whatever other status may be appropriate, at international organizations such as the United Nations, the International Labour Office and so on, and for the formation of what might be called the Vatican's foreign policy. Also under the Cardinal Secretary of State is the Pontifical Ecclesiastical Academy, better known as the 'Pontifical Academy of Noble Ecclesiastics', founded in 1701, which trains young ecclesiastics in the intricacies of diplomacy.

There are several types of Vatican representative, as there are diplomats of other sovereign states. At the head of the list are 'nuncios' or, more correctly, apostolic nuncios. They have the rank of ambassadors, as do apostolic pro-nuncios. The difference between the two ranks is technical. According to article IV of the 1815 Regulation of Vienna, precedence is given to the ambassador in order of date of appointment. However, where there is a papal representative present he takes precedence, the argument being that he represents a spiritual authority rather than a temporal one, and the spiritual has precedence over the temporal. This would mean that, in normal circumstance, the papal representative would be, *ex officio*, dean of the diplomatic corps in the country to which he is accredited. This is not always acceptable to the host government, hence (as in Britain) a pro-nuncio is appointed, who does not take automatic precedence. The term pro-nuncio was originally used of nuncios who had been appointed cardinals, but were awaiting their call back to Rome. It was therefore a temporary title and, according to Mario Oliveri who was appointed counsellor to the Vatican's London representative in the late 1970s, the term pro-nuncio 'continues to indicate that this is considered a temporary situation, at least by the Holy See, in the hope of being able to appoint a Nuncio, to whom recognition of the right of precedence will be given'.[11] Archbishop Luigi Barbarito, appointed pro-nuncio to Britain in 1986, became nuncio in January 1994. In addition to nuncios and pro-nuncios there are, sometimes, internuncios, the equivalent of envoys for particular purposes.

These ranks, as I have said, are all accredited to governments. There is in addition another rank, and one which raises the question of the need for any papal diplomats. When William Godfrey came to London as papal representative in 1938, he came with the title of apostolic delegate. His accreditation was not to Whitehall, but to the Bishops' Conference of England and Wales – which in fact did not want him.[12] The rank was raised to that of pro-nuncio shortly before Pope John Paul II's visit to England in 1982. The reason why apostolic delegates are unpopular is that local hierarchies see them as an intrusion into their own authority. During the second session of the Vatican Council, as Oliveri remarks,[13] criticism of the role of these papal representatives was voiced in the debates because they, or rather their position, cut across the developing ecclesiology, or theory of the Church. According to Vatican II, the whole of the episcopate around the world, the 'college' of bishops, shares with the pope responsibility for the whole Church. In the eyes of very many commentators, the present pope's views, despite the vigorous citing of the Council in which he indulges, also cuts across the ecclesiology sanctioned by Vatican II. It should be no surprise, therefore, that the number of papal diplomatic representatives has rocketed.

In the canon law of the Church the role of papal legates, to use the term employed formally to cover all ranks, is first of all (canon 364) 'to make more firm and effective the bonds of unity which exist between the Holy See and the particular churches'. Among the tasks which are specified are reporting to Rome on the situations in which the local churches find themselves, and both proposing names to Rome for vacant bishoprics, and undertaking enquiries into the lives and characters of those suggested for promotion. There is no clear reason why these tasks should not be undertaken by the bishops' conference in any particular country, and despite the politeness which necessarily exists between papal legates and local bishops, one cannot help thinking that their role is resented. This is especially true with respect to subparagraph 7 of canon 364, 'to work with the Bishops to safeguard, as far as the rulers of the State are concerned, those things which relate to the mission of the Church and of the Apostolic See'. Local bishops may very well feel – though not always, perhaps, rightly so – that they are in a better position to deal with their own governments than are papal legates, whether those in permanent posts as in Britain where Cardinal Hinsley was certainly disturbed by the arrival of Archbishop Godfrey in 1938, or as envoys sent to negotiate with hostile governments, as happened frequently in the course of the Ostpolitik inaugurated, one could perhaps say, by John XXIII when he received the son-in-law of Nikita Khrushchev in 1963.[14] There are plenty of examples of this. In the days when I was going fairly regularly to Poland, the early 1970s, I was frequently told that Rome was sending special envoys to negotiate with the government which was hoping for the establishment of diplomatic relations so as to bypass the anti-Communist intransigence of the Polish primate, Cardinal Stefan Wyszynski – unlike, it would be added, the more politically aware cardinal archbishop of Cracow, Cardinal Karol Wojtyla (the future Pope John Paul II).

Of course, just as the British government may be represented by officials from different ministries and not just the Foreign Office in particular situations, so too is the Holy See. At disarmament conferences, for example, or conferences on Third World debt, or that on cities, the Vatican may well be represented by someone from the Pontifical Council for Justice and Peace. Its under-secretary is a Dublin-born priest, Mgr Diarmuid Martin. In the course of a programme I made some time ago for the BBC,[15] I asked Mgr Martin how much influence he thought the

Vatican could bring to bear on issues facing the international community. His reply, to paraphrase it, was not a lot, but we have to keep on trying.

One has to remember, however, that influence may be indirect. One of the founding members of the Pontifical Commission for Justice and Peace was the English economist Barbara Ward, Lady Jackson, and she was a considerable influence directly upon the policies of the World Bank under Robert McNamara, and on two American presidents, one of whom she very much liked – Lyndon Johnson – and one of whom she cordially disliked, John Kennedy. She was also an indirect influence on world affairs through her writings for *The Economist* and work for the UN and other agencies.

One of the leading members of the Pontifical Commission for Justice and Peace today is Mgr Michael Sabbah, the Latin-Rite Patriarch of Jerusalem, and the first Arab to be appointed to that office, which brings me to what might be termed a case-study in Vatican diplomacy and, from the Vatican's point of view, one of the most problematic: the Middle East.

Case-study 1: the Middle East

The issue, clearly, is the status of the Holy Places, and has been ever since the Muslim conquest in the seventh century. In the Middle Ages the answer had been the crusades, but by the nineteenth century the Church, though still regretting the loss of the Holy Land, had come to an understanding with the Ottoman empire, upon which it could have a considerable influence either directly or through the Catholic states of Europe. Some 10 per cent of Arabs are not Muslims but Christians in communion with Rome – one hesitates to say they are Catholics because though some, like Michael Sabbah, belong to the Latin Rites, others belong to ancient churches with their own liturgies and spiritualities. Part of the significance attached to the Vatican by Jewish leaders arose because the Christians were among the best educated and influential Arabs in Palestine. It is, perhaps, worth dwelling on papal diplomacy in relation to the state of Israel because, whereas much papal activity has perforce to be confined to moral exhortation, in particular situations such as this the papacy can act rather more directly.

In January 1904 Theodor Herzl called on Pope Pius X. There was at that time no mention of the situation of the Arabs in Palestine, but there was a feeling, expressed by the then alarmingly anti-Semitic Jesuit fortnightly *Civiltà Cattolica* – whose views then, as now, reflected those of the secretariat of state whenever political issues were discussed – that the Vatican considered the Holy Places to be safer in the hands of Muslims than, as *Civiltà* put it, 'in the custody of the synagogue'. The day after British troops occupied Jerusalem, the cardinal secretary of state told a French diplomat that the Turks were 'the most equitable guardians of the Holy Places'. That was in 1917. Thirty years later Mgr Montini, the future Paul VI, was telling the British minister that the Vatican wanted a third power, neither Jewish nor Arab, to control the Holy Land. By this time the Vatican had taken up the economic and social problems experienced by Christian Arabs, and could not leave out their Islamic neighbours. But it did not support their political aspirations any more than it supported those of the Jews, in the case of the former because it feared that any Muslim government in Palestine would be less tolerant than the much more secularized Turks had been. In the struggles to found the state of Israel, the Vatican found itself coming to the rescue of Christian Arabs displaced from their homes, some three-quarters of the original Christian Arab population of Palestine. Once again, it was not in practice possible to discriminate between Christians and Muslims: hence the Vatican, which had stayed neutral on the Israeli struggle for independence, now seemed to be siding with the Arabs. The Holy See withheld formal recognition of the state of Israel, despite the fact that an Israeli delegation attended the coronation of Pope John XXIII, and that, during a trip to Israel in January 1964, Pope Paul VI met the Israeli president. That meeting, however, was instructive. The pope never addressed the president as 'President', not even in the telegram of thanks which Paul sent after his return to Rome. The Israeli president lives in Jerusalem: the telegram was addressed to Tel Aviv so that the Vatican would not be seen to be recognizing even implicitly the Israeli claim to Jerusalem as its capital city: it was the Vatican's policy that Jerusalem should be an open city, under international control.

The Israelis kept up pressure on the Holy See. Audiences with Paul VI were granted to Abba Eban in October 1969, and to Mrs Golda Meir in January 1973. That of Mrs Meir was particularly controversial because immediately after the meeting the Vatican spokesman pointed out to journalists that the pope had already received a number of Arab leaders, including King Hussein, that it was Mrs Meir who had requested the audience and it was she who had asked the pope to help the weakest people of the region, in particular the Arab refugees. This apparent playing down by the Holy See of the significance of Meir's visit caused much irritation in Israel. The Israeli prime minister herself commented that Pope Paul had thanked her for Israel's care for the Holy Places.

It should perhaps be said in defence of the Vatican that the chief concern of the Holy See in modern times has been with social and economic rights, rather than with political ones. It has had, moreover, and especially since the 1967 encyclical *Populorum Progressio* and the constitution *Gaudium et Spes* of the Second Vatican Council, a particular concern for people in the developing world – into which category the Palestinian refugees certainly fall, as do very many, if not most, Roman Catholics. Even when, in an address to the College of Cardinals in December 1975, Pope Paul gave implicit recognition to the claims of Jews to the Holy Land, he still spoke more about the Palestinians:

> Although we are conscious of the still very recent tragedies which led the Jewish people to search for safe protection in a state of its own, sovereign and independent [this was the first time a pope had said such a thing], and in fact precisely because we are aware of this, we would like to ask the sons of this people to recognize the rights and aspirations of another people, which have also suffered for a long time, the Palestinian people.

The present pope's policy has been similar, though it might well have been quite otherwise. One of Karol Wojtyla's closest friends as a boy in Wadowice – and indeed, now quite by accident also in Rome – was a Jew. Wojtyla does not appear in any way to have shared the anti-Semitism which was at one time so much a feature of Polish life. When first elected to the papacy John Paul II thought it would be a splendid gesture to fly to Bethlehem for Christmas: the secretariat of state had to persuade him this was rather more complicated than he had imagined. His earliest remarks on the Middle East situation do not dwell, as had Pope Paul's, on the Palestinian issue. He met prominent Jews from around the world, and the Israeli Ministry of Foreign Affairs was moved to comment in April 1979 that, as a result of these encounters, contact with the Vatican would be more frequent. Shortly afterwards a meeting with the Christian Arab mayor of Bethlehem was cancelled, giving offence to Palestinians. The annexation of Jerusalem by Israel on 30 July 1980 radically altered the Vatican's position as it was being expressed by the pope. John Paul began to speak more forcefully about the rights of the Palestinians. In 1981 and again in 1982 a Palestine Liberation Organization (PLO) leader was received at the Vatican, though not personally by the pope. A scheduled visit by the then foreign minister of Israel, Itzhak Shamir, in February 1981, was put off for a whole year. The Israeli invasion of Lebanon pretty well destroyed the sympathy for Israel which John Paul had brought to the papacy.

Lebanon was a particular problem for Vatican diplomacy. It has a large and powerful Maronite Christian community which had for long lived in relative harmony, both politically and socially, with the Muslim community. The Vatican wanted to maintain that harmony, not only for the sake of Lebanon but also as an example of Christian–Muslim relations throughout the Middle East and in North Africa. It therefore wanted to re-establish harmony in Lebanon and did not want what many of the Maronite leaders wanted, a federation of mini-states based on religious faith. A further problem was that the Maronites were unhappy with having Palestinian refugees in their midst, even if some of them were Christian. The Vatican's support for the Palestinians was therefore not welcome among Lebanese Christians. Successive visits by high-ranking members of the secretariat of state, including the late Cardinal Casaroli himself, tried to prevent the Christian militias from siding with the Israelis after the 1982 occupation of southern Lebanon. The Maronite patriarch tried to cool Christian militancy, and as a consequence was attacked in his own home by supporters of General Awn, and forced to kiss the general's photograph.

This last event occurred in 1989. I have been rather telescoping events, but it is against this general background that the Vatican's decision to receive Yasser Arafat in September 1982 has to be set. Arafat's visit was brief, only twenty minutes, and in the official communiqué the PLO was not even mentioned. But Israel was furious:

The Church, which did not say a word about the massacre of the Jews for six years in Europe, and has little to say regarding the killing of Christians in Lebanon for seven years, is now prepared to meet the man who has perpetrated the killings in Lebanon, and who seeks the destruction of Israel in order to complete the work carried out by the Nazis in Germany.

That was Menahem Begin, the Israeli prime minister. The United States was also alarmed, but Western European governments were sympathetic, and the Vatican's standing among Arab governments was considerably enhanced.

Of all the signs in the Vatican's changing attitude to Israel, none was more dramatic than the visit John Paul paid to the Rome synagogue in April 1986. 'With Judaism', he said, 'we have a relationship which we do not have with any other religion. You are our dearly beloved brothers and, in a certain way, it could be said that you are our elder brothers.' He did not, on the other hand, make mention of the 'silences' of Pius XII on the Nazi persecution of the Jews, preferring to dwell on the assistance given by Catholics, even within the Vatican, to Jews during the war.

The signing of the peace accord between the Palestinians and the state of Israel finally changed the attitude of the Vatican, and though it is still concerned with the situation of the Holy Places in general, and Jerusalem in particular, the Holy See has established diplomatic relations with Israel. But one Israeli commentator, admittedly writing just before the 'fundamental agreement' was signed on 30 December 1993, remarks,

The Arabs are perceived as part of the Third World, thus meriting support; Israel in contrast, is considered a satellite of the United States, which should be condemned, or at least kept at a certain distance. Moreover, Pope John Paul II is on record for his friendly policy towards Islam . . . While Islam is daily winning new holds in black Africa, the Catholic Church resigns itself to this fact without any display of will to fight back. Although Islam may attract millions of Christian believers, the Church has no major theological dispute with it. In contrast, contentions with Judaism, which has no interest in converting Christians, abound in many areas.[16]

The same commentator[17] draws attention to a further, outstanding, issue, that of Europe. Israel is very eager to join what he calls 'the European economic space'. If Europe is to be identified as Christian, that presents yet another point of tension for Israel (as for Turkey).

Case-study 2: Europe

Despite the pope's frequent trips around the world, despite the presence of the Holy See at many international conferences and its diplomatic representation in most of the world's capital cities, the overwhelming impression of the present pontificate is one of concentration upon the notion of Europe, and its reunification around a common faith: Christianity. 'If Europe's historical memory does not dig deeper than the ideas of the Enlightenment', Pope John Paul said in Prague, 'its new unity will be based upon superficial and unstable foundations.' Christianity 'is the very root of European culture. The drive towards Europe's new unity cannot but take that into account.'[18]

Without doubt this reflects John Paul's personal concern to encourage the reintegration of the former Soviet bloc countries, particularly Poland, with Western Europe. Very early on in his pontificate he had declared Saints Cyril and Methodius, the ninth-century missionary brothers who proselytized the Slavs, to be patron saints of Europe alongside St Benedict, to symbolize the unity of the then Communist-dominated Eastern Europe with the West. His Europe, as he told UNESCO,[19] stretched from the Atlantic to the Urals, not a concept with which the then USSR could feel at all comfortable. It has, however, been a major concern of the present pontificate, perhaps to the detriment of concern for global issues, papal globe-trotting notwithstanding. It is worth noting that the Holy See has been represented at the United Nations from 1964 only by permanent observers;[20] at the European Union it has been represented at ambassadorial level since 1970.[21]

At its foundation Pius XII regarded the United Nations with suspicion, with memories perhaps of problems with its predecessor, the League of Nations, in the 1930s when the Pius had been cardinal secretary of state. Certainly the UN Declaration on Human Rights was not greeted with the enthusiasm with which it has since been endorsed by Pope Paul VI and, more especially, by John Paul II. Article 18 of the

Declaration speaks of liberty of thought, of conscience and of religion. John Paul II regularly appeals for liberty of religion (one commentator has remarked he commonly omits liberty of thought[22]) throughout the world. In his address to diplomats at the beginning of 1999,[23] for example, he instances offences against religious freedom in Asia and Africa, in Islamic countries, in Europe, because of a 'false idea of the principle of separation between the state and the churches, or as a result of a deep-seated agnosticism', and 'in some countries of Central and Eastern Europe' – the context would suggest that he is thinking of Russia.

It is common for these annual addresses to be a *tour d'horizon* of the world's problems from a Vatican perspective. In 1999 John Paul II gave a strong endorsement to the Good Friday Agreement over Northern Ireland, and to the first tentative moves to a peace process in Spain concerning the armed struggle for Basque separatism. He went on to speak of themes which have been the hallmark of this papacy:

> The transition to one currency and the enlargement toward the East will no doubt give Europe the possibility to become more and more a community with a common destiny, a true 'European community' – this is in any case our dearest wish. This obviously presupposes that the member countries are able to reconcile their history with the same common project, so that they may all see themselves as equal partners, concerned only for the common good.
>
> The spiritual families which have made such a great contribution to the civilisation of this continent – I am thinking especially of Christianity – have a role which seems to me to be more and more decisive. In the face of social problems which keep significant sectors of the population in poverty and of social inequalities which give rise to chronic instability, and before the younger generations seeking points of reference in an often chaotic world, it is important that the churches should be able to proclaim the tenderness of God and the call to fraternity which the recent feast of Christmas has caused to shine out once again for all humanity.

These paragraphs, with the pope's remarkable endorsement of the Euro (which the Vatican City State has decided to join), provide further evidence, were more needed, of papal pre-occupation with Europe. But John Paul's claim for the Church's role is of course far wider. He sees Christianity as having an important part to play in the eradication of 'poverty and social inequalities' world-wide. It is a topic which he has frequently addressed when speaking to the diplomatic corps.

Conclusion

The Catholic Church has a role on the international stage, the present pope affirms, because it stands for the highest of human values, because it refuses to reduce the human person to one single dimension but treats the person as an individual, as social and as transcendent; it has an especial concern for those who have been left on the margins of history – he is thinking of those condemned to death, of those who have been tortured, of refugees and those who have simply disappeared; it has a role because it preaches 'a pedagogy of peace', and because it preaches forgiveness and reconciliation.[24] Even the recently published *Catechism of the Catholic Church* has something to say about the ethics of international relations: 'International solidarity is a requirement of the moral order; world peace depends in part upon this.'[25] As one commentator puts it,

> The new catechism confirms this papacy's plans to invest the Holy See with the role of a worldwide ethical reservoir of unprecedented dimensions . . . St Peter's See, convinced that 'if there is no ultimate truth guiding and orienting political actions, then ideas and beliefs can be made into instruments of power [a quotation from the 1991 encyclical *Centesimus Annus*]' puts itself forward as an ethical beacon at the service of the post-Cold-War international society.[26]

The language may be over-blown – the author is an Italian diplomat – but they represent the position of the Holy See well enough.

This 'ethical reservoir' largely consists of the Church's social doctrine, elaborated by successive popes since 1891 in a series of encyclicals – of which series *Centesimus Annus*, marking the centenary of the first, *Rerum Novarum*, would seem intended to be the last, at least for the present pontificate. John Paul II's writings on social issues, though claiming to be in a hundred-year-old tradition, mark a distinctly more radical turn, particularly with his emphasis on the centrality of religious liberty, a concept which, until the publication of the document *Dignitatis*

Humanae in 1965 at the end of the Second Vatican Council, not many in the hierarchy of the Church would have been ready to embrace, let alone embrace with enthusiasm.

It had seemed that the Church had become wary of its social doctrine, not so much because it was wrong as because it had been accused of being an ideology,[27] something which John Paul has constantly been at pains to deny. In *Octagesimo Adveniens* of 14 May 1971, Pope Paul VI had written, 'In the face of such widely varying situations [around the world] it is difficult for us to utter a unified message and to put forward a solution which has universal validity . . .' Pope John Paul II has no such inhibitions. He, and his curia, have been unfailingly ready to address the general principles of the relief of Third World debt, of religious liberty, of the growing inequality of wealth between North and South, of war and peace, of the destruction of the planet.[28] And more often than not he is speaking over the heads of governments directly to the people. He is fond of talking not of 'states' but of 'nations', defined by their culture, their language – and their religion.

But the inspirational language of the 1980s has become, in the aftermath of the collapse of Communism, 'the inflammatory rhetoric of the 1990s'.[29] The optimism engendered by the collapse of Communism in 1989, which enabled John Paul to talk to young people gathered at Santiago de Compostela in August that year of a world without frontiers,[30] has largely disappeared from the discourses of an increasingly frail pope. Whether his successor will share the Polish pontiff's enthusiasm for the global mission of the Church, or whether he will turn to the growing internal divisions within Roman Catholicism, there can be no way of knowing.

Notes

[1] For purposes of comparison, at the 50th anniversary celebrations of the United Nations in 1995, 185 nations were represented. The text of the discourse can be found in *Origins*, 28, No. 31 (21 January 1999), 534ff.

[2] Strictly speaking, the predecessor of John Paul II was John Paul I, but he died after only a month in office. Karol Wojtyla was elected on 16 October 1978. The figures for diplomatic representation can be found

in the relevant volumes of the Vatican's yearbook, the *Annuario Pontificio.*

[3] *His Holiness,* by Carl Bernstein and Marco Politi (New York and London, Doubleday, 1996) was particularly flattering about the pope's international role, a view sharply criticized by Jonathan Kwitny in *Man of the Century* (New York and London, Little Brown, 1997) though his own book is otherwise generally complimentary. My *Pope John Paul II: A Biography* (London, HarperCollins, 1994) is a good deal less sympathetic to John Paul's perception of his function than either of the above.

[4] I know of only one general history of papal diplomacy, Pierre Blet's *Histoire de la représéntation diplomatique du Saint Siège* (Rome, Archivo Vaticano, 1982), but this comes down only to the nineteenth century.

[5] One papal diplomat has written a book about it: Andrés Carrascosa Coso, *La Santa Sede y la Conferencia sobre la Seguridad y la Cooperación en Europa* (Rome, Libreria Editrice Vaticana, 2nd edn., 1991).

[6] Benedict XV's diplomatic activity during the First World War is examined in detail in Giorgio Rumi (ed.), *Benedetto XV e la pace* (Brescia, Morcelliana, 1990). Nothing comparable exists in English, but cf. John Pollard, *The Unknown Pope: Benedicto XV (1914–1922) and his pursuit of peace* (London, Geoffrey Chapman, 1999), *passim* but especially 123–8.

[7] For the story surrounding this appointment, see Thomas Moloney, *Westminster, Whitehall and the Vatican* (Tunbridge Wells, Burns & Oates, 1985).

[8] H. E. Cardinale, *The Holy See and the International Order* (Gerrards Cross, Colin Smythe, 1976), 83.

[9] Ibid., 85.

[10] For example, Peter Nichols, *The Pope's Divisions* (London, Faber, 1981); George Bull, *Inside the Vatican* (London, Hutchinson, 1982); Peter Hebblethwaite, *In the Vatican* (London, Sidgwick & Jackson, 1986); David Willey, *God's Politician* (London, Faber, 1992); Thomas J. Reese, *Inside the Vatican* (Cambridge, MA, Harvard University Press, 1996).

[11] Mario Oliveri, *The Representative* (Gerrards Cross, Van Duren, 1980), 73.

[12] Cf. Moloney, *Westminster, Whitehall and the Vatican, passim.*

[13] *Representative*, 26–30.

[14] The Ostpolitik had, of course, a longer history. Cf. Hans Jakob Stehle, *Eastern Politics of the Vatican, 1917–1979* (Athens, OH, Ohio University Press, 1981).

[15] *The Pope's Divisions,* an 'Analysis' programme for BBC Radio 4, transmitted on 16 February 1995.

[16] Sergio I. Minerbi, 'The Vatican and Israel', in Peter C. Kent and John F. Pollard (eds.), *Papal Diplomacy in the Modern Age* (Westport, CT, Praeger, 1993), 192.

[17] Ibid., 200.

[18] Discourse, 1 April 1990.

[19] Discourse, 1 June 1980.

[20] It has, however, been represented for longer at the ILO, the WHO and UNESCO, also by permanent observers. It cannot be a member of the UN because it would then have a vote, which could be interpreted as being contrary to the Lateran Treaty.

[21] The first ambassador (nuncio) was Archbishop Cardinale.

[22] Jorge Mejía, 'La Liberté religieuse dans l'enseignement du Pape Jean Paul II', in Joël-Benoît d'Onorio (ed.), *La Liberté religieuse dans le monde* (Paris, Éditions Universitaires, 1991), 79.

[23] Cf. n.1 above.

[24] Jean-Louis Tauran, 'La Doctrine pontificale des relations internationales d'après les discours du Pape Jean-Paul II au corps diplomatique', in Joël-Benoît d'Onorio (ed.), *Le Saint-Siège dans les relations internationales* (Paris, Cerf/Cujas, 1989), 83.

[25] Paragraph 1941.

[26] U. Colombo Sacco, *John Paul II and World Politics* (Louvain, Peeters, 1999), 28.

[27] For a brief discussion of this, with references, see my introduction to *Proclaiming Justice and Peace* (London, Collins, 1991), xx–xxii.

[28] Cf. for these and similar issues, Maura A. Ryan and Todd David Whitmore (eds.), *The Challenge of Global Stewardship: Roman Catholic Responses* (Notre Dame, IN, University of Notre Dame Press, 1997).

[29] Jonathan Luxmoore and Jolanta Babiuch, *The Vatican and the Red Flag* (London, Geoffrey Chapman, 1998), 304.

[30] Ibid., 302.

5

Political Islam and global order

JOHN L. ESPOSITO

Political Islam, commonly referred to as 'Islamic fundament-alism', has often been regarded as a major threat to global order.[1] The Iranian Revolution, hijackings and hostage-taking in the 1980s, the Gulf War, bombings of New York's World Trade Center and locations in Paris, and fears that a 'fundamentalist' takeover in Algeria would have a spill-over effect in North Africa and Europe have reinforced images of an expansive and explosive reassertion of Islam in global politics which threatens global order.

With the triumph of the democratization movement in Eastern Europe and the breakup of the Soviet empire, Islam constitutes the most pervasive and potentially powerful transnational force, with one billion adherents spread out across the globe. Muslims are a majority in more than fifty countries ranging from Africa to South-East Asia, and they exist in growing and significant numbers in the United States and Europe.

For a Western world long accustomed to a global vision and foreign policy predicated upon the superpower rivalry for global influence if not dominance, the all too alluring temptation is to identify another global ideological force, a resurgent 'evil empire', to fill the 'threat vacuum' created by the demise of Communism: 'No matter how and when the war ends, Islamic rage already threatens the stability of traditionally pro-Western regimes from Morocco to Jordan to Pakistan.'[2]

Belief that a clash of world-views, values and civilizations is leading to an impending confrontation between Islam and the West is reflected in headlines and articles with ominous titles like:

'A holy war heads our way',[3] 'Still fighting the crusades', 'Focus: Islamic terror: global suicide squad',[4] 'The new crescent in crisis: the global intafada',[5] 'Rising Islam may overwhelm the West',[6] 'The roots of Muslim rage',[7] and Samuel Huntington's 'The clash of civilizations'.[8] Huntington, in many ways, provides a summary of the major arguments of those who see Islam as a threat to global order and gives them an academic legitimacy. He identifies a 'Confucian-Islamic connection that has emerged to challenge Western interests, values, and power', concluding that 'a central focus of conflict for the immediate future will be between the West and several Islamic-Confucian states'.[9] Huntington sees the impending confrontation as historic and rooted today in a clash of values: 'Conflict along the fault line between Western and Islamic civilizations has been going on for 1300 years';[10] 'Western ideas of individualism, liberalism, constitutionalism, human rights, equality, liberty, the rule of law, democracy, free markets, the separation of church and state, often have little resonance in Islamic [and other] . . . cultures.'[11]

Is Islam a threat to global order? Are Islam and the West on an inevitable collision course? Is there an impending global confrontation between the Islamic world and the West?

The Islamic resurgence

Islam re-emerged as a potent global force during the 1970s and 1980s.[12] The scope of the Islamic resurgence has been worldwide, embracing much of the Muslim world from the Sudan to Indonesia. Heads of Muslim governments as well as opposition groups increasingly appealed to religion for legitimacy and to mobilize popular support. Islamic activist (fundamentalist) organizations have run the spectrum. Many work within the system, such as the Muslim Brotherhoods in Egypt and Jordan, and the Jamaat-i-Islami in South Asia. Islamic activists have held cabinet-level positions in Jordan, the Sudan, Iran, Malaysia and Pakistan. Islamic organizations have constituted the leading opposition parties/organizations in Egypt, Tunisia, Algeria, the West Bank and Gaza, and Indonesia. At the same time, a minority of radical extremists such as Egypt's Society of Muslims (known more popularly as Takfir wal-Hijra, Excommunication and Flight), al-Jihad (Holy War) and the Gamaa Islamiya have resorted to violence, attacking government officials and foreign tourists, killing Coptic Christians in their attempts to overthrow prevailing political systems. Islam has been a significant ingredient in nationalist struggles and resistance movements in Afghanistan, the Muslim republics of Soviet Central Asia, in Kashmir, and in the communal politics of Lebanon, India, Thailand, China and the Philippines.

Much of the 1980s was dominated by fear of radical Islam: Khomeini's Iran and Iran's threat to export its revolution, extremist organizations who used violence, assassinated Egypt's Anwar Sadat, engaged in hostage-taking and terrorism. Although disturbances in Saudi Arabia, Bahrain, Kuwait and Iran's strong backing of a Shiite group, Hizbullah, in Lebanon, as well as the assassination of Sadat, fed the fears of Muslim rulers and the West, no other 'Irans' occurred. The late 1980s and 1990s offer a more complex picture, revealing the diversity of contemporary Islamic movements rather than radical extremism and monolithic threat. While violent extremists continue to exist, Islamic activism has also become more visible as a social and political force operating within the system – part of the institutions and life of mainstream society. Islamically inspired organizations run schools, clinics, hospitals, banks and publishing houses and provide social welfare services. In addition, a new generation of élites, modern educated but Islamically rather than secularly oriented, may be found throughout the professions (physicians, lawyers, engineers, teachers, social workers) seeking to implement their Islamic alternatives or visions in society. In countries like Egypt and Jordan they have emerged in the leadership of professional organizations or syndicates. Most importantly, many Islamic movements joined the chorus of voices calling for political liberalization and democratization.

Democratization

In the wake of the Gulf War of 1991, the issue of political liberalization and democracy re-emerged as an issue in the Middle East and in Western diplomacy.[13] Democracy movements and pressures upon Muslim governments for greater liberalization had predated the Gulf War. As the Soviet Union and Eastern Europe were swept along by the wave of democratization in

1989–90, the demands of Muslim nationalities in the Soviet Union for greater autonomy, the Palestinian *intifada* and Kashmiri Muslim demands for independence from India captured the attention of many in the Muslim world. Secular and Islamic activists increasingly couched their criticisms and demands of their regimes in the language of political liberalization and democracy. In many Muslim countries Islamic activists not only took to the streets but also turned to the ballot box. Both secular and Islamic organizations and political parties pressed for political reforms in Egypt, Tunisia, Algeria, Jordan and Pakistan, and, in the aftermath of the Gulf War, in Kuwait and Saudi Arabia.

Calls for political liberalization and democratization in the Muslim world have brought greater political liberalization in some cases and repression in others. Where governments opened up their political systems, Islamic organizations participated in elections and emerged as the leading opposition in countries like Egypt, Tunisia, Turkey and in Jordan, where they not only won thirty-two of eighty seats in parliament but also held five cabinet positions. In Algeria, the Islamic Salvation Front swept municipal and parliamentary elections in the early 1990s and seemed poised to come to power when the Algerian military intervened. The seeming successes of Islamic movements in electoral politics have led some governments such as Tunisia, Algeria and Egypt to engage in political repression, charging that religious extremists threaten to 'hijack democracy', to use the political system to come to power and then impose their will.

Demands for democratization trouble both autocratic rulers in the Muslim world and many Western governments. The former fear any opposition, let alone one that cloaks itself in values that Western governments officially cherish and preach. For leaders in the West, democracy raises the prospect of old and reliable friends, sometimed referred to as 'client states', being transformed into more independent and less predictable nations. This prospect generates a fear that such nations could make Western access to oil less secure. Thus, global order and stability in the Middle East have often been defined in terms of preservation of the *status quo*.

Lack of enthusiasm or support for political liberalization in the Middle East has been rationalized by the claim that both Arab culture and Islam are anti-democratic. The proof offered is the lack of a democratic tradition, more specifically, the paucity of democracies in the Muslim world. Why the glaring absence of democratic governments? The political realities of the Muslim world have not been conducive to the development of democratic traditions and institutions. European colonial rule and post-independence national governments headed by military officers, monarchs and ex-military rulers have contributed to a legacy which has had little concern for political participation and the building of strong democratic institutions. National unity and stability as well as political legitimacy have been undermined by the artificial nature of modern states whose national boundaries were often determined or drawn by colonial powers and whose rulers were either placed on their thrones by Europe or seized power for themselves. Weak economies, illiteracy and high un-employment, especially among the younger generation, exacerb-ate the situation, undermining confidence in governments and increasing the appeal of 'Islamic fundamentalism'.

Electoral successes of Islamic candidates have fed the fears of nervous rulers. In a climate in which most governments during the post-1979 period were traumatized by the spectre of 'Muslim fundamentalism', this fear has provided an excuse for govern-ments to continue to limit political liberalization and democrat-ization. At best the attitude of many rulers may be characterized, in the words of some Western diplomats, as an openness to 'risk free democracy' or 'democracy without dissent'! Both the Tunis-ian and Algerian governments' management of political liberal-ization as well as that of Egypt reflect this approach. Openness to government controlled and dominated change – yes; openness to a change of government that would bring Islamic activists to power through democratic means – no. Opposition parties and groups, religious as well as secular, are tolerated as long as they remain relatively weak or under government control and do not threaten the ruling party.

A major issue facing Islamic movements is their ability, if in power, to tolerate diversity. The status of minorities in Muslim majority areas and freedom of speech remain serious issues. The record of Islamic experiments in Pakistan, Iran and the Sudan raises serious questions about the rights of women and minorities under Islamically oriented governments. The extent to which the growth of Islamic revivalism has been accompanied in some countries by attempts to restrict women's rights, to separate women and men in public, to enforce veiling, and to restrict their public roles in society strikes fear in some segments of Muslim society and challenges the credibility of those who call for Islamization of state and society. The record of discrimination against the Bahai in Iran and the Ahmadi in Pakistan as 'deviant' groups (heretical offshoots of Islam), against Christians in Sudan and Arab Jews in some countries, as well as increased communal sectarian conflict between Muslims and Christians in Egypt and Nigeria pose similar questions about the future of religious pluralism and tolerance.

If many Muslims ignore these issues or facilely talk of tolerance and human rights in Islam, discussion of these questions in the West is often reduced to two contrasting blocs, the West which preaches and practises freedom and tolerance and the Muslim world which does not. Muslim attitudes towards Christian minorities and the case of Salman Rushdie are marshalled to support the indictment that Islam is intolerant and anti-democratic. Muslim demands for independence are regarded as deceptive and a threat to global order and to minorities:

> What is being pursued, therefore, is not Wilsonian self-determination (though many of these intifadas have adopted its language), because in the Islamic world self-determination is permitted only to Moslems. What instead is being pursued is a pan-Islamic demand for sovereignty over any territory where Moslems form a local majority.[14]

The status of non-Muslims and the implications of political pluralism remain contemporary Islamic issues. Without a reinterpretation of the classical Islamic legal doctrine regarding non-Muslim minorities as 'protected people' *(dhimmi)*, an Islamic ideologically oriented state would be at best a limited democracy with a weak pluralistic profile, whose ideological orientation would restrict the participation of non-Muslims in key government positions and the existence of political parties that represent a competing ideology or orientation: secular, socialist or whatever. Non-Muslims would be second-class citizens with limited rights and opportunities, as is the case in countries such as Iran and Pakistan. However, it is useful to recall that Christianity faced a similar need to reinterpret and reform its tradition to accommodate modern notions of pluralism and tolerance. Indeed, it was at Vatican II that Roman Catholicism officially accepted pluralism. Discussion and debate exist within the Muslim world today as intellectuals and religious leaders grapple with these issues.

Despite democratic tendencies in the Muslim world and among Islamic activists, multiple and conflicting attitudes towards democracy continue to exist and leave the future in question.

Only time will tell whether the espousal of democracy by many contemporary Islamic movements and their participation in the electoral process are simply a means to power or a truly embraced and internalized end/goal, a transformation of tradition which is the product of a process of religious reinterpretation informed by both faith and experience. Based on the record thus far, one can expect that, where Islamic movements come into power, like many governments in the Middle East, secular as well as 'Islamic', issues of political pluralism and human rights will remain sources of tension and debate. Greater political liberalization and participation, the building of strong civil societies, are part of a *process* of change that requires time and experience to develop new political traditions and institutions. However, if attempts to participate in the electoral process are blocked, crushed or negated, as in North Africa, the currency of democracy as a viable mechanism for political and social change will be greatly devalued in the eyes of many.

Conclusion

The lessons from the Soviet experience have a bearing on our understanding of the relationship of Islam and Muslim politics to global order and thus Western policy towards the Muslim world. Celebration of the unravelling of Communism and the victory of democracy have been accompanied by a growing realization of the extent to which fear and the demonizing of the enemy blinded many to the true condition and extent of the Soviet threat. Viewing the Soviet Union through the prism or lens of 'the evil empire' often proved ideologically reassuring, emotionally satisfying, justifying the expenditure of enormous resources and supporting a vast military-industrial complex. However, our easy stereotypes of the enemy and the monolithic nature of the

Communist threat also proved costly. Neither government agencies nor academic think-tanks predicted the extent and rapidity of the disintegration of the Soviet empire. The exaggerated fears and static vision which drove us to take Herculean steps against a monolithic enemy blinded us to the diversity within the Soviet Union and the profound changes that were taking place.

So too today, in understanding and responding to events in the Muslim world, we are again challenged to resist easy stereotypes and solutions. The easy path is to view Islam and political Islam as a threat to global order – to again posit a global pan-Islamic threat, monolithic in nature, a historic enemy whose faith and agenda are diametrically opposed to the West. This attitude leads to support authoritarian governments at almost any cost rather than to risk an Islamically oriented government in power.

Just as simply perceiving the Soviet Union through the prism of the 'evil empire' had its costs, so too the tendency of governments in the West and the media to equate Islam and Islamic fundamentalism with radicalism, terrorism and anti-Westernism has seriously hampered our understanding, conditioned our responses and had a cost. As Patrick Bannerman, a former diplomat and analyst for the British Foreign Office, observed in his *Islam in Perspective*, 'How non-Muslims think of Islam conditions the manner in which they deal with Muslims, which in turn conditions how Muslims think of and deal with non-Muslims.'[15]

The challenge today is to appreciate the diversity of Islamic actors and movements, to ascertain the causes or reasons behind confrontations and conflicts, and thus to respond to specific events and situations with informed, reasoned responses rather than predetermined presumptions and reactions. The failure to speak out forcefully for democratization in the Middle East and to condemn government repression and violations of human rights against Islamic movements in Egypt, Algeria and Tunisia, in effect denies Islamic activists the same rights to political participation and human rights as other citizens and raises serious questions about a 'selective' approach to democratization. At the heart of this 'selective' approach to democratization is a tendency (as in the battle against Communism during the cold war) to define stability in terms of support for the *status quo*, no matter how authoritarian some governments may be.

In some ways, the attitude of the West towards Communism and its threat to global order seems at times transferred to or replicated in the elevation of a new threat, 'Islamic fundamentalism'. Indeed, in the 1990s, the effects of this polarization are expressed by the prevailing tendency of governments in the Muslim world and the West, the media and many analysts, to conclude, without regard to the diversity of Islamic organizations and specific social contexts, that 'Islamic fundamentalism' is inherently a major global threat or danger.

Cognizant of a Western tendency to see Islam as a threat, many Muslim governments use the danger of Islamic radicalism as an excuse for their own control or suppression of Islamic movements. They fan the fears of a monolithic Islamic radicalism both at home and in the West, much as many in the past used anti-Communism as an excuse for authoritarian rule and to win the support and aid of Western powers. The banning of Islamic organizations, imprisonment of activists and the violation of human rights are excused with the plaintive plea, 'We are facing young fanatics threatening our future.'[16] Western stereotypes of a united world-wide fundamentalist movement that threatens the stability of the Arab world and thus of Western interests are exploited by Arab diplomats from states with strong Western ties who declare: 'Fundamentalism is international in scope. It has branches everywhere . . . Fundamentalist expansion will eventually threaten the industrial nations when most Arab countries have been destabilized.'[17] The focus on radicalism and the equation of Islam with an extremism that threatens to confront the West has become commonplace. Too often, we are exposed in the media and literature to a sensationalized monolithic approach which reinforces facile generalizations and stereotypes rather than challenges our understanding of the 'who' and the 'why' of history, the specific causes or reasons behind the headlines. Moreover, like the attitude towards Communism in the McCarthy era, in government and professional discussions, not to be simply dismissive of Islamic fundamentalism is viewed as being biased or sympathetic towards the enemy. The experience of the past decade alerts us to the need to be more attentive to the diversity that is behind the seeming unity of Islam, to appreciate and more effectively analyse both the unity and diversity in Islam and in Muslim affairs. Differing contexts have spawned a variety of Islamically oriented nations, leaders and organizations. The diversity of governments (the Saudi monarchy and Qaddafi's populist state, Khomeini's clerical republic in Iran and the military regimes of Zia ul-Haq's Pakistan or Jafar al-Numayri's and now Omar al-Bashir's in Sudan), their differing relations with the West, and the variety of Islamic movements, are undercut and distorted by the univocal connotation and monolithic image conjured up by the term Islamic fundamentalism.

Muslim states continue to exist in a climate of crisis in which many of their citizens experience and speak of the failure of the state and of secular forms of nationalism and socialism. Heads of state and ruling élites or classes possess tenuous legitimacy in the face of mounting disillusionment and opposition, among whom Islamic activists are often the most vocal and effective. The extent to which governments in predominantly Muslim countries fail to meet the socio-economic needs of their societies, restrict political participation, prove insensitive to the need to effectively incorporate Islam as a component in their national identity and ideology, or appear exceedingly dependent on the West, will contribute to the appeal of an Islamic political alternative. Contemporary Islamic politics is more a challenge than a threat. It challenges the West to know and understand the diversity of the Muslim experience. It is a challenge to Muslim governments to be more responsive to popular demands for political liberalization and greater popular participation, to tolerate rather than repress opposition movements and to build viable democratic institutions. At the same time, it challenges Western powers to stand by the democratic values they embody and recognize authentic populist movements and the right of the people to determine the nature of their governments and leadership. As European and American history and experience reveal, the process of democratization is an experiment whose outcome is unpredictable but one with long-term as well as short-term risks and consequences. Issues of political legitimacy, popular political participation, national identity and socio-economic justice cannot continue to be defined, determined and imposed from above without paying a heavy price, if not now then in the future, in terms of political development and global order.

Notes

[1] This chapter draws on my previous work, in particular *The Islamic Threat: Myth or Reality?* (NewYork, Oxford University Press, 2nd edn., 1995).

[2] Strobe Talbott, 'Living with Saddam', *Time* (25 February 1991), 24.

[3] Fergus M. Bordewich, 'A holy war heads our way,' *Reader's Digest* (January 1995), 76–80.

[4] 'Focus: Islamic terror: global suicide squad', *Sunday Telegraph* (1 January 1995).

[5] Charles Krauthammer, 'The new crescent of crisis: the global intifada', *The Washington Post* (16 February 1990).

[6] 'Rising Islam may overwhelm the West', *New Hampshire Sunday News* (20 August 1989).

[7] 'The roots of Muslim rage', *The Atlantic Monthly*, 226, No. 3 (September 1990).

[8] Samuel P. Huntington, 'The clash of civilizations,' *Foreign Affairs* (Summer 1993).

[9] Ibid., 45–8.

[10] Ibid., 31.

[11] Ibid., 40.

[12] For studies of the Islamic resurgence, see YvonneY. Haddad, John O. Voll and John L. Esposito, *The Contemporary Islamic Revival: A Critical Survey and Bibliography* (NewYork, Greenwood Press, 1991); John L. Esposito, *Islam and Politics* (Syracuse, NY, Syracuse University Press, 4th edn., 1998); John L. Esposito (ed.), *Islam in Asia: Religion, Politics and Society* (New York, Oxford University Press, 1987); James P. Piscatori (ed.), *Islam in the Political Process* (Cambridge, Cambridge University Press, 1983); and Nazih Ayubi, *Political Islam: Religion and Politics in the Arab World* (London, Routledge, 1991).

[13] For an analysis of this issue, see Michael C. Hudson, 'After the Gulf War: prospects for democratization in the Arab world', *The Middle East Journal*, 45 (Summer 1991), 407–26; John L. Esposito and James P. Piscatori, 'Democratization and Islam', *The Middle East Journal* (Summer 1991), 427–40; John O. Voll and John L. Esposito, 'Islam's democratic essence', *Middle East Quarterly* (September 1994), 3–11 with ripostes, 12–19, and Voll and Esposito reply, *Middle East Quarterly* (December 1994), 71–2; Robin Wright, 'Islam, democracy and the West', *Foreign Affairs* (Summer 1992), 131–45; Bernard Lewis, 'Islam and democracy', *The Atlantic* (February 1993), 87–98); and Martin Kramer, 'Islam vs. Democracy', *Commentary* (January 1993), 35–42; 'Can Islam, democracy, and modernization co-exist?', *Africa Report* (September–October 1990), 9.

[14] Charles Krauthammer, 'The new crescent of crisis', 2.

15 Patrick Bannerman, *Islam in Perspective: A Guide to Islamic Society, Politics and Law* (London, Routledge, 1988), 219.
16 'Tunisia warns of Islamic radicals', *Washington Times* (25 October 1991).
17 Ibid.

II

From the 'Old' to the 'New' Order

6
Religion and the fall of Communism

PAUL BADHAM

In his book *The Christian Church in the Cold War*, Britain's leading church historian, Owen Chadwick asked the question 'To what extent was the persistence of Christianity responsible for toppling of the regimes in most of Eastern Europe?' His answer in 1992 was 'Hardly at all . . . the Revolution did not need the Churches.'[1] This was not quite the whole of his response for he qualified his judgement with the phrase 'And yet' and went on to indicate ways in which the Churches did indeed contribute to the events that took place in 1989. But Chadwick's central view was that Communism was bound in the end to collapse because it could not deliver what it claimed to be able to offer. In his more recent *History of Christianity* Chadwick has modified his original verdict and, in looking for causes of the breakdown of the Soviet empire, he argued that 'in Hungary, Romania, Czechoslovakia and East Germany, and especially in Poland, the religious convictions of the people helped to precipitate that breakdown'.[2]

Interestingly, however, just as Chadwick has changed his mind in one direction, so pope John Paul II has changed his in the reverse direction. Shortly after the events of 1989 the pope was reported on television as claiming 'God has won in Eastern Europe' and he certainly said at one point that 'Divine providence caused the fall of communism'. However, in his 1994 work *Crossing the Threshold of Hope* the pope took a quite different line and insisted that Communism 'fell by itself, because of its own inherent weakness'.[3] Here, however, the pope may be being too modest. For there is a strong case for saying that he gave it a decisive push. At least that is the view of Mikhail Gorbachev. His verdict is quite unequivocal: 'What has happened in Eastern Europe . . . would not have been possible . . . without the great role – including a political one – which John Paul II played in the events.'[4] But of course it was not the individual man, Karol Wojtyla, who mattered. It was rather that as pope, John Paul II could personify the ongoing strength of Polish Catholicism, and at a crucial moment of history become the voice of the voiceless in opposing an alien imposed regime.

Poland: catalyst and turning point

In Poland more than any other country in Europe atheistic Communism totally failed to win the hearts and minds of the people and, despite forty years of state support for an atheistic ideology, Catholicism not only declined to wither away but steadily grew stronger. It is of course extremely hard to separate the sense in which it was really religious rather than national feeling which inspired Polish Catholicism. Historically the two are probably inseparable, no less during the period we are considering than they had been in earlier periods of Polish history. We must also note that the identification of Polishness with Catholicism had been enhanced by the new post-war boundaries of Poland which made it a much more ethnically and religiously unified state. However, although we note the nationalistic influence on Polish Catholicism we must also recognize the reality of its actual church commitment. Anton Pospieszalski has pointed out that in 1937 Poland had 11,000 priests and 7,000 churches but by 1972 it had 18,000 priests and 13,000 churches, and this despite the large number of churches destroyed during the Second World War, and the thousands of priests killed in Nazi concentration camps. Popular support for the Catholic Church also remained high, with 77 per cent of the population attending mass in towns and 87 per cent attending mass in the countryside.[5]

This continuous expansion of the Church's influence had been in the face of every effort made by the state to minimize it. In the early years of Communist rule many clergy had been arrested and imprisoned including the bishops of Katowice, Pelplin and Kielce and from 1953 to 1956 the primate of Poland, Cardinal Wyszynski, had also been imprisoned for his and the whole episcopate's refusal to accept state interference in major church appointments. However, in 1956, recognizing the strength of popular support for Wyszynski the government backed down; he was released from prison and later that year when Gomulka came to power the government appealed to Wyszynski for his help in stabilizing the country. From that time onwards the Church was never in danger again and in 1966 celebrated the millennium of Polish Catholicism with great enthusiasm.

The election of Archbishop Karol Wojtyla as pope in 1978 was of immense importance to Poland. He was not only the first Polish pope in history he was also the first Slavonic pope, a point to which John Paul II attaches almost mystical significance because of ancient Polish hopes for such a person. In 1979 the pope made a triumphal return visit to Poland and the millions who assembled to greet him became conscious of their strength *vis-à-vis* the ruling minority. That set the stage for the events of 1980 when Solidarity was born and for sixteen months carried the hopes of the Polish people for a new order. After the suppression of Solidarity and declaration of martial law in December 1981 it was the Church in Poland which kept alive the spirit of freedom. For the next decade churches and church halls were places where independent thought and culture could survive and the licensed Catholic press kept the flame of freedom burning. At one time there were up to 700 Catholic periodicals in circulation, providing the one channel for alternative viewpoints to Communist ideology.

During the 1980s a church boom continued in Poland, with more and more churches opened, and more and more ordinands coming forward to train for the priesthood. Atheistic Communism increasingly lost ground. The most famous centre of Catholic resistance to Communism was Fr Jerzy Popielusko's parish church of St Stanislaw Kostka in the centre of Warsaw. At his monthly Masses for the Fatherland Popielusko drew crowds in the thousands with his patient appeal for resistance, and his assertion that defiance of authority was an obligation of heart, of religion, manhood and nationhood.[6] His assassination by agents of the secret police did not end the appeal of his message, for when the manner of his death became known the authorities were forced to prosecute and sentence his murderers. Popielusko became a martyr. His funeral mass was conducted by Cardinal Glemp with hundreds of thousands of the people of Warsaw in attendance. Subsequently his grave became a shrine and a place of pilgrimage for people from all over Poland. I myself have vivid memories of going to see his grave six years later covered in a mass of fresh flowers and with a throng of pilgrims all come to pay tribute to the example of his life and his faithful resistance to the Communist authorities.

But the key to the strength of the Polish resistance to Communism was the Polish pope. On each of his three visits to his homeland he stirred up the longing for a new future. According to the former Polish president, General Jaruzelski, it was the pope's first return visit to Poland that spelt the beginning of the end of the old regime.[7] Preaching in all the main religious centres of Poland over a nine-day tour he was heard by thirteen million of his fellow Poles. In all cases his theme was the dignity of humanity, the need for renewal and change, and the right of each nation to self-determination and to its own culture. Inevitably this would imply resistance to the Communist establishment and indeed the pope explicitly taught that 'The future of Poland will depend on how many people are mature enough to be nonconformist.'[8] These themes were to be re-echoed in May 1983 when, at a time when Poland still languished under martial law, Pope John Paul preached against demoralization and prayed for perseverance in hope. He also dedicated the church of St Maximilian Kolbe in Nowa Huta, with its vivid altar cloth inscribed to Mary with the words: 'Mother of Solidarity pray for us.' In 1987 he preached a series of sermons on the philosophical and theological meanings of the concept of solidarity, which his social encyclical of 1987 re-echoed on his return to Rome.

Weigel claims that Pope John Paul's private and unscheduled meeting with General Jaruzelski at the conclusion of his 1987 tour laid the foundation for the round table talks between leaders of the Church, the state and the Solidarity union in the following year. These talks led directly to the agreement to allow 35 per cent of the seats in the lower house and all the seats in the Senate at the next election to be open to genuine electoral choice. During the election campaign church halls throughout Poland became the campaign centres for Solidarity candidates, and church presses printed their election leaflets. The result was beyond the wildest dreams of anyone, with Solidarity winning all 161 of the openly available seats in the lower house and ninety-nine out of a hundred Senate seats. The traditional allies of the Communist party, the Democrats and the United Peasants party announced a switch of their allegiance in the light of this overwhelming demonstration of the national mood, and Poland became the first country of Eastern Europe with a non-Communist prime minister.

I have focused a lot on Poland because what happened in Poland was the key to the unravelling of the Soviet empire in Eastern Europe. If the path of liberation was to be stopped, it was in Poland that the tanks should have been sent in. Yet Poland highlighted the cost of such a course because the papal pilgrimages had demonstrated that the loyalty of the Polish people belonged to Polish Catholicism rather than Soviet Communism, and the endorsement of this in the election landslide meant that any invasion would have entailed the crushing of the spirit of a whole people. This was not a path that Gorbachev or Shevardnadze were prepared to take. This decision once taken implied a willingness to let other nations also take upon themselves their own destiny.

It seems to me, on surveying the course of the Polish struggle, that religion, or at any rate a self-identification with Catholicism, played a decisive part in the events leading up to the overthrow of the former Communist regime. There was no deep-rooted aversion to the economic theories of Communism, as can be seen in the subsequent election of a social democratic mode of Socialism to a majority in parliament. But there was a refusal to accept Communism in the form of a foreign and atheistic ideology which conflicted with Catholic and Polish ideals and traditions. And there was deep pride in the election of a Pole to the papal throne. To this extent it seems to me demonstrable that what happened in 1989 would not have happened as it did without the impact of religion. In Poland at least I would argue against Chadwick and with Gorbachev that the revolution did need the Church.

Other main East European cases

However, it must be recognized that Poland is much the strongest instance of religion playing a key role. In other contexts its contribution was much less obvious, and much less important, even if in almost every case it did make at least some contribution. What is important is that in every country of Eastern Europe as in the Soviet Union itself the ideology of atheism and a negative evaluation of religion was part of the package which had been taken on board with the imposition of Communism. In every state of Eastern Europe restrictions had been placed on Christian activity, financial resources had been to a greater or lesser extent removed from the churches, access to the media and education had been made more difficult, and a policy of cultural strangulation had been adopted to encourage the gradual disappearance of religion as older generations passed on. The harshness with which such policies were applied varied from state to state, but in all of them an anti-Christian approach was perceived to be part of what being a Communist implied.

Albania was unique in resorting to total persecution, with all churches and mosques closed and all clergy executed, imprisoned or exiled. In all other countries the churches were allowed to continue to minister to the spiritual needs of their present members, but with the hope and expectation that they would in due course fade away. We should not minimize the effect of this. A generation has grown up with a very diminished awareness of Christianity. There has been a decisive break in the centuries of Christian culture. Nevertheless, the fact that Christian institutions were allowed to continue in every country but Albania did mean that an alternative ideology continued to be available. Dialectical materialism was not the only possibility. This had important consequences in that as it became clear that Communism was not working, even in the material sphere, there was a known alternative ideology to hand – a Christian ideology – and an alternative culture – the heritage of Christianity. There was also in every country an alternative publication network in church newspapers, parish magazines, encyclical letters. There was also a national and an international network of ecclesiastical organizations, with synods, councils and committees where ideas could be exchanged. There were also church buildings and church halls in which, when the opportunity ultimately arrived, alternative political parties could meet.

East Germany provided the clearest example of where a Christian Church could provide an alternative communication network and an alternative ideology which could help at a crucial time, though it is interesting that, unlike some other countries, Christianity helped forward the revolution of 1989 without there being in any real sense a revival of religion in that country. The most important contribution the Church made throughout the

Communist era was in offering an alternative ideology. It had a different message to that offered by the Marxist state, and it was the only different message which could be heard. In sermons, in synod meetings, in Bible classes, comments were made about the nature of society and the problems facing people in their daily lives. This tradition became important as disillusionment with Marxism grew, for the churches could provide a context in which discussion could happen.

Professor Gottfried Kretzschmar argues that the role of the ancient churches of Leipzig was very significant here. From 1980 onwards a tradition had grown up of holding 'peace prayers' in the Saint Nikolai church every Monday and a tradition grew up of associating these meetings with discussions of such topical issues as peace and disarmament, the environment, Third World development, justice and human rights. In 1988 these Monday prayer meetings increasingly became the meeting place for people wishing to leave East Germany. Throughout 1989 attendance at the Monday meetings steadily grew: though the church could actually seat 2,500, it would be full to overflowing by 4.30 p.m. and hundreds, later thousands, would be left outside. Another Leipzig church, St Luke's, hosted a church congress in July 1989 to which 5,000 young people came for Bible study, hymn singing and prayer, and then went on to discuss with one another the growing crisis in their country and their hopes and fears for the future.

What stimulated the crisis in East Germany was partly what had just happened in Poland, but also the fact that on 11 September 1989 the Hungarian government removed its barriers on the border between Hungary and Austria, so it became possible for any East German to travel via Czechoslovakia, Hungary and Austria to West Germany, where under Federal law they all had a right to citizenship. As thousands began to vote with their feet the government grew more and more worried. On 7 October 1989 the East German government celebrated its fortieth anniversary but its guest Gorbachev commented that it needed to change far more quickly, for 'life punishes those who come late'. Two days later at the St Nikolai church in Leipzig the attendance at the Monday prayers reached over a hundred thousand and they began to assert their role with the slogan 'We are the people', but also to encourage each other to avoid violence. Faced with demonstrations on this scale Honecker resigned on 18 October, the Berlin Wall fell on 9 November 1989 and the pressure for reunion with the West became irresistible.

According to Kretzschmar the part played by the Protestants of East Germany during the turn-round of 1989–90 was essentially that of midwife to change. At the time of the turn-round the churches were full to capacity, and the number of subscribers to church periodicals rose dramatically. But this was a temporary phase during the change of direction of East German society. There was no religious awakening or revival in East Germany as there was in some of the countries of the former Soviet Union or in Poland; it was simply that people turned to the Church at a time of national crisis and the Church responded by offering temporary leadership and support until other democratic bodies could re-emerge.

During the time of the turn-round the Church assumed an important support function. Forty years of Communist rule had left no other locus of authority outside the socialist framework. The Church was therefore the only institution left to step into the breach to prevent anarchy. It was thus church officials who negotiated with the former state power and who called for moderation from the incensed masses. The quasi-parliamentary experience of church men and women who had served in synod conferences or church board meetings and their experience of leading discussions and in group dynamics fulfilled an urgent but temporary need in the re-establishing of democratic principles. In some cases this led to ministers being elected to the new parliament and a continuing role in the new society. But these were relatively exceptional. In essence the role of religion in East Germany was supportively enabling, temporarily fulfilling an altruistic but important function, namely of responding to a national need and offering assistance in the management of change.

In other countries of Eastern Europe the Catholic Church played an important role in providing leadership which came to symbolize the fact that there was an alternative to atheistic Communism. In some cases it was a case of Catholic churches led by obstinate old men who simply made it clear to all that they had no sympathy with Communism. Cardinal Wyszynski of Poland, Cardinal Mindzenty of Hungary and Cardinal Tomasek in Czechoslovakia are three names that spring to mind. In the case of Poland we have already seen how the election of Wyszynski's younger episcopal colleague to the papacy eventually proved decisive. In Hungary and Czechoslovakia the long years of primatial resistance also eventually bore fruit. Mindzenty died in exile in 1975 fifteen years before the ending of Communism in Hungary. Yet one of the first acts of the new regime in February 1990 was to celebrate a requiem in his memory and to name the main square of Estergom, Mindzenty square in his memory, with the acting president praising his heroic resistance. In Hungary both Protestants and Catholics played a role in the resistance movement to Communist oppression and both shared in the religious revival which helped to discredit the Communist regime.

In Czechoslovakia Cardinal Tomasek lived to see and to contribute to the velvet revolution of 1989. For decades he had been a symbol of resistance. The Communists often referred to him as a 'general without an army', rather as Stalin had earlier referred to the pope's lack of divisions. But Catholic support rallied and from 1985 onwards Catholic participation in Civic Reform and in Public against Violence became intense. In the great rally in Wenceslas Square which determined the success of the velvet revolution and where a crowd of 250,000 cheered Vaclav Havel and Alexander Dubcek, Cardinal Tomasek issued a totally unequivocal pledge of the support of the whole Catholic community, which was read out to the cheering crowds by Fr Vaclav Maly. Part of the cardinal's declaration to the peoples of Bohemia, Moravia and Slovakia read as follows:

> I must not remain silent at the very moment when you have joined together in a mighty protest against the great injustice visited upon us over four decades. It is impossible to have confidence in a state leadership that is unwilling to speak the truth, and that denies basic rights and freedoms . . . these people cannot be trusted. We are surrounded by countries that in the past or presently have destroyed the prison bars of the totalitarian system . . . we must not wait any longer. The time has come to act. We need a democratic government. We are with you friends in the struggle for freedom. With God's help our destiny is in our hands.[9]

Not surprisingly, after the success of the revolution the ceremonies for Havel's installation as president involved a service in the cathedral of St Vitus on 29 December 1989, to sing a Te Deum in honour of the victory.

That Czechoslovakia should celebrate its freedom from Soviet power by singing a Te Deum in a historic cathedral reminds us of the deep roots Christianity has had in Eastern European history, thought and culture. Consequently, after the 'modern' experiment of Communism had been abandoned, people looked back to the situation as it was before the imposition of Communism. Christianity came to be viewed through rosy spectacles as part of the way of life that Communism had sought to replace. So as Communism came to be discredited there was a revived interest in Christian culture, literature and music. Towns which had once been named after saints were given their old titles back, churches and cathedrals were reopened, choral traditions were revived. The heritage of Christendom was perceived to be part of the self-identity of an Eastern European.

To this extent one can say that a return to a sense of a Christian identity was a contributory factor in the disenchantment felt towards Communism, and to a greater or lesser extent this helped towards the rejection of Communism, at least in its atheistic and Soviet form. I had a vivid experience of this in Bulgaria in 1993 when I stayed at the seaside resort known as Droubza throughout the Communist period but recently restored to its pre-Communist name of St Constantine's. Every tour on offer seemed to include a visit to a church or cathedral and there was a tremendous emphasis on the Christian heritage of Bulgaria and its long struggle against the Turks and more recently against atheistic Communism. One had a tremendous sense of a self-consciously Christian heritage being rediscovered through the process of liberation from Soviet rule.

In Romania a revived consciousness of a Christian identity played a central role in the sudden overthrow of the Ceauşescus. It was not simply that it was the protest of one Protestant minister, Lazlo Tokes, which sparked off the revolution, but also that religious feelings spurred on the people to take their courage in their hands. I vividly remember watching the television coverage of the occasion when an enormous crowd of some 200,000 gathered in the opera square of Timisoara in defence of Tokes. It is highly significant that they encouraged each other to stand firm by shouting out together 'God exists'. Seeing the defiance of the crowds Ceauşescu recognized that he had lost control of the country, abruptly left the podium and made his vain attempt to flee from the wrath of his compatriots.

Change in the USSR

Let us now turn to the revival of religion in Russia and the role played by religion in the recent changes. The first distinct sign of change came in 1988 with the celebration of one thousand years of Russian Christianity. Originally planned as a low-key event this developed into a major celebration. The state permitted an official televised ceremony attended by government officials and by guests from all over the world. This event brought out into the open and into union two trends which had been developing unnoticed. The first was a revival of interest in religion, the second a revival of interest in Russian identity. The thousandth anniversary of Russian Christianity reminded Russians of how much Christianity had shaped their history and culture. From the time of the millennium onwards the checks on Christian practice were increasingly ignored and then in 1991 totally abolished. The revival of Christianity went hand in hand with the gradual opening up of society under Gorbachev's policy of glasnost. Glasnost means openness – a willingness to let ideas circulate and flourish. This went very much with religious revival. Throughout the Soviet era the churches had continued as the one area of life not wholly controlled by the totalitarian regime. Hence as more and more people became disenchanted with Communism so they turned to the one surviving institution which was not identified with Marxist ideology. Many turned to religion not because they knew much about it, but because they could no longer go on with Communist ideology. This was naturally helped by the fact that many of the early dissidents in Soviet society had been dissidents on religious grounds. As disaffection with the Soviet system grew so did the influence of those who had first sought to oppose it.

In many ways the revival of religion in Russia came as a complete surprise. I had a little first-hand experience of this in that in November 1991 I was invited to speak to the Russian Academy of Sciences on the case for religion.[10] Introducing the discussion the head of the Russian Institute for Philosophy, Pavel Gurevich commented: 'The power of the religious revival had not been

anticipated by any of our futurology.' This is almost an understate-
ment in that in the first three years of Gorbachev's secretaryship
more than 5,000 churches were reopened. This almost doubled the
number of available churches. Since then the process has
continued unabated, with ambitious plans for the rebuilding of the
Cathedral of Christ the Saviour in the centre of Moscow. Sunday
schools and adult Christian schools have been opened and in
public life religion is now given a respected place. Likewise in the
media. Whereas in the past Christianity was almost wholly
excluded, except for reports of priestly misdemeanours, now
Christian programmes and church services are regularly broadcast.

In public life, too, the patriarch has been restored to a respected
and honoured place. Following Yeltsin's election as president of the
Russian Republic, a ceremony was held in which the orchestra
played 'A life for the Czar' while the patriarch stepped forward to
shake Yeltsin's hand and greet him as president in the name of the
Russian people. Moreover this role was not entirely ceremonial, for
a year later, at the time of the August *coup*, the patriarch played an
absolutely central role in tipping the balance away from the
conspirators. In the West we tend to think with hindsight that the
coup was bound to fail, but I was assured in Moscow in 1991 that it
could easily have gone either way.

In his discussion of the part played by the Russian Orthodox
Church in the collapse of the *coup*, Michael Bourdeaux points out
that the attempted *coup* took place on the Orthodox date of the
Feast of the Assumption while the patriarch was celebrating the
liturgy in the newly opened and freshly restored Dormitian
Cathedral in the Kremlin itself. In the course of the liturgy he
omitted the standard petition for the army and next day issued a
declaration which read: 'These events confuse the conscience of
millions of our fellow countrymen who are confronted with the
question of the legality of the newly formed State Committee.
Consequently we declare it to be essential at this time to hear the
voice of President Gorbachev and to find his relations to the
events which have occurred.' Later that night the patriarch came
out even more strongly against the *coup* leaders and the threatened
use of the army. In words which were later televised on every
channel the patriarch declared: 'The Church does not and cannot
bless illegal, violent and bloody acts. I beg you all dear people do
all you can to extinguish the flame of civil war. Stop!'[11]

Michael Bourdeaux claims that, 'unquestionably' this appeal 'played a part in undermining the resolve of the coup leaders and the army'. This might be hard to document without, for example, ascertaining whether or not General Lebed was aware of the patriarch's appeal and how far he was or was not influenced by it. However, it is clear that in addition to the role of the patriarch, ordinary Russian Orthodox clergy appeared very prominently in television coverage of the crisis as they issued forth from the 'White House' to bless the soldiers in the tanks. I vividly recall the CNN pictures of Fr Gleb Yakunin helping Yeltsin on to the tank to make his statement of defiance against the *coup* leaders. We do know that the decision of the military was finely balanced and that it was a heroic step for Lebed to refuse to obey the direct orders he had been given. In this context it would seem reasonable to suggest that the patriarch's appeal and the visibility of Orthodox opposition to the *coup* may well have made a significant contribution to the climate in which the decision against the *coup* could be made and the confidence of the ordinary soldier could be kept.

There is no doubt that a major change has taken place in the public attitude towards religion. From my perspective as a philosopher of religion it was fascinating to hear the comments of speaker after speaker at the 1991 Conference on Religion and Culture at the Russian Academy of Sciences. Let me cite some quotes I noted at the time: 'Our fight against God destroyed our society. We need to repent. Only spiritual resources can now help'; 'The barbaric attitude to religion in Russia in the twentieth century has killed everything that used to be the spiritual wealth of our country'; 'Such grounds for optimism as exist, exist in spiritual renewal.'

However, it is important not to overstate the depth of this apparent revival of concern for religion. The impact of seventy-five years of official atheism remains a significant factor in Russian society. The ambiguity of the present situation can be illustrated by looking at two figures published in a survey cited in the *Keston Newsletter* for December 1996 from the Russian newspaper *Today*. What the survey found was that, while 65 per cent of Russians say that they believe that the Russian Orthodox Church is vital for Russia, only 6 or 7 per cent actually attend any of its services.[12] In other words, while there has been a dramatic change in the public avowal of the value of religion, there has been no significant change in regular personal participation since the attendance percentage is not significantly different from the figures that used to be cited during the Soviet era, and suggests that existentially continuity may be more significant than change

I have focused here on Russia, but it is important to notice the role of religion in other countries of the former Soviet Union. First let us note the Baltic States of Lithuania, Latvia and Estonia. In Lithuania the population is predominantly Roman Catholic and its Catholicism was central to the revival of its sense of national identity. When the struggle for independence was at its height one noted how often reference was made to the president worshipping in the cathedral. Yet for almost forty years prior to 1988 the cathedral had been closed by the Soviet authorities. Its reopening and rededication by Cardinal Steponavicius, recently released from exile, was broadcast on Lithuanian radio and television in February 1989, and was a crucial stage in the growing public sense of nationhood and separateness from the Soviet Union. The same is true of the Lutheran populations of Estonia and Latvia. In Latvia the restoration of the Latvian Lutheran cathedral in 1988 was also an important step in the renewal of a national sense. For the Latvian Lutheran Church began to revive and grow again at the same time as the national movement developed. The Latvian Lutheran synod unequivocally called for restoration of national independence and the Catholic Archbishop Gailitis was a fervent supporter of the Latvian National Independence Movement whose founding congress he opened with prayer.

In Estonia individuals of all the main churches played a significant part in the independence movement and the Ecumenical Council of Churches of Lutherans, Orthodox, Methodists, Baptists and Adventists in 1989 presented a united front in seeking change to the laws on religion as applied there. In all three Baltic States religious revival has been central in the movement for independence and moves towards complete religious freedom have been part of their earliest independent measures. For example, all three Baltic States declared Christmas, Easter and All Souls Day public holidays in 1989 and sought to restore rights and properties of churches confiscated in the Soviet era.

In the Ukraine the Uniate Church was an important factor in the national independence movement. The Uniate Church is a church with a similar liturgy to that of the Orthodox Church but which accepts the authority of the pope. Under Stalin the Uniate Church had been compelled to unite with the Orthodox Church, but Gorbachev's decision to restore its previous separation was a significant stage in the recognition of a powerful sense of Ukrainian identity, an identity stirred further by a sense of indignation at the way in which the millennium of Russian Christianity had actually hi-jacked an anniversary of the Ukrainian nation, since it was the baptism of Vladimir, prince of the Kievan Rus peoples, which was actually being commemorated.

In the states of the Caucasus, Georgia has re-emerged as a self-conscious Christian state and Shevardnadze as the first president of Georgia has sought baptism to identify himself with his country's Christian heritage. Armenia is Christian and Azerbaijan is Muslim and this difference plays a major role both in their distinctive sense of nationhood and in the conflict between them over disputed territories. Within the Soviet Union as a whole the new nations that have emerged have in each case tended to be identified to a considerable extent by their dominant religion, with the Muslim states of Asia being very conscious of their difference from the predominantly Christian Slav nations. The falsity of a supposed Soviet identity is shown by its failure to survive the ideology which gave birth to it, and with the disenchantment with that ideology, older identities based on religion and culture have re-emerged.

In the years since the heady days of 1989 and 1991 we have come to recognize that the changes have not been an unequivocal good. We know that in Ngorno Karabakh there has been six years of warfare between Christian and Muslim in a formerly secular state. And in former Yugoslavia the situation has been far worse with ethnic strife, 'ethnic cleansing' and massacres in Croatia, Serbia and Bosnia as Catholics, Orthodox and Muslims reassert divisive religious identities as against the notion of a united but secular state for all the southern Slavs.

The pope's assertion that the finger of God could be seen at work in Eastern Europe is less attractive now as we see the negative implications of what has happened, not only in ethnic strife but in the revival of religious bigotry and authoritarianism. To try to replace totalitarian Marxism with an authoritarian Catholicism in Poland (by some Catholic leaders) seems a far cry from the time when the Catholic pope became the voice of the voiceless in a struggle for human freedom. A simple appeal for no divorce, no contraception and no abortion is a long way from the vastly more visionary presentation of the Christian challenge to an atheist Communist society. It would be a tragedy if the hopes for Eastern Europe turned to ashes, and if the dream of a renewed society were to be buried in nostalgia for a past and very different civilization. Christianity in Eastern Europe may be being offered one brief window of opportunity for significant revival. If this chance is not taken new processes of secularization and political division may well destroy the dream of a new beginning.

Notes

My discussion of Poland, East Germany and the Baltic States is indebted to contributions prepared for my book co-edited with V. Arzenukhin, *Religion and Change in Eastern Europe*, by Anton Pospieszalski, Gottfried Kretzschmar and Marite Sapiets respectively.

[1] Owen Chadwick, *The Christian Church in the Cold War* (Harmondsworth, Penguin, 1992), 207.

[2] Owen Chadwick, *A History of Christianity* (London, Weidenfeld & Nicolson, 1995), 258.

[3] Pope John Paul II, *Crossing the Threshold of Hope* (London, Jonathan Cape, 1994), 132.

[4] Michael Bourdeaux, *The Role of Religion in the Fall of Soviet Communism* (London, Centre for Policy Studies, 1992).

[5] Anton Pospieszalski, 'The Catholic Church in Poland 1945–89', in Paul Badham and V. Arzenukhin, *Religion and Change in Eastern Europe* (Basingstoke, Macmillan, 2000).

[6] George Weigel, *The Final Revolution* (Oxford, Oxford University Press, 1992), 149.

[7] Desmond O' Grady, *The Turned Card* (Leominster, Gracewing, 1995), 7.

[8] *Final Revolution*, 135.

[9] Ibid., 160.

[10] Conference on Religion and Culture, Moscow, 21–23 November 1991; Institute of Philosophy, Russian Academy of Sciences. My paper was published as 'The relationship between faith and reason', *Faith and Freedom* (April 1992), 3–7.

[11] Bourdeaux, *Role of Religion*, 21.

[12] 'The right to believe', *Keston Newsletter* (October–December 1996).

7

Religion and the political and social order in the Middle East

SIMON MURDEN

Introduction

The Middle East is the historic birthplace of the world's three great monotheistic religions, and Judaism, Christianity and Islam have long had a definitive influence on the construction of social identities, the nature of politics and the battle-lines of conflict in the region. Islam has been the most important religious influence. The expansion of Arab civilization in the seventh century heralded an era of Islamic empires that lasted until the abolition of the Ottoman Caliphate in 1924.

For the last two centuries, the dominant issue for the Muslim states and societies of the Middle East has been the rise of European and American hegemony in the international system, and the model of progress that the West brought. During the twentieth century, the Middle East was overtaken by modernization. Pioneered in Europe, modernization combined an industrial and technological revolution with a philosophical, political and social revolution. One of the most important manifestations of modernity was secularism: the exclusion of religious ideas and organizations from positions of political and social authority. The European model of modernity produced the secular territorial state, and the relocation of ultimate political legitimacy from the divine to the human.

Modernization has had an enormous impact on Middle Eastern societies, but as the twenty-first century dawns, the Middle East can be seen to be confounding a number of the expectations associated with the process of modernization. The power of religion to shape beliefs and behaviour has not been swept away by some irresistible tide of secularism. Religious doctrines and organizations continue to play a major role in constructing social and political identities, and in creating boundaries of belonging and exclusion. Today, the stability of Middle Eastern politics and society is inextricably linked to religion.

Religion and the state system in the Middle East

The final demise of the Ottoman empire in the First World War put an end to the reality of an Islamic government ruling over a multi-ethnic union of Muslim peoples. Britain and France went on to preside over the construction of a new system of territorial states in the Middle East that included the creation of Iraq, Syria, Palestine and Jordan. The new state system was the setting for a future that pointed away from religion, and towards nationalism and secularism. Turkish, Iranian and Arab nationalisms became the dominant political ideas for new state-based élites that tended to believe that Islamic culture was at the root of backwardness and decline. The model of a nationalist élite aspiring to essentially Western forms of culture and organization emerged in the Turkey of Mustafa Kemal, in the Iran of Reza Pahlavi and in the Arab world. Arab nationalism was never quite so hostile to Islam as Turkish or Iranian nationalisms, but Gamal Abdul Nasser's regime in Egypt after 1952, and the Ba'ath party regimes in Syria and Iraq represented solidly nationalist and socialist experiments in modernization.

Modernity and secularism penetrated the politics of key Middle Eastern countries, but the influence of religion far from disappeared. In the less developed parts of the Arab world, Islamic-centred culture remained powerful. The expansion of the Saudi Kingdom in the 1920s was supported by a puritanical Islam, and the Islamic state that was formed enforced a rigorous interpretation of Islamic *sharia* law. Meanwhile, even in the more modern parts of the Middle East, politics was closely associated with sectarian divisions between religious and cultural solidarity groups. In Iraq, Sunni Arab clans ruled over the majority Shia Arab and Sunni Kurdish populations under the cover of Arab nationalism and socialism. Similarly, in Syria, the Ba'athist state fell under the control of Alawite army officers, who proceeded to uplift their minority Islamic sect in the face of the traditional Sunni establishment. The emerging state system in the Middle East also met the 'solidarity group' in the form of Zionist Jews. The founders of the Israeli state were nationalists and socialists, but they were inextricably rooted in Jewish culture, and the whole Zionist project was justified by reference to an ancient religious claim to the Land of Israel.

The crisis of modernization in the Middle East

Notwithstanding the undercurrents of religion and solidarity groups, the idea of modernity represented the political main-stream in many Middle Eastern countries. By the late 1960s, however, the whole process of modernization was in crisis, and Middle Eastern societies were on the verge of a major sea change in attitudes. The shattering Arab defeat in the Six Day War of 1967 acted as a catalyst for the deeper crisis. Many Arabs had responded to pan-Arab nationalism, but the repeated failure of the Arab states that propagated it meant that its prestige faded. Behind the façade of secular ideologies was, as James Bill and Robert Springborg observed, a 'mosaic' of more deeply ingrained religious, ethnic and linguistic identities.[1] Above all, Islam had remained a key component in the identity of many Middle Easterners, and the most widely accepted reference point for political and social legitimacy. The waning of Arab nationalism opened the way for one of the great phenomena of the twentieth century: the Islamic revival of the 1970s.

The crisis of modernization in the Middle East was rooted in the strains of the development process, and in the failure of secular states to develop stable forms of political legitimacy. The Middle Eastern state was bureaucratic and ineffective, and state-led development projects did not live up to expectations. Economic progress failed to keep pace with the demands of explosive rates of population growth, with rural to urban migration, and with the growing expectations of the new urban population. For far too many Middle Easterners, modernization meant an urban experience of poverty, underemployment, poor housing and services, and few prospects. With the traditional forms of com-munity and civility disappearing in the process of urbanization, social alienation was one of the major features of city life.

The secular state responded slowly to the development crisis, and the economic reform that was introduced often worsened the underlying tensions. The launching of the *infitah* (opening) by the regime of Anwar Sadat in Egypt in the 1970s was an experience shared in many Middle Eastern countries. The idea of the market and of engaging with international capitalism was embraced, but reform was very patchy and the benefits did not extend deep enough into society. The state and business élite that emerged from the *infitah* aspired to Western values and lifestyles that were far removed from the lives of most ordinary people. As the secular élite essentially abandoned the masses, a vacuum of leadership and common interest opened up into which Islamic values and organizations moved. Where the state failed, Islam provided. Benevolent Islamic organizations offered welfare hand-outs, health care and education to Muslims in their local communities. The young, especially the recently urbanized and educated lower middle classes, turned to Islam, and became the leaders of a broader frustration amongst the urban poor. Islam offered dignity and hope in the midst of the Middle Eastern city, where there had seemed to be none.

The growing role of Islam as an opposition to the modernizing state was reinforced by the coercive practices of the state. The secular opposition to most Middle Eastern governments was often effectively repressed, but those opposing the state could find some shelter in Islamic language, communities and institutions. The mosque, and especially the tens of thousands of small religious meeting places that exist in Middle Eastern countries, became a political platform that few secular states could completely control. Islam gradually emerged as the principal opposition, and pressed its case for a return to 'authentic' Islamic values and to a more just society.

The doctrines of the Islamic revival

The Islamic revival after the 1970s manifested itself in numerous ways. Many Muslims reaffirmed their relationship with Islamic culture. More men went to mosque, more women covered themselves with the *hijab*, and religious celebrations were more fully observed. Islamic resurgence also took place in the realm of ideas, although the intellectual substance of the Islamic revival was by no means monolithic. Islam was interpreted for the modern world in diverse ways, and the debate within Islam is a complex one, with particular thinkers and groups synthesizing different perspectives. Yet, as Mir Zohair Husain has outlined, Islamic opinions can be broadly categorized into four positions: the traditionalist, fundamentalist, modernist and pragmatist.[2]

The pragmatist's position is that held by the non-practising Muslims who have dominated the secular regimes of the modern Middle East. The pragmatists continue to hold state power, notably in Iraq, Syria, Egypt and Algeria, but the attraction of the nationalism and socialism that underpins their rule has waned, and even they are increasingly prone to clothe their language and actions in Islam *gharb*. Saddam Hussein may now use Islamic language, but the Iraqi state is still far from Islamic. The modernists also sought to adapt Islam to the modern world, often referring to Marxism and socialism, but within a more genuinely Islamic world-view than the pragmatists. The modernist's objective is to incorporate essentially Western notions of democracy, economic justice and human rights into Islam. Whilst the modernists have had an influence on Middle Eastern politics, notably in the form of Ali Shariati and Abolhassan Bani-Sadr in the Iranian Revolution, they have been peripheral to the Islamic revival. Muslim societies have been resistant to modernist reformulation of basic Islamic doctrines, and some modernists have fared very badly indeed. Modernists often tread a path that borders on heresy.

The dominant streams in the Islamic revival were the traditionalist and fundamentalist ones. Traditionalists and fundamentalists share the vision of a society ruled by an Islamic state that rigorously enforces *sharia* law, but beyond this common ground tend to part company. The traditionalists are immersed in the classical and medieval heritage of Islam and Islamic jurisprudence, and largely oppose further adaptation. The heart of traditionalism is the established clergy and members of the ruling élite in the Arab kingdoms, and so many traditionalists are hostile to the use of Islam as an instrument of political mobilization. On the other hand, most fundamentalists are more political ideologues than Islamic scholars, and are interested in what Islam can do for Muslims in the modern world. Fundamentalists believe that Muslims have been attacked and subordinated by alien powers and beliefs, and that only a return to the basic texts of Islam can rescue Muslims from their decline in the world. The struggles to purify Muslim societies from within and to combat the forces of corruption from the outside involve taking on a contemporary political agenda. In fact, fundamentalists are often hostile to the established Islamic clergy, whom they condemn for their political passivity, and are prepared for doctrinal innovations that make the idea of rebellion against existing states more thinkable.

Islam has a long history of puritanical revivals. The twentieth century has witnessed many such revivals. From the emergence of the Saudi state in the early part of this century to the rise of the Taliban in Afghanistan in the 1990s, localized Islamic revivals have played an important role in many parts of the Middle East. The Islamic revival that took shape in the 1970s, though, was unusual in that its influence was so widespread across the Muslim world, and because it has lasted for so long. The Islamic revival was also unusual because it was not the product of a struggle within a tribal or traditional society, but was generated in the modern urban setting.

Modern political Islam can trace its roots back to Hasan al-Banna and the development of the Muslim Brotherhood (*Ikhwan al-Muslimin*) in Egypt from the end of the 1920s. Al-Banna proposed the re-Islamization of Muslim societies as a prelude to an Islamic state, and established the Muslim Brotherhood to set about this task. Much of the time, the Muslim Brotherhood provided social welfare to Muslims in their communities, but it also turned to politics and even to violence to achieve its objectives. Indeed, Muslim Brothers have been involved in violent agitation against every Egyptian regime since the 1930s. The Muslim Brotherhood in Egypt represented a model that spread to many Middle Eastern countries, and with it came organized political resistance to the secular state.

The fundamentalist revival was subsequently shaped by the status of a number of prominent Islamic thinkers, the most important of which were Sayyid Qubt (d. 1966) in Egypt, Abu al-Ala al-Mawdudi (d. 1977) in Pakistan and Ruhollah Khomeini (d. 1989) in Iran. The militant Islam that such figures promoted in the 1960s and 1970s was no longer prepared to wait for the re-Islamization of society, and spoke of an Islamic struggle in the language of revolution, martyrdom and *jihad*. The moral corruption and tyrannical government of the modern world – for Qubt, a new age of ignorance (*jahiliyya*) – had to be overcome. The enemies of Islam – secular Muslims, Islamic modernists, and the West and Israel – were identified, and the struggle engaged.

The mission of the new Islamists was political: the forging of a revolution by a vanguard élite, the seizure of the state and the creation of a new Islamic order. The ultimate destination was even more radical, for Islam is a universal religion, and such fundamentalists made claims to sovereignty that superseded the legitimacy of national and state boundaries. The unification of the Muslim people, the *umma*, was the ultimate dream. Militant Islamists, then, were not only an opposition to the ruling regimes of the state system, but also to the existing system of states itself.

The crescendo of Islamic revivalism

The political and social stability of many Middle Eastern countries was shaken by the Islamic revival in the 1970s and 1980s. The triumphant moment of the Islamic revival was the Iranian Revolution in 1978–9. The rebellion against the Pahlavi monarchy arose from the tensions and conflicts generated by modernization. The values of the secular élite and the centralized character of capitalist development ran into the interests of the traditional merchant class and the Shia clergy. The Shah's authoritarian regime was overthrown by a populist coalition that included Islamic traditionalists, Islamic modernists, Marxists and liberals, but it was the radical Shia clergy, led by Grand Ayatollah Ruhullah Khomeini, that emerged as the most dynamic force. In the following years, the real Iranian Revolution was played out. In a struggle for power, 1979–83, the militant clergy moved to system-atically destroy their partners in the rebellion against the Shah in order to consolidate their religious vision of politics and society.

The real Iranian Revolution, then, was the Islamic project led by Ayatollah Khomeini. The Revolution established an Islamic state by unifying political and religious authority in the form of the *velayet-e faqih* (the rule of the Islamic jurist) and other institutions that ensured the political power of the Shia clergy. Khomeini himself was to be the *faqih*, a constitutional position that possessed enormous powers over the workings of the Islamic state. The Revolution also embodied a view of Islam's purpose in the world that shared much with other Third World populisms.[3] Dismantling exploitative capitalism, achieving social equality, and resisting the penetration of Western cultural and economic imperialism were embodied in the mission.

The Iranian Revolution had significant implications for international security. Few revolutionaries had much respect for existing national boundaries. In fact, the Revolution was ideologically hostile to the conservative Arab monarchies, but also disdained the secular nationalism of the Arab states that had considered themselves radical and progressive. The export of the Revolution was pursued by clerics from within the new Islamic state, but also by those acting in a freelance capacity through personal and religious networks that extended across the Middle East. The impact of the Revolution was most pronounced amongst the other Shia communities of the region. The Gulf States faced serious Shia agitation, particularly in Bahrain and Kuwait. In Iraq, a violent conflict between the Baathist regime and Shia militants eventually helped set Saddam Hussein on a path to a full-scale invasion of Iran in September 1980. In Lebanon, the emergence of the Shia militancy of Amal and Hizbullah, especially after the Israeli invasion in 1982, changed the balance of the Lebanese political system, and went on to give Israel the most serious military set-back in its history. Shia militants from Lebanon were also behind a wave of international terrorism in Europe and the Middle East directed at Israel, the United States and the Gulf States.

The wider resonance of the Iranian Revolution, though, was limited. The bloody power struggle in Iran between 1979 and 1983 and the outbreak of the Iran–Iraq War did much to diminish its appeal in the Arab world. The basic divisions between Persian and Arab, and between Sunni and Shia sects within Islam, were another limitation: the more so because Sunni fundamentalists were committed to returning to the basic texts of Islam and to eliminating all deviations, including Shi'ism. With many Sunni fundamentalists actually hostile to the Iranian Revolution, the significance of what had happened in Iran was that of an example. The mobilization of Islamic faith on a massive scale had overthrown the Shah's regime and its powerful army; what had been thought impossible had been achieved.

The direct appeal of the Iranian Revolution may have been limited, but as an example it did energize Islamic militants, and so generated a real sense of crisis in the Middle East of the 1980s. The Islamic dissidence that broke out was not a part of some transnational Islamic revolution, but a crescendo of violent opposition shook established Arab regimes. The violent seizure of the Grand Mosque in Mecca by a messianic group led by Juhayman al-Utaiba in 1979, the assassination of the Egyptian president, Anwar Sadat in 1981, the uprising of the Muslim Brotherhood in the Syrian city of Hama in 1982, and the start of an Algerian civil war between the old secular regime and the Front Islamique du Salut (FIS) were but the most extreme manifestations of Sunni activism. Even in the most developed and secularized Middle Eastern societies, such as Turkey and Tunisia, a militant Islam established itself on the political stage.

The politics of managing Islamic militancy has been an experience shared by most Middle Eastern states. Whilst Islamic militants tend to agree over objectives – an Islamic state ruled by *sharia* law – many differ over means, and this has shaped the way that the states have dealt with the Islamic challenge. The situation was perhaps most stark in Egypt where the Muslim Brotherhood was reluctant to engage in an all-out war against the secular state, and instead concentrated on increasing its influence in national politics and civil society. The Muslim Brotherhood's moderation over means stands in contrast to more radical groups, notably al-Jihad and al-Jamaat al-Islamiyya, committed to a violent war against the Egyptian state and other infidels. Keeping the mainstream Muslim Brotherhood away from the smaller more radical groups has been the key dynamic of political management for the state.

Differing combinations of re-Islamization, political reform and coercion have been the means by which Middle Eastern states have managed Islamic militancy. In Egypt, political reform and coercion has inhibited the formation of alliances between the Muslim Brotherhood and extremist secret societies. In Saudi Arabia, the state met the challenge of the Iranian Revolution and the Juhayman revolt by reinforcing its attachment to a state-centred fundamentalist Islam. In Jordan, mainstream Islamists were brought into a reformed political system to diffuse much of the threat. In Algeria, the mishandling of political reform culminated in the intervention of the military to prevent the Front Islamique du Salut winning national elections in December 1991, and so brought mainstream and extremist Islamists together against the old regime to produce a terrible civil war.

The faltering march of Islamic activism

The Islamic revival has dominated the political agenda in the Middle East since the 1970s, and represents the principal political challenge to many Middle Eastern governments. That said, despite the real force behind the Islamic revival, it has left the system of territorial states unchanged and has failed to actually overthrow an established government since the Iranian Revolution. Islamic revolutionaries have been confined within the borders of the state, and have substantially met their match at that level.

What happened in Iran is perhaps indicative of what is likely to happen to Islamists even when in power. Faced with the realities of managing a state and society, the revolutionary clergy produced its pragmatists in the mid-1980s, led by Hashemi Rafsanjani, that were mindful of the interests of the Iranian state. For the Islamic Republic's pragmatists, the overriding priority was not the export of some universal revolution, but fighting a conventional war against Iraq and finding ways of dealing with Iran's serious social and economic problems. The election of a liberal cleric, Mohammed Khatami, as Iranian president in May 1997 emphasized the trend. Islam continues to be a defining influence in Iran, but Iranians are increasingly concerned with domestic issues, such as the role of foreign capital, the place of women and the value of democracy. In sum, the Iranian Revolution has taken on the form and language of a territorial nation-state.

Militant fundamentalism as an opposition also seemed to be changing by the 1990s. Grand dreams of revolution and of seizing the state were fading, and were being replaced by more fragmented and localized social struggles: what Olivier Roy calls the drift from Political Islamism to Neo-fundamentalism.[4] The political Islamism of the 1970s and 1980s was promoted by a self-proclaimed vanguard that did not reject modernization in its entirety, but rather the secularism and Westernization associated with it. Political Islamism, though, was a mixture of the traditional and the modern, and as the 1980s went on, it was the rediscovery of the traditional that was coming to preoccupy many Islamic militants. What emerged was a form of militancy that held a highly conservative vision for society, but one that was less political. Neo-fundamentalism is less interested in the state and in political revolution, and more concerned with puritanical preaching aimed at re-Islamizing society as a prelude to the organic re-emergence of Islamic rule.

The drift to Neo-fundamentalism in the 1980s was supported by an international network that combined Saudi money, Arab Muslim Brotherhoods, radical Pakistani and Afghan groups, a variety of Islamic educational, financial and social organizations, and an international brigade of militarized activists, many of whom had participated in the anti-Soviet *jihad* in Afghanistan. Veterans from the war in Afghanistan returned home to preach a brand of puritanical Islam in Arab countries, notably in Algeria and Egypt. Afghanistan veterans also brought new violence to the struggle.

Recreating the 'authenticity' of the Prophet Muhammad's ideal Islamic society was the concern of the Neo-fundamentalist, even down to adopting more traditional styles of dress.[5] Women had no place in the public arena. The austere 'authenticity' imagined by Neo-fundamentalists was one that they sought to carve out within existing society, and they were prepared to wage violent struggles within local communities to do it. Such violence could sometimes look pointless, but was rationalized in terms of the righteousness of purifying society. The violence of Jamaat-i Islamiyya in southern Egypt and much of the savagery in the Algerian civil war had little to do with seizing state power: it was more about what Islamic activists were prepared to do for God in their personal *jihad*, and about local social struggles, right down to who runs village life.

Neo-fundamentalist violence proved difficult for the state to control. Tinkering with political and legal reform in an effort to appease militant Neo-fundamentalists is irrelevant, whilst repressive measures have not been easy to apply because of the Neo-fundamentalist's social situation. The Neo-fundamentalist tends to be, as Olivier Roy observed, a 'vagabond' intellectual operating on the fringes of society, and often not particularly well integrated into any Islamic organization or institution.[6] Thus, whilst Islamic militancy was becoming a less coherent challenge to the state, it often represented a low-level but endemic instability, including political and social violence. In some places, notably Algeria and Egypt, the Islamic challenge is capable of seriously threatening the security of the state and society, but most Middle Eastern states have adapted to the Islamic impulse, and for the time being another triumphant Islamic revolution seems unlikely, much less any transnational Islamic upheaval. The influence of Islam still percolates through Middle Eastern societies, but largely through the activities of Muslim groups in national politics, legal reform, professional associations and welfare provision.

Religion and international security in the contemporary Middle East

Many of the flashpoints of international conflict in the Middle East have been related to religious resurgence, or are prone to be interpreted in religious ways. The end of the cold war produced all sorts of conflicts involving Islam. The Gulf War of 1991 was rooted in the *raison d'état* of the Iraqi regime, but the arrival of Western troops in Saudi Arabia and the demolition of Iraq led to a wave of anti-Western sentiment in the Muslim world. For Saudi Arabia, the Gulf War weakened its influence in the Islamic world's network of Muslim Brotherhoods, but also precipitated the emergence of an urban and educated Islamic opposition in Saudi Arabia itself that has caused political and social agitation, as well as some violence.[7]

Usama Bin Laden – a millionaire businessman – was perhaps the best-known example of the new Saudi militant, eventually leaving the kingdom to find refuge in Sudan and in the Taliban's Afghanistan. The huge bomb attacks on the US embassies in Kenya and Tanzania in August 1998 that killed 240 people, mostly local Africans, were linked to Bin Laden. The US had found a target amongst its Islamic terrorist enemies, and responded by firing Cruise missiles at sites associated with Bin Laden in Afghanistan and Sudan. A tit-for-tat war between the USA and the 'Bin Laden militants' seemed a real possibility. Bin Laden certainly became a symbolic figure for both sides, with other wealthy Saudis reported to be helping to finance his anti-Western *jihad*.[8]

The pressure on Muslim states to do something about the predicament that many Muslims seemed to be facing in the post-cold war world represented a continuing challenge to their legitimacy. Conflicts in Afghanistan, Kashmir, Bosnia, Sudan, Chechnya, Indonesia, Kosovo and parts of Central Asia progressively reinforced the sense of crisis, and strengthened the idea that Islamic peoples were beset with enemies. The belief that Islam was locked in a great civilizational struggle with the West – not to say with other religious opponents, Hindus as well as Jews – found a significant audience in the Muslim world.

The rise of religious militancy in the Israel–Palestinian conflict had particularly significant implications for the stability of the Middle East. The secular and nationalist mainstream of both Israeli and Palestinian societies were challenged by growing religiousness in society at large and by religious militants. Within Israel, the capture of the West Bank and Gaza in the Six Day War of 1967 focused a religious Zionism that saw reclaiming Eretz Israel (Land of Israel) as an act of redemption that legitimized the entire project of founding the state of Israel. A number of belligerent settler groups, notably Gush Emunim (Bloc of the Faithful), assumed an influence in the Israeli political system, but also introduced unofficial violence to settlement activity. When the Labor party lost power to the Likud Bloc in 1977, and Labor's governing alliance with the religious Zionists of the National Religious party dissolved, the gap between secular and religious forces in Israel widened.[9] By the 1980s, those Israelis that identified themselves as secular and modern were increasingly running into both the belligerent political agenda of religious Zionist-settlers and the conservative social agenda of newly assertive ultra-orthodox Jews. The merging of the two streams of religious Zionism and of the ultra-orthodox was a particularly dangerous development in Israeli politics, and one that Shmuel Sandler argues eventually culminated in the assassination of the Israeli Prime Minister, Yitzhak Rabin.[10]

Meanwhile, the Israeli occupation in the West Bank and Gaza, especially after the outbreak of the Palestinian's *intifadah* rebellion from late 1987, contributed to the development of the Islamic resistance of Hamas and Islamic Jihad. Islamic resistance reinfused the Israel–Palestinian conflict with new militancy and violence, and challenged the efforts of the Palestinian Liberation Organization (PLO) leadership to adopt a more flexible political strategy. When the Israel–PLO peace process did emerge in the 1990s, religious-inspired violence dogged the development of the process. Competing claims to sacred sites, especially in Jerusalem and Hebron, produced serious outbreaks of killing. Two events proved particularly disastrous for the peace process: the assassination of Yitzhak Rabin by a Jewish militant in early November 1995, and a series of Hamas and Islamic Jihad bus bombings in Israel in February and March 1996. The subsequent election of Benjamin Netanyahu and the Likud Bloc to power in Israel went on to increase the influence of religious Zionists and conservative orthodox Jews in the government of Israel. The forces of the Palestinian National Authority (PNA) clashed with Hamas and Islamic Jihad, but the Netanyahu government's contention that the PNA was not doing enough to control the Islamic opposition looked like stalling the peace process indefinitely.

Yet, the election of a new Labour-led government under Ehud Barak in May 1999 seemed to prove the adaptability of some of the orthodox religious parties in Israel. The orthodox Sephardic religious party, SHAS, established a position as easily the third largest party, raising its share of the vote to over 13 per cent and its number of Knesset seats from ten to seventeen.[11] SHAS had been a supporter of the Netanyahu government, but after ditching its leader, Aryeh Deri, recently convicted on bribery and fraud charges, went on to enter into a broadly based coalition with the Barak government.[12] The National Religious Party – with five seats from 4.2 per cent of the vote – also swapped sides in order to take positions in Barak's cabinet.[13]

The state of the Israel–Palestinian peace process continues to be one of the most serious threats to domestic and international stability in the Middle East. The Arab–Israeli conflict remains capable of firing intense religious and national feelings, and of undermining the legitimacy of established Muslim regimes. Israeli settlement activity around Jerusalem has been a particularly explosive issue. The Arab states most associated with the West and most committed to the peace process – Egypt, Jordan and the Gulf States – had the most to lose from the absence of a just solution to the Arab–Israeli conflict, let alone any catastrophic failure that rolled back the advances made by the Palestinians. The Barak government brought a commitment to press on with the peace process, and so promised to relieve some of the pressure that the conflict exerted on politics in the Middle East.

Religion in perspective

The Islamic revival that followed the 1970s was one of the great ideological and political phenomena of the twentieth century. Religion retains its power to define Middle Eastern politics, and Islam will be in the driving seat of political opposition in important states such as Algeria, Egypt, Jordan and Saudi Arabia well into the next century. The deep social and economic problems embodied in the modernization process, as well as the lack of political legitimacy, are far from being resolved in many Middle Eastern societies. As long as so many young Middle Easterners, especially young men, are condemned to a future with no resources, no voice and no hope, Islamic militancy will be an ideological and organizational refuge for the disaffected. The selfishness and indifference of established secular élites, and the repressive force of American and European hegemony in the international system are the self-evident enemies of Islamic militants.

Religion is central to the understanding of Middle Eastern politics, but, as Fred Halliday has argued, it is important to avoid a myopic view on Islam when thinking about the region, because other factors are at play.[14] Indeed, the radical alternative that the Islamic project of the 1970s and 1980s represented has faded: the Iranian Revolution has adapted to the territorial nation-state, and political Islamism is changing into Neo-fundamentalism. What Halliday highlighted was the power of great social and economic structures to influence the behaviour of both individuals and states. For all the claims that 'Islam is the solution', religious faith alone is unable to really address the social and economic crisis that gave rise to the Islamic revival in the first place. Religious belief cannot solve the urban crisis in the Middle East, or address the myriad deficiencies – low productivity, weak currencies, over-regulation – that prevent Middle Eastern countries from participating more effectively in the global market-place. Nor can faith really alter the subordinate position in which Muslims find themselves in the international system.

Navigating a path between historic faith and functioning successfully in the contemporary world is a difficult task, and one no better demonstrated than in the Islamic Republic of Iran. The Islamic Republic has always embodied tensions between tradition and modernity, a feature that was emphasized by the landslide election of Mohammad Khatami in 1997. Khatami represented a more moderate Islam as well as a constituency, of the young, of the middle class and of women, that wanted change. The ferment going on in Iranian politics witnessed dramatic outbursts, such as the explosion of student anger in Tehran and other major cities over six days in July 1999.[15] Tired of restrictions on the freedom of the press – in particular, a court order banning the moderate newspaper *Salam* – and of the arbitrary interference and brutality of both official and unofficial religious enforcers, large numbers of students became involved in some of the most serious civil disturbances in Iran since the revolution.[16] The emotions unleashed were very deeply felt. Many young people in Iran wanted more political and social freedom, whilst others were determined to stop them having it. The conservative establishment organized a heavy-handed crackdown and the mass mobilization of 'hard-line' supporters to put a stop to the demonstrations. The Khatami government was certainly not helped by its own supporters during the student protests, but no matter the outcome of particular battles, Iran's future will hardly be unaffected by the cultural preferences and economic imperatives of the global economy. The clash is not over.

The same tensions between tradition and globalized modernity are likely to be played out in differing ways across the Arab Middle East. Most Muslims are not militants and the urge to consume the material goods of the global market is very strong. Islam has been contained by the state and the world economy, and there is little sign that Muslims are about to throw off these powerful structures. Indeed, Muslim countries are increasingly faced with the prospect of making some important cultural and political choices in order to respond to the challenges of the global market. Finding a path for Islam in a global setting will substantially define the future of Middle Eastern politics and society.

Notes

1 James Bill and Robert Springborg, *Politics in the Middle East* (New York, HarperCollins, 4th edn., 1994), 34.
2 Mir Zohair Husain, *Global Islamic Politics* (New York, HarperCollins, 1995), 11.
3 Fred Halliday, *Islam and the Myth of Confrontation: Religion and Politics in the Middle East* (London, I. B. Tauris, 1995), 73.
4 Olivier Roy, *The Failure of Political Islam* (London, I. B. Tauris, 1994), 26.
5 Ibid., 82.
6 Ibid., 95.
7 See R. Hrair Dekmejian, 'The rise of political Islamism in Saudi Arabia', *Middle East Journal*, 48, No. 4 (Autumn 1994), 627–43.
8 Julian Borger, 'US fears Bin Laden plans new attacks', *Observer* (11 July 1999), 22.
9 Shmuel Sandler, 'Religious Zionism and the state: political accommodation and religious radicalism in Israel', in Bruce Maddy-Weitzman and Efraim Inbar (eds.), *Religious Radicalism in the Greater Middle East* (London, Frank Cass, 1997), 133–54.
10 Ibid., 149.
11 'Israeli elections May 1999'. Reported by Israel's Ministry of Foreign Affairs Internet site.
    http://www.israel-mfa.gov.il?mfa/go.asp?MFAH0epu0
12 'Arafat and Barak make peace pledge', BBC News, 19 May 1999.
    http://news.bbc.co.uk/hi/english/world/middle_east/newsid_347000/347380. stm
13 '28th Government of Israel'. Communicated by the Government Press Office.
    http://www.pmo.gov.il/english/gpo/press-releases/070799/070799–4.html
14 Halliday. *Islam and Myth of Confrontation*, 12–16 and 195–8.
15 'Iran unrest "under control"', BBC News, 14 July 1999.
    http://news.bbc.co.uk/hi/english/world/middle_east/newsid_394000/394026. stm
16 Gary Sick, 'Mullahs in full cry to turn back time', *The Sunday Times*, (18 July 1999), 23.

Further Reading

As'ad AbuKhalil, 'The incoherence of Islamic fundamentalism: Arab Islamic thought at the end of the 20th century', *Middle East Journal*, 48, No. 4 (Autumn 1994), 677–94.
Joel Beinin and Joe Stork (eds.), *Political Islam: Essays from Middle East Report* (Berkeley, University of California Press, 1997).

John Esposito, *The Islamic Threat: Myth or Reality?* (Oxford, Oxford University Press, 1992).

Graham Fuller and Ian Lesser, *A Sense of Siege: The Geopolitics of Islam and the West* (Boulder, CO, Westview, 1995).

Laura Guazzone (ed.), *The Islamist Dilemma* (Reading, MA, Ithaca Press, 1995).

Sohail H. Hashemi, 'International society and its Islamic malcontents', *Fletcher Forum of World Affairs*, 20, No. 2 (Winter/Spring, 1996), 13–29.

Gema Munoz (ed.), *Islam, Modernism and the West* (London, I. B. Tauris, 1999).

Abdel Salam Sidahmed and Anoushiravan Ehteshami (eds.), *Islamic Fundamentalism* (Boulder, CO, Westview, 1996).

8

Renaissance of political religion in the Third World in the context of global change

JEFF HAYNES

The chapter offers a perspective on the relation between religion, politics, conflict and identity in the 'Third World',[1] in the context of global change and the pursuit of global order. Using a range of cases from various parts of the Third World, it examines the complex ways in which religious values, beliefs and norms stimulate and affect political developments and vice versa; the social conditions which give rise to religious movements as well as how such movements are promoted and sustained over time; and the links between 'political' religion in the Third World and global order.

The defining characteristic of the contemporary relationship of religion and politics in the Third World, it is argued, is the increasing dissatisfaction with established, hierarchical and institutionalized religious bodies. Many contemporary religious movements seek to find God through personal searching rather than through the mediation of institutions. They also focus on the role of communities in generating positive change in members' lives through the application of group effort. In this regard, religion's interaction with political issues carries an important message of societal resurgence and regeneration, which may challenge the authority of political leaders and economic élites.

The chapter is organized in four parts. The first provides an overview of the relationship between religion and modernization. It surveys the contradictory effects of modernization on social values in different cultural and religious settings. Given the uneven impact of modernization in Third World countries, the relationship between religion and politics has always been a close one. Political power is underpinned by religious beliefs and practices, while political concerns permeate to the heart of the religious sphere: as a result, virtually all organized religion is 'political' in the Third World. Attempts in many countries to separate politics from religion have largely been unsuccessful, especially as economic crisis and global restructuring often undermine social and political cohesion.

The second part examines the political significance of identity in the context of religion. Precisely how religious conflicts relate to development is not clear, although, as Hettne suggests, it is highly likely that 'the differential outcome of both [economic] growth and stagnation [has] an impact'.[2] What is clearer is that social, political and economic change in the Third World comes about as a result of a complex interaction of both domestic and external developments over time. The contemporary political importance of religion is an integral facet of wider 'identity crises', involving serious threats to national integration and to the process of economic development, which revolves around the existence of 'cleavages' within societies. The concept of a cleavage refers to the alignment of the population around social dimensions which are conducive to conflict.

The third part examines the problematic of the political role of Third World religion in the post-cold war global order. It argues, against the arguments of Huntington and others, and while recognizing the potential of political religion to impinge upon the domestic politics of a number of states, that the political renaissance of religion in the Third World does not pose a serious threat to a global order which is dominated by a handful of Western states, including the United States and Japan.

The final part presents a typology of religious movements in order to demonstrate the political and social significance of religion in the Third World. Four types of movements are highlighted, based on whether religion is used as a vehicle of opposition or as an ideology of community development. Groups which link religion to the pursuit of community development are categorized as 'community-orientated' while oppositional movements are classified as 'culturalist', 'fundamentalist' and 'syncretistic'. Threats from powerful outsider groups or from unwelcome symptoms of modernization largely sustain the oppositional movements; community movements on the other hand derive their *raison d'être* from failures of social welfare development.

Religion and modernization

The concern here is with the role of religious establishments (institutions and officials) as well as of socio-political groups and movements whose *raisons d'être* are to be found in religious concerns; examples are the conservative Roman Catholic organization, Opus Dei, Algeria's reformist Front Islamique de Salut, and India's Hindu-chauvinist Bharatiya Janatar party. The impact of religious ideas and values in shaping social and individual behaviour also comes into the reckoning. An individual's religious belief – in a personal spiritual sense – can lead them to join groups which strive after socio-political reform, particularly so in the Third World.

One of the most resilient ideas about societal development after the Second World War was that nations would inevitably secularize as they modernized. The idea of modernization is strongly linked to urbanization, industrialization and to an accompanying rationalization of previously 'irrational' views, such as religious beliefs and ethnic separatism. Loss of religious faith and secularization dovetailed with the idea that technological development and the application of science to overcome perennial social problems of poverty, environmental degradation, hunger and disease would result in long-term human progress. With the decline in the belief in the efficacy of technological development to cure all human ills came a wave of popular religiosity with political ramifications in the Third World. Examples include: the Iranian Islamic Revolution of 1978–80; the widespread growth of Islamic 'fundamentalism' in the Middle East and elsewhere; Protestant Evangelical sects in Latin America whose followers helped to elect two 'born again' presidents in Guatemala in the 1980s; internecine conflict between Hindus and Muslims in India, Buddhists and Hindus in Sri Lanka and Buddhists and Communists in Tibet; Sikh and Muslim separatists in Punjab and Jammu-Kashmir respectively; and religious syncretistic groups in sub-Saharan Africa and elsewhere whose aim is community protection.

Because of the importance placed here on the explanatory value of the role of modernization, it may be appropriate to say a little about it. Throughout the Third World, with the important exception of post-revolutionary states such as China and Iran, the general direction in which social change has taken place is usually referred to as 'modernization'. That is, social change is understood to lead to significant shifts in the behaviour and prevailing choices of social actors, with such particularistic traits as ethnicity or caste losing importance in relation to more generalistic attributes such as nationalism and statism. Growth of formal organizations (for example, state bureaucracy, political parties) and procedures (for example, 'the rule of law'), it is believed, reduces the central role of clientelism and patronage. More generally, the advent of social change, corresponding to a presumed process of modernization, would lead to a general jettisoning of older, traditional values and the adoption of other, initially alien, practices.

In many respects, however, the adoption of Western traits in many Third World states is rather skin deep: Western suits for men rather than traditional dress, the trappings of statehood (flag, constitution, legislature, etc.), a Western lingua franca and so on. The important point is that social change will not be even throughout a society; social and political conflicts are highly likely, owing to the patchy adoption of modern practices. Social change destabilizes, creating a dichotomy between those who seek to benefit from wholesale change and those who prefer the *status quo*. New social strata arise whose position in the new order is decidedly ambiguous. Examples include recent rural–urban migrants in Middle Eastern, African, Latin American and other Third World societies, who find themselves between two worlds, often without an effective or appropriate set of anchoring values. Such people are particularly open to political appeals based on religious precepts.[3]

Generally, religion is an important source of basic value orientations. It may have a powerful impact upon politics within a state or region, especially in the context of ethnicity or religious fundamentalism. Ethnicity relates to perceived shared characteristics of a racial or cultural group. Religious belief may reinforce ethnic consciousness and inter-ethnic conflict, especially in the Third World (but not only there, think of Northern Ireland or former Yugoslavia). Religious fundamentalism, on the other hand, connotes a 'set of strategies, by which beleaguered believers attempt to preserve their distinctive identity as a people or group' in response to a real or imagined attack from those who apparently threaten to draw them into a 'syncretistic, areligious, or irreligious cultural milieu'.[4] Sometimes such defensiveness may develop into a political offensive which seeks to alter the prevailing social, political and on occasions economic, realities of state–society relations.

The political significance of identity

Precisely how ethnic and religious conflicts relate to Third World modernization is not clear, although, as noted above, they often seem to be connected to the effects of economic growth or stagnation. The contemporary political importance of ethnicity and religion are integral facets of wider Third World 'identity crises', associated with the problematical and linked process of national integration and economic development.[5]

Identity and politics

Modernization entails a cultural transformation in the direction of national state identity, a new focus of loyalty. Growing economic advancement and political sophistication are assumed to foster a sense of life satisfaction and lead to generally positive attitudes about the prevailing social and political environment. The orientations and sentiments people have towards politics in general and toward existing political arrangements in particular are formulated within the context of the views they have of themselves and their concept of their own identity. As already noted, two of the most important for these in the Third World are ethnicity and religion. As Kamrava notes, 'it is their sense of identity which largely determines how people behave politically and in turn view their own political environment'.[6] The absence of widely accepted, enduring arrays of norms and social values may make it difficult for many people in the Third World, subject to dramatic change over the last two decades or so, to form cogent opinions about what exactly their socio-political identity is, whether personally or nationally. The identity crisis which follows often focuses on unsatisfactory governments, many of which in the Third World are not only fragmented and incoherent but also sectarian and highly changeable.

The social and political characteristics of many countries in the Third World have not only failed to result in a strong sense of national identity and life satisfaction but have also fostered feelings of disappointment and identity crisis. Political repression, rapid industrialization, the growth of urban-based populations, economic dislocation and social change prompt people in the Third World to question not only their predominant social and political values but also their identity as part of an often putative nation. It would not be an exaggeration to say that identity crisis has become a ubiquitous facet of politics in much of the Third World.

The extent and intensity of cleavages within countries may have a strong impact upon political stability and the formulation of national identity. Sometimes the pursuit of national identity takes the extreme form of 'ethnic cleansing' whereby the desire for ethnic purity is the 'justification' for large-scale atrocities toward so-called internal enemies, that is, groups with a different ethnic or religious identity. As we have recently seen in former Yugoslavia, Rwanda and Burundi, such atrocities exacerbate domestic conflicts where the aim is domination of one ethnic and religious community.

Global order and the Third World

Such conflicts have an impact upon the pursuit and attainment of global order, a condition which Murphy defines as any 'concrete historical, political and economic system'.[7] In international relations theory three broad perspectives regarding global order – the realist, the liberal/pluralist and the Marxist – vie with each other.

The realist perspective contends that the state is *always* the most important actor in international relations because there is no higher authority; international organizations are regarded as always subservient to the state. The global system is a global *states* system grounded in competition, conflict and co-operation. States must rely upon their own resources to achieve the power they need to thrive, even if they are prepared, as most are, to collaborate with others to achieve general goals. Serious conflict is not the usual status of the international system because peace is maintained through local and global balances of power. Realism emphasizes how hegemonic powers, such as the USA, have an important role in establishing and maintaining order in the international system and stresses that the structure of power in the international system shapes the character of the political order.[8] In short, realist analysis places great stress on the significance of military power, and states must ultimately rely on their own efforts to achieve their goals.

In contrast, the liberal/pluralist paradigm begins from the premiss that the state is no longer automatically the primary actor in world politics. The growth of transnational relations points to the significance of non-state actors, especially transnational corporations and international organizations of various kinds which are often deemed to be independent of any individual state's or group of states' control.[9] Indeed, the state itself is not regarded as a unitary actor. Rather, it consists of a body of bureaucratic organizations and institutions. The global system is perceived as an aggregate of different issue areas, such as trade, finance, energy, human rights, democracy and ecology, in which domestic and international policy processes merge. The management of global interdependencies is carried out through processes of bargaining, negotiation and consensus-seeking. Order is maintained not by a balance of power, as realists contend, but by the consensual acceptance of common values, norms and international law. In other words, global order is maintained because states have a vested interest in so doing while the global political process does not involve states alone but also includes a variety of non-state actors.

In the Marxist view, political processes at the global level are viewed primarily as expressions of underlying class conflicts on a global scale. Marxists differ from the realists in not conceiving of global order as based upon the structure of military power, nor sustained by networks of interdependence as the liberal/pluralists do. One of the dominant characteristics of the global order for Marxists is the structural differentiation of the world into core, peripheral and semi-peripheral centres of economic power. While, traditionally, this was regarded as the division between the 'North', 'South' and the Communist Eastern bloc, the emergence of the East Asian Newly Industrializing Countries and the demise of the Eastern bloc has comprehensively undermined the simple (and increasingly simplistic) three-way international economic division. In short, for Marxists, global order is preserved through the power of the leading capitalist states, by international agencies, such as the United Nations, by transnational corporations, and by international regimes which together serve to legitimate a global diffusion of a dominant ideology of liberalism and Western-type modernization.

In each of the three perspectives a degree of stability or predictability in world politics – that is, global order – is achieved, whether by a balance of power (realists), by mechanisms of collective security such as the United Nations (liberal/pluralists) or by a shared liberal-capitalist ideology (Marxists). Nevertheless, despite the existence of (imperfect) mechanisms for building and maintaining global order, one of the defining features of the post-cold war period is the extensive religious and ethnic conflict enveloping not only several Third World regions – sub-Saharan Africa, South Asia and the Middle East – but also the erstwhile Soviet Union and former Yugoslavia. Given the high profile of religious and ethnic conflicts in the current era, coupled with the apparent perplexity with which the traditional international relations paradigms view them, it is necessary to examine in the next section to what extent ethno-religious conflicts are the chief problematic of global order.

Fukuyama, Huntington and global order optimism

The Gulf War of 1990–1 was a defining moment in the debate about global order. Before the conflict President Bush spoke confidently about the birth of a 'new world order'; after the defeat of Iraq, optimism appeared dashed: the aim henceforward was to maintain a global stability rather than strive for a qualitatively *better* order. The aggression of Muslim Iraq against Kuwait, a Western ally, crystallized for some the chief threat to global order: the Third World.

The dual shift from optimism to pessimism and from seeing 'the enemy' as the Soviet Union to the Third World is clearly shown in the work of Fukuyama. In 1989, he was the epitome of optimism: the 'end of history', he maintained, would be a period of increasing liberal democracy and capitalism. For Fukuyama, the sudden collapse of East European Communism indicated the passing of a particular period of history, the unabashed victory of economic and political liberalism as the final form of human government, and the arrival at the end-point of humankind's ideological evolution.[10] For Fukuyama, the Western way of life represents a pattern of universal validity, a ray of hope not only to itself but also to non-Western societies still struggling 'in history'. In relation to the Third World, there would, no doubt, be minor internal conflicts within states which would remain 'in history' – because they were subject to archaic conditions fostering nationalist, religious or ethnic disputes – but in the longer run they too would tread the path of economic and political liberalism. In sum, the post-cold war global order would be a liberal order, only mildly and intermittently troubled by tiresome, yet essentially irrelevant, disputes between Third World peoples who had not (yet) developed the same levels of tolerance, consensus and uniformity of value systems as those in the West.

In his book, *The End of History and the Last Man*, published three years later in 1992, Fukuyama was much more circumspect about the prospects for a liberal post-cold war global order: he had become, in effect, a global order pessimist. In 1989, economic and political liberalism were to govern the world in the long run; in the 1992 version, however, liberal democracy had become only a transitory historical form, the process of whose dissolution was already proceeding.[11] This was because 'the broad acceptance of liberalism, political or economic, by a large number of nations will not be sufficient to eliminate differences between them based on culture,[12] differences which will undoubtedly become more pronounced as ideological cleavages are muted'.[13] The spectre of 'clashing cultures' was also the theme of an article by John Mearsheimer, published in 1990.[14] Mearsheimer argued that the end of the cold war would lead to the revival of traditional state rivalries not only between Third World countries but also between the nation-states of Europe. It was, however, Samuel Huntington, with his 'clash of civilizations' thesis, who was to attract most recent scholarly attention.[15]

Huntington believes that an era of cultural conflict is dawning between the West and the 'anti-democrats' of the Third World.[16] The core of Huntington's argument is that the 'Christian', democratic West will find itself in conflict with a group of Third World countries, united in their antipathy to the West, and inspired by the non-democratic religious and cultural dogmas of 'Islamic fundamentalism' and 'Confucianism'. The intellectual affinity between (the later) Fukuyama, Mearsheimer and Huntington is pronounced. Each believes that the post-cold war order will be one in which conflict between the West and the Third World is increasingly likely, notwithstanding a trend towards the creation and consolidation of broadly democratic political systems in many areas of the world. Cultural – that is, ethnic and religious – competition between countries will be the main area of antagonism.

The chief threats to international stability, according to Huntington and Fukuyama, come from two non-Christian cultures, Islam and Confucianism. Christianity, on the other hand, is deemed by Huntington to be a religion which spawns a culture which is highly efficacious to the growth of liberal democracy. The collapse of dictatorships in southern Europe and Latin America in the 1970s and 1980s, followed by the development of liberal democratic political norms (rule of law, free elections, civic rights), is regarded by Huntington as conclusive proof of the synergy between Christianity and liberal democracy, both foundations of global order.

Confucianism and global order

To what extent are the Confucian[17] countries a threat to the West? Several countries in East Asia – including China, Japan, South and North Korea, Singapore, Taiwan and Vietnam – have cultures rooted in Confucianism. China, North Korea and Vietnam are, of course, three of the few remaining Communist countries, while Japan, South Korea, Singapore and Taiwan are staunch allies of the West. What seems to be the chief shared cultural characteristic of these countries is that they are community-orientated rather than individualistic. '[T]he community-orientedness of Asian cultures', Fukuyama argues, '(often) originates in doctrines like Confucianism that have acquired the status of religion from being handed down through centuries of tradition'. Confucianism is regarded by many Western scholars as a 'value system most congruent with Oriental authoritarianism';[18] it is 'hierarchical and inegalitarian'.[19]

Between the seventh and tenth centuries AD, a period of strong growth of Confucianism in Korea, it was a 'system of government and not a religious or philosophical system which affected the social and cultural aspects of the nation's life'.[20] As Weber notes, in China, 'Confucianism was the status ethic of prebendaries, of men with literary educations who were characterized by a secular rationalism.' It was important to belong to the *cultured* stratum; if one did not, he (much less she) did not count. The result was that the Confucian status ethic of this stratum determined the Chinese way of life far beyond the stratum itself and, by extension, in those areas which came under Chinese influence.[21]

Over the last few years, two of the most economically important Confucian countries, Taiwan and South Korea, have moved towards real democratization and enhanced human rights involving meaningful and extensive competition for government power through regular elections. There are now significant opposition parties and considerable – although incomplete – civil and political liberties, including increasing freedom of expression, of the press, to form organizations and to demonstrate and strike.[22] In three of the 'Confucian' countries – South Korea, Taiwan and Japan – democratization and enhanced human rights seem increasingly entrenched. The tiny island state of Singapore is heavily pro-Western, although non-democratic, while both Vietnam and China are increasingly opening up to Western influence. Only North Korea retains its Communist aloofness, although even here things may be changing. In sum, the differences between the 'Confucian' states are more important than alleged authoritarian similarities. There is very little – if anything – in the spectre of a 'Confucian' threat to global order.

Islamic radicalism and the West

One of the most serious threats to the West, according to Fukuyama, is Islamic fundamentalism which, he believes, has a 'more than superficial resemblance to European fascism'.[23] It is one thing to argue that various brands of political Islam have qualitatively different perspectives on liberal democracy than some forms of Christianity but it is quite another to claim that the Islamic countries *en masse* are poised to enter into a period of conflict with the West. The raising of the Muslim bugbear has more to do with the bigotry of some Western analysts than with the threat of Islam *per se*. The latter – like Confucianism – is usually interpreted by Western analysts as a decidedly undemocratic, often reactionary, set of ideas. The concept of an Islamic state, for example, suggests to many the clear antithesis of democracy. The West's response to the struggle in Algeria for democracy is a good illustration of this way of thinking.

In December 1991 Algeria held legislative elections which most independent observers characterized as amongst the freest ever held in North Africa or the Arab Middle East. The following January, however, Algeria's armed forces seized power to prevent an overwhelming victory in the elections by the reformist Front Islamique du Salut (FIS). The assumption was that if the FIS achieved power it would summarily close down Algeria's newly refreshed democratic institutions and political system. A respected London-based weekly news magazine posed the question which was on many people's lips: 'What is the point of an experiment in democracy if the first people it delivers to power are intent on dismantling it?'[24] The answer might well be: this is the popular will, it must be respected whatever the outcome. Algeria's army nevertheless had its own ideas. The FIS was summarily banned, thousands of supporters were incarcerated and more than 30,000 people have died in the ensuing civil war (which has also involved a bombing campaign in France[25]).

It is important to see the struggle in the Islamic world of groups like the FIS as directed primarily against their own rulers rather than at the West. It was the intransigence of the support of Western states – especially France – for the military junta in Algeria which served to export the civil war to Europe. Mardin asserts that since the beginning of Islam, Muslim critics of the *status quo* have periodically emerged in opposition to what they perceive as unjust rule.[26] Contemporary Islamists (that is, politically organized, radical, Muslims) are the most recent example, characterizing themselves as the 'just' involved in struggle against the 'unjust'. The dichotomy between 'just' and 'unjust' in the promotion of social change throughout Islamic history, according to Mardin, parallels the historic tension in the West between 'state' and 'civil society'.[27] The implication is that the 'unjust' inhabit the state while the 'just' look in from the outside, aching to reform the corrupt system.

The goal of the Islamically 'just' historically has been to form popular consultative mechanisms in line with the idea that the Muslim ruler was open to popular pressure and would seek to settle problems brought by his subjects. The concept of *shura* (consultation) should not be equated closely with the Western notion of popular sovereignty because sovereignty resides with God alone. *Shura* is a way of ensuring unanimity from the community of Muslims, 'which allows for no legitimate minority position. The goal of the 'just' is an Islamically based society.'[28] Thus, some – but not all – Islamists oppose Western interpretations of democracy, where sovereignty resides with the people, because it is seen as a system which negates God's own sovereignty. It is partly for this reason that Islamists (who, by definition, are in conflict with conservative, 'unjust' Islamic establishments) have been conspicuous by their absence in current demands for Western-style democratic change. Yet, despite an unwillingness to accept any sovereignty other than God's, Islamic radicals often accept the need for earthly rulers to seek a mandate from their constituency. For example, Dr Abdeslam Harras, leader of the Moroccan radical Islamic movement, Jama'at al-Da'wa al-Islamiyah, asserts that the ruler of an Islamic country should be elected by a majority of the people.[29]

The rise of Islamism in virtually all of the Muslim states of North Africa and the Middle East is the result of the failure of modernization to deliver its promises. Etienne and Tozy argue that Islamic resurgence in Morocco carries within it 'the disillusionment with progress and the disenchantments of the first twenty years of independence'.[30] This argument can be extended. Faced with state power which seeks to destroy or control the former communitarian structures and to replace them with an idea of a national citizenry based on the link between state and individual, popular (as opposed to state-controlled) Islam emerges as a vehicle of political aspirations. The Muslim awakening should be seen primarily in relation to its *domestic* capacity to oppose the state: 'It is primarily in civil society that one sees Islam at work.'[31] It does not translate into a wider threat to *global* order.

To summarize this section: the end of the cold war was followed by an eruption of ethnic and religious conflicts which served to cast serious doubt on the probability of moving from an old order rooted in bipolarity, nuclear deterrence and ideological division to a new global order where the pursuit of peace, prosperity and co-operation would be paramount. New threats to world order, some claim, were to be found in both Confucianism and Islam. I have argued that such fears are without foundation. In the case of Islamism, domestically orientated groups threaten the incumbency of their rulers rather than the global system, while as for Confucianism the differences between the 'Confucian' states are more important than alleged authoritarian similarities. There is very little – if anything – in the spectre of a 'Confucian' threat to global order.

In the final section of this chapter I want to broaden the analysis by offering a typology of political religion in the Third World in order to examine whether the various types of religious groups either individually or collectively pose a threat to contemporary global order.

A typology of political religion in the Third World

> Attempts to salvage the secularization model have interpreted evidence of burgeoning religiosity in many contemporary political events to mean that we are witnessing merely a fundamentalist, antimodernist backlash against science, industrialization, and liberal Western values . . . Religious fervour is often dismissed as ethnic hostility . . . typically explained away as an isolated exception to unremitting trends of secularization and seldom recognized as part of a larger global phenomenon.[32]

The quotation suggests two areas where religion is of particular importance in understanding recent political and social developments in the Third World: ethnicity issues and 'religious fundamentalism'. Yet this is only part of the story: we also need to be aware of the political importance of religious syncretism and of community-orientated religious groups (whose position may be bolstered by a national religious hierarchy's institutional voice of opposition during dictatorship), in order to understand fully what has been happening in recent times in the sphere of religious-political interaction in the Third World and any effects this has had upon global order.

Each of the four categories of religious movements – 'culturalist', 'fundamentalist', 'community-orientated' and 'syncretistic' – has two common factors. First, leaders of each type utilize religious precepts to present a message of hope and a programme of action to actual and putative followers, which may have a political impact. Second, the religious movements tend to be inherently oppositional in character. Leaders seek to capitalize

Types of Religious Groups and Political Interaction

	Culturalist	Syncretist	Fundamentalist	Community-Oriented
Objective	To use cultural separateness to seek to achieve autonomy in relation to centralized state Examples: Sikhs, Tibetans	To achieve higher political standing within national culture of diverse groups. Examples: Napramas, Holy Spirit Movement	To protect self-proclaimed groups of the 'religiously pure' against governmental attempts to belittle religion. Examples: Gush Emunim, Hamas, Islamic Salvation Front (FIS)	To direct community activities for enhancement of local groups' self-interest. Example: Basic Christian Communities
Perceptions of state and society	Aggregation of diverse groups with state structure dominated by one particular group	Society comprises diverse groups with one or a few often dominating at state level	Society is dichotomized between 'believers' and 'non-believers'. State aims to extend its power at the cost of believers.	Society comprises diverse interests. Local groups need to be aided so that self-interest can be protected and furthered
Perception of role of government	To prevent the full flowering of diversity	Seen as hostile or indifferent	Regarded as seeking to undermine religion's role in society	Seen as hostile or indifferent to plight of local communities
Role in political process	May use vehicle of political party if government permits; non-constitutional means may also be employed	Will often remain outside any formal political process pursuing goals through direct action, negotiation and lobbying	May fight elections if permitted. In addition, a wide range of means of gaining political ends may be employed	Formally uninvolved although activists may ally themselves with most progressive political parties
Citizen participation	Active participation of group members will be encouraged by group leaders in seeking political goals	Individual interests seen as synonymous with community goals	Individual interests seen as subordinate to the interests of the religious entity	Popular participation essential to offset élite dominance of politics and society
Tactics to achieve objectives	Any means necessary considered – constitutional or non-constitutional – including terrorism	Defensive mobilization of community interests which may become more aggressive	Depending on the ideology of the fundamentalist group most tactics would be regarded as legitimate	Lobbying of political élites, and as widespread as possible popular mobilization

upon dissatisfaction with the *status quo* in order to focus and direct organized societal opposition. It is important to note, however, that not all of the four groups target the governing regime in an overtly politicized manner. Fundamentalist and culturalist groups have as their *raison d'être* an inherent antipathy to government; community-orientated and syncretistic groups, on the other hand, tend to be more diffuse in character, often rurally based and more concerned with self-help issues rather than emphasizing straightforward opposition to government policies. The table sets out in schematic form the relationships which each has with government.

Culturalist groups
Culturalist groups emerge when a community, sharing both religious and ethnic affinities, perceives itself as a powerless and repressed minority within a state dominated by outsiders. The mobilization of the opposition group's culture (of which religion is an important part) is directed towards achieving self-control, autonomy or self-government. Examples include Sikhs and Kashmiri Muslims in India, southern Sudanese non-Muslim peoples (such as the Dinka and the Nuer fighting both Islamization and Arabization), Tibetan Vajrayana Buddhists in China and Muslim Palestinians living in both the Gaza Strip and in Israel's West Bank. In each case, the religion followed by the ethnic minority provides part of the ideological basis for action against representatives of a dominant culture whom the minority perceives as aiming to undermine or to eliminate their individuality.

Political culture is an important variable in analysis of culturalist groups, as it suggests underlying beliefs, values and opinions which a people holds dear. It is often easy to discern close links between religion and ethnicity. Sometimes, indeed, it is practically impossible to separate out defining characteristics of a group's cultural composition when religious belief is an integral part of ethnicity. Both are highly important components of a people's self-identity. It would be very difficult to isolate the different cultural components – religious and non-religious – of what it means to be, for example, a Sikh, a Jew, a Tibetan, a Somali or an East Timorese.

Syncretistic groups

A second type of religious entity, found predominantly among certain rural dwellers in parts of the Third World, especially sub-Saharan Africa, is of religious syncretistic groups, that is, those involving a fusion or blending of religions.[33] They typically feature a number of elements found in more traditional forms of religious association, such as ancestor worship, healing and shamanistic practices. Sometimes ethnic differentiation forms an aspect of syncretism. A syncretistic community uses both religious and social beliefs to build group solidarity in the face of a threat from outside forces – often, but not invariably, the state.

During the colonial era many syncretistic groups flourished in sub-Saharan Africa in the context of widespread dissatisfaction with aspects of European rule. On occasion, erstwhile foes – such as the Shona and the Ndebele in colonial Rhodesia (Zimbabwe) – combined to resist British colonialism. Religious identification was an important facet of such organization. Spirit mediums used 'medicines' to enhance warriors' martial efforts. They created a national network of shrines to provide an agency for the transmission and co-ordination of information and activities, a structure which was re-established during the independence war of the 1970s. The use of medicine also helped galvanize the anti-colonial Maji-Maji rebellion of 1905–7 in German controlled Tanganyika. The diviner and prophet, Kinjikitili, gave his followers medicine which was supposed to render them invulnerable to bullets. He anointed local leaders with the *maji* ('water') which helped to create solidarity among about twenty different ethnic groups and encouraged them to fight together in a common anti-European cause. In northern Uganda, the cult of Yakan amongst the Lugbara, which also centred on the use of magic medicine, galvanized the Lugbara in their short war against Europeans in 1919.[34] The list of such religio-political movements could be extended; the point, however, is already hopefully clear: many cults arose, led by prophets, stimulated by colonialism and the social changes to which it led. They employed local religious beliefs as a basis for anti-European protest and opposition.

After the colonial period syncretistic groups appeared in a variety of Third World countries as a result of the effects of an unsatisfactory and in many cases partial modernization. Examples include the cult of Olivorismo in the Dominican

Republic and, according to some, Sendero Luminoso in Peru, whose ideology, a variant of Maoism, also utilizes aspects of indigenous (pre-Christian) cultural-religious belief to attract peasants in Ayacucho; the *napramas* of north-eastern Mozambique who combine traditional and Roman Catholic beliefs, and were temporarily successful in defeating the then South African-supported guerrilla movement, the Mozambique National Resistance (Renamo) in the early 1990s; and the two 'Alices' – Lakwena and Lenshina – who led syncretistic movements in the post-colonial period, respectively in Uganda and Zambia, involving a fusion of mainstream Christian faith and traditional beliefs, against their governments in pursuit of regional autonomy.

Religious fundamentalism

Like many followers of syncretistic religions in the Third World, religious fundamentalists also feel their way of life under threat from unwelcome alien influences. As a result religious fundamentalists aim to reform society in accordance with religious tenets: to change the laws, morality, social norms and sometimes the political configurations of their country. They seek to create a traditionally orientated, less modern(ized) society and tend to live in population centres – or are at least closely linked with each other by electronic media. They also fight against governments because the latter's jurisdiction encompasses areas which the former hold as integral to the building of an appropriate society, including education, employment policy and the nature of society's moral climate. Fundamentalists struggle against both 'nominal' co-religionists whom they perceive as lax in their religious duties and against members of opposing religions or ideologies (Marxism, liberalism) whom they perceive as evil, even satanic. Examples of fundamentalist groups are to be found among followers of Christianity, Islam, and Judaism (the Abrahamic 'religions of the book') and also among Hindus and Buddhists.

The character and impact of fundamentalist doctrines are located within a nexus of moral and social issues revolving around state–society interactions. The main progenitor of recent fundamentalist movements has been a perception on the part of both leaders and followers that their rulers are performing inadequately and, often, corruptly. Religious fundamentalism is often (but not always: Buddhist and Hindu fundamentalisms are exceptions) strongly related to a critical reading of religious texts, and the relating of God's words to believers' perception of reality. The significance of this from a political perspective is that it supplies already restive peoples with a ready 'manifesto' of social change leading to a more desirable goal, which their leaders use both to berate their secular rulers and to propose a programme for radical reform of the *status quo*.

Community-orientated groups

Community-orientated groups utilize aspects of their religious faith to inspire themselves primarily toward self-help improvements in their lives; this may or may not involve overt conflict with government. Especially prominent in this category are the Basic Christian Communities (BCCs), mostly Roman Catholic in inspiration, which have mushroomed over the last twenty-five years, especially in Latin America, but also in the Philippines, Haiti and parts of sub-Saharan Africa. Many – but not all – derive their ideas from the tenets of radical 'liberation theology', a set of ideas with a core of belief that true religious struggle involves striving to change the political here and now.

In Latin America, the origins of the BCCs can be traced back to the moves towards popular community development which developed from the early 1960s, encouraged by radicalized clergy at the grassroots. Such priests organized their followers for self-help and spiritual purposes, guided by a vision of the Christian promise of redemption which directly linked the temporal sphere with the spiritual. Social change in the present was seen as integral to people's long-range spiritual redemption. Concretely, this meant the full participation of ordinary people in the shaping of their own lives. Profound dependence and passivity had to be replaced by full participation and self-determination in the economic and political spheres. To achieve these goals, radical priests became spokesmen for a broad political programme with two main aims: participatory democracy and practical development to deliver desirable social goods, including electricity, schools, health posts, clean water, roads and latrines. BCCs occasionally produced leaders for mass movements, such as trade unions and Brazils' labour-orientated political party, which were important in the process of popular mobilization that ultimately helped to undermine the credibility and viability of the country's military dictatorship, forcing it to hand over power to elected civilians in 1985.[35]

These four broad categories are not mutually exclusive. For example, some fundamentalist groups may also be community-orientated, while a number of culturalist groups may also be syncretistic. The purpose of differentiating between them in what is inevitably a somewhat ideal fashion is to seek to identify the nature of their relationship with other religious or ethnic groups and with government. By separating the four types of religious groups it is possible to arrive at some conclusions relating to the way in which each copes with the stresses and strains of modernization, as well as their potential for conflict with others.

To conclude

Over the last twenty years or so religion has had considerable impact upon politics in many regions of the Third World. Confidence that the growth and spread of urbanization, education, economic development, scientific rationality and social mobility would combine to diminish significantly the socio-political position of religion was not well founded. Two broad trends have been observable: religion used as a vehicle of opposition or as an ideology of community self-interest. In the first category are the culturalist, fundamentalist and, in part, the syncretistic, religious entities. Threats emanating either from powerful, outsider groups or from unwelcome symptoms of modernization (such as apparent decline in moral behaviour or alleged over-liberalization in education and social habits) galvanized religious reactions. In the second category are the BCCs and other community-orientated groups. The failure of governments to push through their programmes of social improvement led to the founding of these groups helping to develop a religious ideology of solidarity and development.

Developments within the Third World make it plain that one of the most resilient ideas about societal development – that nations would inevitably secularize during modernization – was misplaced. What is clear is that technological development and aspects of modernization left many people with a feeling of loss rather than achievement. One result was a wave of popular religiosity which often had political ramifications. When such a loss of faith in central government was writ large, in that it galvanized large portions of discrete culturalist groups, then religion often assumed a central tenet of political opposition to the state. Hopes of national co-operation as a result of modernization were replaced by widespread ethno-religious conflict in the Third World, especially since the end of the cold war.

The chapter has also examined the problematic of the political role of Third World religion in the search for global order. It argued that, against the arguments of Huntington and Fukuyama, the political renaissance of religion in the Third World does not pose a serious threat to the extant, Western-dominated global order. In the Third World, however, religion offers for many people a rational alternative to a modernization which is widely deemed to have failed to deliver its main goals of social development. Religion's interaction with politics over the medium term is likely to be of especial importance, carrying a serious and seminal message of societal resurgence and regeneration in relation to political leaders. Religion – often in tandem with ethnicity – will probably play a considerable role in the politics of many Third World countries in the years to come. There is considerably less likelihood of Third World countries, under the banner of Islam or Confucianism, seriously threatening the post-cold war global order based on a market capitalism largely sustained by Western states and their allies.

Notes

[1] The term 'Third World' was invented in the 1950s to refer, on the one hand, to the large group of economically underdeveloped, decolonizing countries and, on the other, to Latin American states, mostly granted their freedom in the early nineteenth century but still economically weak. The Third World is a useful shorthand term to refer to this group of now more than 150 countries, whilst recognizing that, despite a generally shared history of colonization, there are also important economic and political differences between Third World states.

[2] Björn Hettne, *Development Theory and the Three Worlds* (Harlow, Longman, 1995), 6.

[3] For extended discussions of this issue, see Jeff Haynes, *Religion in*

Third World Politics (Buckingham, Open University Press, 1993); *Religion, Fundamentalism and Identity: A Global Perspective* (Discussion Paper, 65; Geneva, United Nations Research Institute for Social Development, May 1995) and *Religion and Politics in Africa* (London, Zed Books, 1996).

4   Martin E. Marty and R. Scott Appleby, 'Introduction' in Marty and Scott Appleby (eds.), *Fundamentalism and the State: Remaking Politics, Economies, and Militance* (Chicago, University of Chicago Press, 1993), 3.

5   Jürgen Habermas, *Legitimation Crisis* (London, Heinemann, 1976).

6   Mehran Kamrava, *Politics and Society in the Third World* (London, Routledge, 1993), 164.

7   Craig N. Murphy, *International Organization and Industrial Change* (Cambridge, Polity Press, 1994), 8.

8   Hedley Bull, *The Anarchical Society* (London, Macmillan, 1977).

9   For an examination of transnationalism, see Anthony G. McGrew, 'Conceptualizing global politics' and 'Global politics in a transnational era', both in A. McGrew and P. Lewis (eds.), *Global Politics* (Cambridge, Polity Press, 1992).

10 Francis Fukuyama, 'The end of history', *National Interest*, 16 (Summer 1989), 3–18.

11 Francis Fukuyama, *The End of History and the Last Man* (London, Penguin, 1992).

12 'Culture' is a contested term. I take it to mean people's feeling of separateness based on ethnicity, nationalism, religion and/or language.

13 Fukuyama, *End of History*, 233.

14 John Mearsheimer, 'Why we will soon miss the cold war', *The Atlantic Monthly*, 266, No. 2 (August 1990), 35–50.

15 For two trenchant critiques of Huntington's argument see Adam Tarock, 'Civilisational conflict? Fighting the enemy under a new banner', *Third World Quarterly*, 16, No. 1 (March 1995), 5–18, and Jacinta O'Hagan, 'Civilisational conflict? Looking for cultural enemies', *ibid.*, 19–38.

16 Samuel Huntington, 'The clash of civilisations?', *Foreign Affairs*, 72, No. 3 (Summer 1993), 22–49.

17 Confucius was a Chinese philosopher who lived from 551–479 BC.

18 Ambrose Y. C. King, 'A nonparadigmatic search for democracy in a post-Confucian culture: the case of Taiwan, R.O.C', in Larry Diamond (ed.), *Political Culture and Democracy in Developing Countries* (Boulder, CO, Lynne Rienner, 1994), 141.

19 Fukuyama, *End of History*, 325, 217.

20 James H. Grayson, 'Korea', in Stuart Mews (ed.), *Religion in Politics* (Harlow, Longman, 1989), 153.

21 Max Weber, 'Major features of world religions', in Roland Robertson (ed.), *The Sociology of Religion* (Baltimore, Penguin, 1969), 21.

22 King, in Diamond, *Political Culture*, 141.

23 Fukuyama, *End of History*, 236.

24 *The Economist* (2 January 1992), 3.

25 Paul Webster, 'Capital of terror', *Guardian* (6 September 1995).

26 S. Mardin, 'The venture of democracy in the Middle East', cited in S. Dorr, 'Democratization in the Middle East', in R. Slater, B. Schutz and S. Dorr (eds.), *Global Transformation and the Third World* (Boulder, CO, Lynne Rienner, 1993), 151.

27 Ibid.

28 Dorr, 'Democratization in the Middle East', ibid.

29 Ibid., 152.

30 B. Etienne and M. Tozy, 'Le Glissement des obligations Islamiques vers le phénomène associatif à Casablanca', in *Le Maghreb Musulman en 1979* (Paris, Centre de Recherches et d'Études sur les Sociétés Mediterranéennes, 1981), 251.

31 Christian Coulon, *Les Musulmans et le pouvoir en Afrique Noire* (Paris, 1983), 49.

32 Emile Sahliyeh, 'Introduction', in E. Sahliyeh (ed.), *Religious Resurgence and Politics in the Contemporary World* (Albany, NY, State University of New York Press, 1990), 19.

33 See Haynes, *Religion and Politics in Africa*, esp. chap. 7.

34 Tim Allen, 'Understanding Alice: Uganda's Holy Spirit Movement in context', *Africa*, 61, No. 3 (1991), 379–80.

35 Kenneth Medhurst, 'Brazil' in Stuart Mews (ed.), *Religion in Politics: A World Guide* (Harlow, Longman, 1989), 25–9.

III

Critiques and Visions

9

Buddhist response to global development

SULAK SIVARAKSA

The central teaching in Buddhism is the four noble truths and the first truth is the Truth of Suffering. If one avoids that, one cannot really practise Buddhism. Global development today seems the celebration of a way of a life that not only leads away from this truth but also discourages people from even believing this truth exists. Global development springs from a civilization that claims to adore life, but actually starves it of any real meaning; a civilization that endlessly speaks of making people 'happy', but in fact blocks their way to the source of real peace and happiness.

It is abundantly clear that the material benefits of modernization have been (and remain) unfairly distributed between the people of this planet: industrial capitalism has been built upon the violence of conquest, genocide, slavery, debt and bondage. Even today extermination continues, especially that of indigenous and ethnic people. But economic exploitation takes new forms. These include Third World debt, the International Monetary Fund, the structural adjustment policies of the World Bank, the General Agreement on Tariffs and Trade (now World Trade Organization) and the North American Free Trade Area.

These policies are increasing income and wealth disparities between the industrialized North and the exploited South. Currently one-quarter of the global population lives in the North, consuming over 60 per cent of the world's food, 85 per cent of the world's wood and 70 per cent of the world's energy. At the same time, over one billion people in the South, or so-called 'Third World', live in absolute poverty without access to basic survival necessities. Disparities between social classes are increasing in both the South and the North. In Brazil, the top 20 per cent of the population receive twenty-six times the income of the bottom 20 per cent. In the USA, the middle classes are slowly disappearing, with 2.8 per cent of the population controlling 27.8 per cent of the wealth and 11.1 per cent with no wealth at all. Gender disparities relating to resources and income are also increasing, with women and children being disproportionately the poorest across the world.

Inequality and exploitation lead to tension and conflict. Although many conflicts are expressed in ethnic terms, the underlying issues are often class-based and rooted in the social structures of the global economic system. As social disparities and resistance increase, people have to be managed more and more through violent repression. Thus, we have a situation where the global economy includes a large military economy, and the world's leading nations are producing the weapons. The five permanent members of the UN Security Council – USA, UK, France, Russia and China – export over 85 per cent of the world's arms, with the USA being the biggest exporter of weapons of mass destruction. France is proud of testing nuclear bombs despite protests around the world.

The proliferation of weapons has created an extremely volatile global situation. More and more regions of the world, from Central America to Africa, to Southern Asia and Eastern Europe, are losing any semblance of law and order. As reigns of terror spread across the world, 'disappearances', torture, rape and killing become commonplace. In many places people are afraid to speak the truth. They fear for their jobs, their lives and the lives of their families. These conditions are not peculiar to the Third World. Professors at the University of Hawaii speak and research on any subject, except the presence of the American naval base on the island of Honolulu. There is a dramatic increase in violence in the homes, the streets and the schools of Western industrialized countries. Much of this violence is directed against people of colour, the poor and women.

Resistance and repression cannot be understood at the level of militarism alone. We have to grasp the logic of 'techno-capitalism' and the military-industrial complex. From the beginning technology and capital have been inextricably linked: technological advancement determines capitalist competition and growth. Everywhere, the processes of 'commodification' and mechanization move simultaneously. There is little research on these issues, particularly from a religious perspective.

Techno-capitalism is ultimately illogical, destroying the natural integration of planetary life and threatening the very survival of life. Subsistence is undermined as people are forced to produce for export markets rather than their own needs. Tropical forests and coral reefs are destroyed in the name of economic growth and development. Agribusiness, industrial manufacturing, nuclear weaponry and toxic dumping pollute the earth, air and water. Around the globe rivers are dammed, posing severe threats to eco-systems and the survival of people and their cultures. The twin forces of technology and capitalism are tearing people away from each other by destroying traditional communities. Human relationships are replaced with impersonal commercial, technological and bureaucratic connections. Modernization has increased alienation, distrust and fear among people, making it easier for multinational corporations and international agencies to manipulate and control people.

In the years ahead the control of both human and non-human planetary life will broaden and deepen as biotechnology and genetic engineering are more widely used. Already corporations are controlling the genetic materials of plants and animals and claiming patent rights or ownership to these manufactured products. Local producers, including indigenous people and farmers, are rapidly losing control of original genetic material. The global biodiversity treaty adopted at the Earth Summit in Rio may further help these trends. We must be aware of 'green capitalism', that is, environmentalism as defined and managed by dominant global interests.

Technology and capital are also making rapid inroads into the sphere of human reproduction. As artificial reproduction advances, human beings, like the earth itself, will lose the capacity to reproduce naturally. There is a close parallel between the conquest of Mother Earth and the conquest of the female body that bears life. Population control when coupled with age-old patriarchal traditions results in sex-selective abortions and female infanticide. In China and India, the two most populous countries in the world, amniocentesis is routinely used for sex selection and female foetuses are aborted in large numbers. Many female infants are also killed or abandoned at birth. Already, the sex ratios in China and India are skewed in favour of males over female.

There are also growing numbers of babies exported from the South to the North, an increase in surrogate mothering and a booming trade in human foetus and body organs for scientific experimentation. These practices benefit the wealthy classes, in places like India and Egypt, whilst poor people are forced to sell their kidneys so that their families can buy enough to eat. Life loses its sanctity as it increasingly becomes a commodity and an appendage to the machine. As the world created by humans increasingly undermines the natural 'eco-sphere', our own tensions, fears, hatreds and separateness increase. We are not machines but an aspect of nature and we must honour the laws of nature above the laws of the machine. These are some of the costs of technological and market expansion.

There are now movements across the world for peace, social justice and ecology. These include Thai Buddhist monks ordaining trees to preserve the forest, the struggles of native people against deforestation and the damming of rivers, the struggles of local farmers against biotechnology corporations, the protests of 'Mothers Fronts' against disappearances and killings. These struggles need to be better integrated and their common agenda must be firmly placed on a non-violent and spiritual path. This is the only way they can overcome the violence and destructiveness of the dominant world order. The teaching we need in order to walk this path already exists. The challenge facing humanity is not the development of more and more technology, markets and bureaucracies *but the spiritual development of wisdom and compassion.* From the Buddhist viewpoint all this suffering is directly or indirectly linked with greed, hatred and delusion.

Today, greed is clearly personified in capitalism and consumerism. Human beings are taught to worship money, worldly sciences and technological advance, at the expense of human development and the spiritual dimension of men and women. Descartes said, 'Cogito ergo sum' (I think therefore I am). I believe that he started the Western dilemma that has now come to be the core concept of consumerism: I buy therefore I am. Without the power of purchasing, modern people become nobody.

In Buddhism we could say, I breathe therefore I am. We breathe in for the first time as we enter the world from our mothers' wombs and we breathe out the last time when we expire from life. Yet we do not take care of our daily breathing, we breathe in suffering, anxiety, hatred and greed. You do not have to believe in Buddhism; if you are a Christian, you can breathe Christ in to you and be happy. Through breathing exercises we can be mindful and synchronize the head and the heart. We will then have understanding and compassion rather than arrogant, intellectual knowledge. We can have a personal transformation, become less selfish and care more for others. We can also develop critical self-awareness and awareness of social ills, in order to find our true potential to face suffering both mentally and socially.

From a Buddhist perspective, for human beings to live happily there must be freedom on three levels. The first freedom is the freedom to live with and share in nature and the environment. We could call this physical freedom. This is freedom from want and deprivation: an adequate supply of the four basic necessities of life: food, clothing, shelter and medicine. This also includes freedom from natural dangers and the ability to deal with such dangers as they arise. The second freedom exists in our relationship with fellow humans. We must have social freedom so that we can live safely together without being exploited by others. But these two kinds of freedom will not be truly effective if they are not connected to inner freedom; this is freedom on the personal level. Having physical and social freedom, people must learn how to live independently, to be happy and contented within themselves.

The most important kind of development is human development on the personal level leading to inner freedom. This is a happiness that is independent of externals; with it we are no longer dependent on exploiting nature or our fellow beings. We become more and more capable of finding contentment within our own minds and through our own wisdom. The ability to be content without exploiting nature or our fellow humans can also be called the ability to be content independent of natural and social conditions. With a more independent kind of happiness, social and physical freedom will be preserved and strengthened. Human beings will then have the best possible relationship with both the natural environment and human society.

Currently, and especially in the West, the predominant approach to curing social ills is by the use of social engineering; this form of pseudo-science operates from a purely intellectual base. By contrast, operating from a Buddhist base, we synchronize our heads and hearts, develop inner peace, plant seeds of peace and use critical self-awareness to tackle social problems non-violently. Buddhism, through insistence on the interrelatedness of all life, its teachings of compassion for all beings, its insistence on non-violence and – as with many indigenous spiritual teachings throughout the world – its caring for all existence, has even been leading some Westerners to broader and deeper interpretations of the relationship between peace and social, environmental, racial and sexual justice. When we talk about inter-faith dialogue, it would have a real meaning if people of different faiths joined together in working against our common enemies: greed, hate and delusion. From the Buddhist standpoint, after the Truth of Suffering one must go on to the second truth: the Cause of Suffering, which is greed, hatred and delusion. If we could overcome these, through the noble eightfold path, or other non-violent means, we can really achieve the other two noble truths: the cessation of suffering and the way to achieve the cessation of suffering. In Siam we are currently working on two projects to help confront the difficulties of global development.

Alternatives to consumerism – visionary voices tell spiritual stories

This is a project in which the Santi Pracha Dhamma Institute is collaborating with fellow Buddhists, Christians and Muslims, in order to pinpoint consumerism as a new demonic religion in global development. We work together using our spiritual traditions as well as scientific approaches in order to have alternatives to consumerism. Amongst many others we are working with John Cobb, a leading Christian theologian from Claremont College, California, David Chappell, a Buddhist scholar from the University of Hawaii, and Chandra Muzzaffer, a leading Muslim from the Just World Trust, Malaysia.

If we do not have an alternative to consumerism, our traditional religions will remain at the periphery of the new dominant value system that reduces human beings to being at the mercy of greed. In today's world, the desire to earn more and more money and consume more and more unnecessary goods is a dominant force at the expense of spiritual growth and contentment. Through the clever use of advertisements and media the multi-national corporations strongly influence and in many cases mercilessly exploit people around the world. Nightly news programmes project violence into our homes. Television advertisements lull us away from this violence and delude us, using greed and lust as means to stir our thirst to possess more and more.

The Alternatives to Consumerism project will record the inspiring stories of *sustainable alternatives to the Western consumer model from different spiritual motivations.* An inter-religious, non-violent approach is advocated and initiatives chosen for recording will generally have strong spiritual values from one of the world religions or indigenous peoples underpinning their activities. Co-ordinators will work closely with a diverse selection of movements, communities and projects whose common aim is working for a sustainable society. From these liaisons, it is hoped to empower the communities whilst telling their unique tales.

The ancient art of story-telling transcends many cultures and will be the core medium for recording vivid images of the difficulties and successes of approximately ninety attempts to live more sustainably. Story-telling will be aided by traditional song, music and drama. Books, videos, photography and reports, much younger relatives of the ancient arts, will be used to record and pass on the wisdom. The resulting material will become a well of information that will be inspirational for existing and potential projects, educational for a broader audience and a unique source of material for further research. It is hoped that the project will help to facilitate a movement with a variety of sustainable value systems to counteract the present threat of a consumer mono-culture.

Spirit in Education Movement (SEM)

In this desolate modern world heading towards a consumer monoculture that destroys spiritual and environmental diversity, there is little time and thought for education of the heart and soul. Mainstream education in the West concentrates on the intellect and is becoming more and more business-like and competitive. As the Eastern countries jump gaily onto the consumer bandwagon, their education systems are emulating the narrow, unconnected fields of Western education. Unbalanced, modern education regularly produces short-sighted and selfish so-called 'new ideas', often borrowed out of context from old traditions and indigenous wisdoms. An example of this is the patenting, as new wonder drugs, of native herbal remedies that have been used by local people for centuries. Here is a challenge for alternative education. With help from concerned friends the Spirit of Education Movement has been formed to respond to these challenges. The founding group included several prominent alternative thinkers and educationalists aspiring to counteract these negative trends and offer in a small way an alternative to mainstream education.

SEM began without buildings, money or extensive forward planning. Initially the movement plans to run on a course-by-course basis at several different, predominantly rural locations in Siam. In a few years enough interest and momentum may be raised to think about a campus and building. SEM philosophy believes synchronicity will follow the commitment of people with good intentions and wisdom. We aspire to offer a spiritually based, ecologically sound, holistic alternative to mainstream education with its narrow, unconnected fields.

Our philosophy is underpinned by Buddhist wisdom and green principles but also welcomes and associates with other spiritual and ecological wisdom. We aspire to create an environment to awaken Buddha nature and cultivate wisdom as well as intellect. We will creatively use the wisdom of interconnectedness, particularly the practical application of the four noble truths and the eightfold path. We aspire to benefit people, initially mainly Asians, by increasing individual and collective confidence in their traditional heritage. We will aid individuals and groups, who resist structural violence and greed, to build up courage, confidence and compassion and give long-term support for their projects.

We hope to move any individual from selfishness to compassion, from a lack of meaning in life to fulfilment and from negativity to positiveness. We will involve students and teachers with current projects concerning ecological balance and social justice. This is a long-term process for a Buddhist approach to global development. We will link together action, meditation, art and intellectual learning. We will use a wide variety of media and senses – art, books, videos, performance, meditation, seeing, feeling, hearing, understanding with the heart. We will create a friendly, nurturing, happy learning environment in spiritually rich places close to nature. We seek to attract students from all walks of life without discrimination on grounds of race, gender, religion or financial status. Indeed, the pricing policy encourages the practice of Dana, where wealthier students can sponsor appropriate students with less financial means.

The Spirit in Education Movement aims to be a happy learning experience! Time to grow, learn from each other, relax and have fun. Through a diverse range of courses, teachers and students, we aim to cross barriers and create inspiring visions. We hope everyone involved takes away the skills and creativity for a more balanced self, hope for a better society, skills to improve present projects and innovative ideas for new beginnings for personal growth, social equity and ecological balance. Where possible courses will be open to international participants, although some will be more suitable for Thai or other Asian participants, or offered to specific target groups, often in response to difficult local causes and conditions.

The courses use a holistic approach to education by learning for head and heart, body and emotions and the inter-connectedness of all beings. We believe that the setting for learning is important and are careful in choosing locations for courses. This is likely to be a simple forest monastery or rural ashram to allow close contact with nature. Natural surroundings are often damaged in the name of progress, and part of the SEM philosophy is to appreciate and learn from nature. Enjoyment and making new friends with like-minded people is as important as the lectures. SEM learns and links with other spiritual education organizations. In the East these include the Siamese Buddhist Universities and the Institute for Total Revolution in India. In the West the recent emergence of alternative colleges with some strong roots in Eastern philosophies, such as the Naropa Institute, USA, and Schumacher College, UK, is an encouraging sign that our approach has a global resonance.

Friends in the West like Adam Curie, Barbara Schumacher, Maurice Ash and Bob McCloy have been very helpful in this venture. I hope some readers who are concerned with education for the spiritual dimension of global order may be sympathetic to our idea of Spirit in Education Movement. For me, this is one of the very positive responses with a view to the next phase of global development. I would certainly welcome any comments, criticism and suggestions. Indeed, for anybody in the West interested in linking up with SEM, whether as teachers or students, there would be a warm welcome, to develop and experience together, across religions and cultures, the realization of this new and necessary vision for global order.

10

Judaism and global theology

DAN COHN-SHERBOK

In the modern world with its multiplicity of faiths, there has been an increasing interest in the relationship between the world's religions. Within Judaism, however, only a few thinkers have grappled with the issue of religious pluralism. A notable exception to this general neglect is a discussion by the Jewish theologian Louis Jacobs in his *A Jewish Theology*. In a chapter entitled 'Judaism and other religions', Jacobs stresses that Judaism has always endorsed the view that there is only one God and that the Torah has not been superseded by any other religious tradition. Such a conviction, he believes, compels Jews to declare that the positions of other religions are false if they contradict the Jewish faith:

> Far Eastern faiths are either polytheistic or atheistic. The Christian concept of God is false from the Jewish point of view. Judaism similarly denies that Mohammed received a revelation from God which made him the last of the prophets with the Koran in the place of the Torah.[1]

Despite such an uncompromising stance, it would be a mistake for Jews to conclude that God has not revealed himself to others or that other religions do not contain any truth. On the contrary, he asserts, the position one should adopt is that there is more truth in Judaism than in other religions. Another contribution to this topic is by the Israeli Jewish theologian David Hartman. In 'On the possibilities of religious pluralism from a Jewish point of view',[2] he maintains that the Bible contains two covenants – that of creation and that of Sinai. The creation covenant is with all

humanity; it is universal and for all generations. The Sinai covenant, on the other hand, is with Israel; it is a parallel covenant and
embraces other communities. On the basis of this scheme,
Hartman argues that God has revealed himself to different
groups of peoples at various times in history. In a later work,
Conflicting Visions, he stresses that revelation in history is always
fragmentary and incomplete since divine–human encounters
cannot exhaust God's plenitude.

More recently the Orthodox British scholar Norman Solomon
discussed the issue of religious pluralism in *Judaism and World
Religion*.[3] In a chapter entitled 'The plurality of faiths', he contends that Judaism is a religion with a mission to all people. In
times of persecution, he states, this universal goal has been overlooked; yet it has never disappeared. In bad times it focuses on
the messianic task; in enlightened eras it is expressed in the
Jewish quest to work for the improvement of humanity. In pursu-
ing this goal, the 'covenant of Noah' (as expressed in the Seven
Noachide Laws) offers a pattern to seek for others without
requiring their conversion to Judaism. What is demanded instead
is faithfulness to the highest principles of justice and morality. In
this context, the dialogue of faiths becomes an imperative which
emerges through our common mission with other religions.

Despite these recent contributions, there is a pressing need to
formulate a comprehensive Jewish theology of other religions. This
chapter is intended to provide a basis point for such an endeavour.
The obvious starting-point for the formulation of such a Jewish
theology of religious pluralism is the Hebrew scriptures. In biblical
times the religion of Israel was essentially exclusivist in orientation; none the less pagan people were not condemned for
their beliefs and practices. Further, the prophets believed that in
the final days all people would accept that the God of Israel is the
Lord of creation. During the rabbinic period, this attitude of
general tolerance continued to animate Jewish life; according to
the rabbis all non-Jews who follow the Noahide laws (laws given to
Noah) are acceptable to God. A number of medievalists continued
this tradition, and in the modern period there has been an
increasing acknowledgement of the integrity of other faiths,
particularly Christianity. In nearly all cases Jewish thinkers have
espoused various forms of inclusivism, assuming that although
Judaism is the superior faith other traditions embody religious

truth. For nearly four millennia, then, Judaism has in various ways espoused a generally indulgent attitude toward other religions.

Given the largely tolerant attitude of Judaism to other faiths, should Jews move beyond such openness? The difficulty with the Jewish inclusivist ideology of previous ages is that it appears to suffer from a number of serious theological defects: Jewish inclusivists appear to affirm two incompatible convictions – the belief in God's universal concern and the conviction that he has definitively revealed himself to a particular group. Yet if God is truly concerned with the fate of all humanity, it seems inconceivable that he would have disclosed himself fully and finally to a particular people, allowing the rest of humanity to wallow in darkness and ignorance. Arguably what is required today is an even more open approach to the world's religions. To use a model of the universe of faiths formulated by the Protestant theologian John Hick, a Copernican Revolution is now required in our understanding of religion. In the past even the most liberal Jewish thinkers retained the conviction that Judaism contains the fullest divine disclosure; while recognizing the inherent value of other religions – particularly Christianity – they were convinced that Judaism is humanity's future hope. These Jewish thinkers were like scientists who previously endorsed a Ptolemaic view of the universe in which the earth is at the centre.

In the modern world, however, where Jews continually come into contact with adherents of other religious traditions, it is difficult to sustain such a narrow vision. Instead a Copernican revolution is currently required in our understanding of the universe of faiths. Instead of placing Judaism at the centre of the world's religions, a theocentric model should be adopted – such a transformation demands a paradigm shift from a Judaeo-centric to a theocentric conception of religious history. On this basis, the world's religions should be perceived as different human responses to the one divine Reality. In previous ages religions understood this one Reality either theistically (as a personal deity) or non-theistically (as non-personal), but such differences were in essence the result of historical, cultural or psychological influences. This shift from a Judaeo-centric to a theocentric model is represented diagrammatically in Figure 1 (p. 206).

On this view there is one ultimate Reality beyond all religious expressions. To use Jewish mystical terminology, the Godhead is

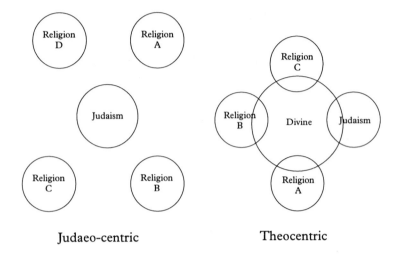

Figure 1

the Ayn Sof – the Infinite beyond human comprehension. The Godhead is the eternal Reality which provides the inspiration for all religions including Judaism. This ultimate Reality is interpreted in a variety of different modes, and these different explanations of the one Reality have inevitably given rise to a variety of differing and competing conceptions.

Such a view of the divine in relation to the world's religions can be represented as well by the image of alternative paths ascending a single mountain – each route symbolizes a particular religion with divine Reality floating like a cloud above the mountain top (Figure 2, p. 207). The routes of these faith communities are all different, yet at various points they intersect: these intersections should be understood as those areas where religious conceptions within the differing traditions complement one another. Thus, as pilgrims of different faiths ascend to the summit, they will encounter parallels with their own traditions. But the divine Reality they all pursue is in the end unattainable by these finite quests. As the Infinite, it is unknowable and incomprehensible. It is the cloud of unknowing. Such a pluralistic model implies that conceptions of the divine in the world's religions are ultimately human images – they represent the myriad ways of approaching

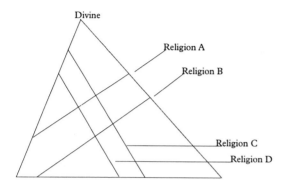

Figure 2

the one indescribably divine Reality. Doctrinal differences (such as the Judaeo-Christian belief in one life in this world as against the Indian doctrine of reincarnation) reflect differences in the historical, social and cultural factors lying behind these convictions. Not only does this pluralistic framework offer a more comprehensible theoretical basis for understanding differences between religious systems, it also provides a wider forum for inter-faith encounter. Instead of assuming, as Jewish inclusivists have in the past, that Judaism embodies God's all-embracing truth of which other religions possess only a share, Jewish pluralism encourages Jews to engage in fruitful and enriching dialogue with members of other traditions.

This new pluralistic model further reflects our current understanding of the world in which no truth is viewed as unchanging. Rather, truth-claims by their very nature must be open to other insights. They prove themselves not by triumphing over other belief systems, but by testing their compatibility with other truths. Such a conception of relational-truth affords a new orientation to our understanding of truth in religion; on this view, religious truth is not static but instead undergoes continual interaction and development.

This model of truth-through-relationship allows each religion to be unique – the truth it contains is uniquely important for religious adherents. But it is not true in a universal sense. Religious truth is relevant only for those who subscribe to it. Judaism thus should not be conceived as the one true faith for all human beings, as a number of previous Jewish inclusivists have argued. Rather, Judaism is true only for the Jewish people. It might be objected that such a relativistic conception of religious truth would inevitably diminish one's commitment as a Jew; however, one can be totally committed to the Jewish faith while at the same time being genuinely open to other religions. Using the analogy of marriage, the American theologian Paul Knitter argues that in expressing devotion to one's spouse, one is not making any kind of universal claim:

> One can be totally and faithfully committed to one's spouse, even though one well knows that there are other persons in this world equally as good, intelligent, beautiful – yes even when one makes the acquaintance of and enjoys the friendship of such persons. Absolute exclusivity, in attitude or practice is neither honest, or healthy in any commitment.[4]

Further, Knitter argues that the deeper the commitment to one's spouse and the more secure the marriage, the more one can appreciate the truth and beauty of others – similarly the deeper one's commitment to Judaism, the greater can be one's openness to other faiths.

Given this new pluralistic framework, how are the absolute claims of the past to be understood? Distancing themselves from the traditionalist perspective of Orthodox Judaism, those who subscribe to this new vision of divine Reality should view religious beliefs as human conceptions stemming from the religious experience of the ancient Israelites as well as later generations of Jewish sages: Jewish monotheism – embracing a myriad of formulations from biblical through medieval and modern times – is rooted in the life of the people. In all cases pious believers and thinkers have expressed their understanding of God's activity on the basis of their own personal as well as communal encounter with the divine. Yet given that the Real as-it-is-in-itself is beyond human comprehension, this Jewish understanding of the God-head cannot be viewed as definitive and final. Rather, it must be seen as only one among many ways in which human beings have attempted to make sense of the Ultimate. In this light, it makes no sense for Jews to believe that they possess the unique truth about God and his action in the world; on the contrary, universalistic truth-claims about divine Reality must give way to a recognition of the inevitable subjectivity of beliefs about the Real.

The same conclusion applies to the Jewish belief about God's revelation. According to tradition, the Hebrew scriptures were communicated by God to the Jewish people. The medieval Jewish philosopher Moses Maimonides argued that this belief is a central tenet of the faith. The Torah, he wrote, is revealed from Heaven – this implies that the whole of the Five Books of Moses was disclosed to Moses on Mount Sinai and is of paramount authority. Further, the rabbis maintained that the expositions and elaborations of this Written Law were also revealed by God to Moses; subsequently they were passed on from generation to generation, and through this process additional legislation was incorporated. Hence traditional Judaism affirms that God's revelation is twofold and eternally binding.

A theory of Jewish pluralism, however, calls such convictions into question. Instead of affirming that God uniquely disclosed his word to the Jewish people in scripture and through the teachings of the sages, Jews should acknowledge that their Holy Writ is only one record of divine communication among many. Both the Written and the Oral Torah have special significance for the Jewish people, but this does not imply that these writings contain a superior divine communication. Instead the Tanakh and rabbinic literature should be perceived as a record of the spiritual life of the people and a testimony of their religious quest; as such they should be viewed in much the same light as the New Testament, the Qur'an, the Baghavad Gita, the Vedas and so forth. For the Jewish people this sacred literature has particular meaning – yet it should not be regarded as possessing ultimate truth.

Likewise the doctrine for the chosen people must be revised from a pluralistic viewpoint. Throughout history the belief that Israel is God's chosen people has been a central feature of the tradition. Through its election, Jewry believed it had been given an historic mission to bear divine truth to humanity. God's choice of Israel thus carries with it numerous responsibilities: Israel is obligated to keep God's statutes and observe his laws, and doing so, the nation will be able to persuade others that there is only one universal God. By carrying out this task, Israel is to be a light to the nations.

Here again, Jewish pluralism must draw attention to the inevitable subjectivity of these claims about Israel's relationship with God and its universal role in a divine providential plan. Although Jews have derived great strength from such convictions, they are based on a misapprehension of Judaism in the context of the universe of faiths. Given that the Real as-it-is-in-itself transcends human understanding, the conviction that God has selected a particular people as his agent is nothing more than an expression of the Jewish people's sense of superiority and impulse to spread its religious message. Yet in fact there is simply no way of knowing if a specific people stands in a special relationship with the Divine.

Again, a pluralistic approach challenges the traditional Jewish conviction that God has a providential plan for the Jewish people and for all humankind. The Bible asserts that God controls and guides the universe – such a view implies that the manifestation of a wise and benevolent providence is found everywhere. Subsequently the doctrine of divine providence was developed in rabbinic literature, and the belief that God is concerned with each individual as well as the world in general became a central feature of Jewish theology.

From a pluralistic point of view, however, such a religious conviction must be seen as simply one way of interpreting Reality. The belief that God's guiding hand is manifest in all things is ultimately a human response to the universe – it is not, as Jews have believed through the ages, certain knowledge. This is illustrated by the fact that other traditions have postulated a similar view of providence, but maintain that God's action in history has taken an entirely different form. In other cases nontheistic religions have formulated conceptions of human destiny divorced from the activity of God or the gods. Such differences in interpretation highlight the subjectivity of all these beliefs.

The Jewish doctrine of the Messiah must also be seen in a similar light from a pluralist perspective. Throughout history the Jewish people longed for a messianic figure who would redeem the nation from exile and inaugurate a period of peace and harmony. Within a pluralist framework such longing must be perceived as a pious hope based on personal and communal expectation. Although this conviction has served as a bedrock of the Jewish faith through the centuries, it is inevitably shaped by human conceptualization. Like other doctrines in the Jewish tradition, it has been grounded in the experience of the Jewish people and has undergone a range of changes in the history of the nation. Because the Real as-it-is-in-itself is beyond complete comprehension, there is simply no way of ascertaining whether this belief in a personal Messiah accurately mirrors the nature of ultimate Reality.

Finally Jewish pluralism demands a similar stance regarding the doctrine of the afterlife. While the set of beliefs regarding the eschatological unfolding of history has been a cardinal feature of the Jewish faith from rabbinic times to the present, it is simply impossible to ascertain whether these events will unfold in the future. In our finite world – limited by space and time – certain knowledge about life after death is unobtainable. Belief in the hereafter, in which the righteous of Israel will receive their just reward, has sustained the nation through suffering and tragedy, but from a pluralistic outlook these doctrines are no more certain than any other feature of the Jewish religious heritage.

A pluralist confessional stance is thus both certain and open-ended: it enables Jews to affirm the uniqueness of their faith while urging them to recognize the validity of other traditions. Jewish inclusivism – with its insistence on completeness and finality – simply does not fit in with what is being experienced in the arena of religious diversity. In place of a Judaeo-centric conception of God's activity, divine Reality must be placed at the centre of the universe of faiths. Within such a context, Judaism can be seen as an authentic and true religious expression. Here then is a new framework for positive encounter and religious harmony: if Jews can free themselves from an absolutist stand-point in which claims are viewed as possessing ultimate and universal truth, the way is open for a radically new vision of Jewish dialogue with the world's faiths.

The formulation of such a theology of Jewish pluralism hinges on two major preconditions. First, Jewish theologians must learn about other faiths than their own. Jewish pluralism requires religious thinkers to explore what the world's faiths have experienced and said about the nature of divine Reality, the phenomenon of religious experience, the nature of the self, the problem of the human condition and the value of the world. Second, Jewish theologians should attempt to enter as best they can into the thought-world as well as religious experiences of those of other faiths; this can only be done by becoming an active participant in their way of life. Jewish thinkers must thus enter into the subjectivity of other traditions and bring the resulting insights to bear on their own religious understanding. Such theological reflection calls for a multi-dimensional, cross-cultural, inter-religious consciousness.

Jewish pluralism is most suited to such a multifaceted approach in which all religions are conceived as interdependently significant. Given the quest for a global perspective, it is important for Jewish pluralism that the theological endeavour occurs in a trans-religious context. This enterprise calls for religious encounter in which Jews confront others who hold totally different truth-claims; such individuals can help Jewish thinkers to discover their own presuppositions and underlying principles. In this process the Jewish partners should be able to recognize the limitations of their own traditions, and as a result make a conscious effort to discover common ground with other faiths.

Given this shift from Jewish inclusivism to Jewish pluralism, the way is now open to inter-faith encounter on the deepest level. Pre-eminent among areas in which Jewish pluralists can participate with members of other religions in a global context is the sphere of prayer. No longer should Jews feel constrained to stand aloof from attending the worship services of other faiths or participating in joint prayer. Rather, a pluralist standpoint in which all faiths are recognized as authentic paths to ultimate Reality would encourage adherents of all the world's religions, including Jewry, to engage in common religious activities. In this regard it is important to distinguish between three major types of inter-faith worship.

1. Services of particular religious communities in which adherents of other faiths are invited as guests. On such occasions, it is customary to ask a representative of the visiting faith-community to recite a suitable prayer or preach a sermon, but the liturgy remains the same.

2. Inter-faith gatherings of a serial nature. At such meetings representatives of each religious community offer prayers or readings usually on a common theme. Those present constitute an audience listening to a liturgical anthology in which the distinctiveness of each religion is recognized, but everyone is free to participate as well.
3. Inter-faith gatherings with a common order of service. In such situations, all present are participants and there is an overarching theme. Possibly a unifying symbol – such as the lighting of candles – is used.

These various services possess their own particular characteristics. In the first type of service the organizers are not setting out to make converts; rather, there is a conscious recognition of the integrity of other traditions. In such a gathering Jewish pluralists should feel completely comfortable: a pluralist outlook would encourage the process of learning and sharing, and ideally Jewish guests at another faith-community's worship service should strive to enter into the religious experience of those praying. In this regard Jewish pluralists should not feel constrained reciting prayers or singing hymns whose truth-claims contradict the truth-claims of their own faith. Given that the Real as-it-is-in-itself is unknowable, the various liturgical formulations in the world's faiths should be understood as human constructions which attempt to depict the nature and activity of a divine Reality – as models of the divine, they guide the believer to the Ultimate. From this perspective, Jewish pluralists should have no hesitation in joining with Christians, Muslims, Buddhists, Hindus, Sikhs, as well as adherents of all the world's religions in the recitation of their respective liturgies. Similarly, in the second type of worship service Jewish pluralists ought to welcome the opportunity to share their liturgical tradition with others and should feel no reluctance in joining in the liturgy from other traditions when appropriate. In accord with a pluralist stance, such serial services are based on mutual respect and afford each faith-community an equal role in worship. Frequently such gatherings take place in order to affirm the common humanity of all the world's faiths – this, for example, has been the basis of the World Day of Prayer for Peace at Assisi. Jewish pluralism would embrace and encourage such initiatives.

Turning to the third type of worship service, in which there is a shared liturgy, Jewish pluralists can be open to the opportunity to pray together in this way with members of other faiths. In such contexts participants are frequently invited to worship the One Eternal One – the ultimate ground of being to which all religious dogma and ritual point as the divine mystery. This form of service is particularly amenable to a pluralist theology in which final Reality is conceived as the unknowable Infinite that cannot be fully expressed in any particular faith. In services of this type the distinctiveness of each religion is accepted; there is no attempt to replace the regular liturgy with prayer of the individual faith communities. Yet there is the implicit assumption that in worship the adherents of all faiths stand before the Ultimate to which they have given different names. The third form of worship then is consonant with the principles of Jewish pluralism; it affirms other faiths while at the same time recognizing the limitation of all human conceptualizations of the Real.

A second area in which Jewish pluralists are able to join members of other faiths is the sphere of global theological exploration. In the past Jewish theologians insisted that Judaism is the superior faith – even the most liberal inclusivists maintained that in the future all human beings will recognize the truth of Jewish monotheism. In this sense Jewish theology throughout the centuries was Judaeo-centric in character. Today, in our religiously diverse world, however, it is no longer possible to sustain this view. What is required instead is a complete redefinition of the theological task. In the modern world Jewish thinkers must recognize that theology can no longer be practised only within a single tradition. The pursuit of religious truth now calls for a dialogical approach in a global context.

At the beginning of the twenty-first century, then, Judaism stands on the verge of a new awakening. Drawing on centuries of tolerance, the way is now open for Jews to formulate a complete reorientation of the Jewish faith in relation to other religious traditions. With a shift from inclusivism to pluralism, there is no longer any need to interpret other religions from a Judaeo-centric standpoint; rather, with the divine at the centre of the universe of faiths, Jewry can acknowledge the inevitable subjectivity of all religious beliefs, including those contained in the Jewish heritage. Jewish pluralism thus demands the recognition that all religions constitute separate paths to divine Reality – yet at the summit of this ascent, the Real as-it-is-in-itself, remains beyond human comprehension: it is the cloud of unknowing beyond human grasp[5].

Notes

[1] Louis Jacobs, *A Jewish Theology* (New York, Behrman House, 1973), 289.
[2] David Hartman, 'On the possibilities of religious pluralism from a Jewish point of view', *Immanuel* (1983).
[3] Norman Solomon, *Judaism and World Religion* (London, Macmillan, 1992), 224.
[4] Paul Knitter, *No Other Name* (New York, Orbis, 1985), 201–2.
[5] See also Dan Cohn-Sherbok, *Judaism and Other Faiths* (Basingstoke, Macmillan, 1994).

11
Theology, ecology and the idea of global order

JOHN HAUGHT

In examining the question of religion's relationship to global order, an indispensable condition for the establishment of order among nations is an integral global environment. Without the co-operation of all political bodies in efforts to reverse the present trend of massive ecological degradation, any prospect of 'global order' will be finally irrelevant. So it is quite appropriate, when we are thinking about religion and politics, to ask about the relationship of religion and politics to ecology.

However, bringing ecological considerations into such a con-versation compels us to think once again about the universe, and this requirement, in spite of the influence of modern science, is not something that either theologians or political experts are accustomed to doing very well. Even though the natural world is the context in which our political and religious activities take place, it is no secret that modernity has allowed us to lose a deep sense of the universe. This is certainly true in the case of modern theology, which has handed over to science the task of under-standing nature while leaving to itself the task of interpreting human life and history. But a deep sense of the universe is also foreign to the social sciences, especially to economics and politics.

Certainly every discipline must abstract to some degree from the totality of the cosmos in order to gain control of its chosen terrain. Yet the abstraction can never be complete, and it is instructive to observe how the universe that has been bracketed still functions in the background as we engage in our various regional inquiries. What sense of nature or the universe, for example, tacitly frames our economic and political studies? Does the natural world show up at the corners of our consciousness as anything more than an endlessly abundant resource for human consumption, transformation and enjoyment?

It is not an overgeneralization to say that our academic disciplines lack a deep sense of our species' rootedness in the cosmos. For this reason the recent emergence of public concern about the welfare of nature, though still not a major focus of university education, is a potentially salutary development for both theology and political science. It invites us to think about religious and political affairs in a more cosmic way than we usually do. And so, as we ponder the prospects for global order today it may not be prudent to suppress completely the questions about what kind of universe it is that we live in, what our true relationship with it might be, and what our moral attitude toward its well-being should be.

And yet, can we honestly address these matters without bringing up once again the more imposing question as to whether this fifteen-billion-year-old cosmos has any transcending purpose to it? In modern times, of course, unlike in previous ages, it has become not only acceptable to purge our scholarly discourse of any such broad and apparently unanswerable considerations; indeed, in academic circles, the bracketing of such a fundamentally religious concern is generally considered to be an essential condition of open discussion. Is it conceivable, however, that in the alleged interest of civility and scientific openness, we scholars have wrested our discussions of politics and religion so violently from their cosmic setting that we have deprived these disciplines of an essential dimension of depth? Do our concerns about the connection of religion to politics perhaps still have something to learn from fresh reflection on ancient questions about the nature of the cosmos and whether it has any 'point' to it?

Many if not most scientific thinkers today, of course, are convinced that any vision of purpose in the universe is archaic and illusory. Our former inklings of a wider than human purpose to cosmic events (or 'cosmic teleology') seem to be projections of a childish human longing for permanent significance onto a universe which in itself remains quite 'pointless'. Only by breaking free of our religious or philosophical preoccupations with cosmic purpose, after all, did physics grow up into a truly illuminating science. And only after biologists turned their attention to the impersonal laws of natural selection, and more recently to the bare chemistry of life, and ceased appealing to vitalistic miracles or myths of purpose and evolutionary progress, did biology finally come to birth as a genuine science. Today the so-called human sciences look enviously to the way in which the apparent maturation of physics and biology could occur only after fruitless questions about cosmic purpose were shoved aside. Perhaps in order to gain comparable respectability they too must thoroughly cleanse themselves of any hazy conjectures about the nature of the universe in which we humans live.

A crucial test of the integrity of modern science is the earnestness with which it expels any traces of teleology from its methods of explanation. Natural scientists today usually express utter contempt for any in their community who suggest, sometimes even when they are not speaking as scientists, that a purposive influence may somehow be shaping the evolution of the universe. They fear that if the slightest hints of teleology creep back into scientific discourse, the whole of science will be poisoned once again by human subjectivity. Only by tracing purely physical causes back into a completely impersonal and unintelligent past can we arrive at an accurate, objective understanding of how nature really works.

The question we must ask in an age of growing sensitivity to the travail of nature, however, is just how far we may fruitfully carry this sterilizing of intelligent discourse from 'contamination' by questions about value, importance, meaning and purpose. Even if the suspension of such concerns is essential in physics and perhaps even biology, should it characterize the totality of thought and education? What, we might ask today, are the ecological implications of our expunging any sense of inherent purpose, meaning or value from nature?

In one of the most frequently quoted lines of recent scientific writing, physicist Steven Weinberg states that, as the universe has grown more comprehensible to science, the more 'pointless' it has also become.[1] And even though other scientists generally display less anguish about this massive loss of meaning than Weinberg does, many agree that science has irretrievably brought home to us the purposelessness of the universe. When asked to comment on Weinberg's statement, the astronomer Sandra Faber, for example, replied:

... I think the universe was created out of some natural process, and our appearance in it was a totally natural result of physical laws in our particular portion of it – or what we call our universe. Implicit in the question, I think, is that there's some motive power that has a purpose beyond human existence. I don't believe in that. So I guess ultimately I agree with Weinberg that it's completely pointless from a human perspective.[2]

Responding to the same statement of Weinberg, physicist Marc Davis mused:

I try not to think about the question [of cosmic purpose] too much, because all too often I agree with Steven Weinberg, and it's rather depressing. Philosophically, I see no argument against his attitude, that we certainly don't see a point. To answer in the alternative sense really requires you to invoke the principle of God, I think. At least, that's the way I would view it, and there's no evidence that He's around, or It's around. On the other hand, that doesn't mean that you can't enjoy your life.[3]

Harvard astronomer Margaret Geller reacted in this way to Weinberg's gloom:

I guess my view of life is that you live your life and it's short. The thing is to have as rich an experience as you possibly can. That's what I'm trying to do. I'm trying to do something creative. I try to educate people. I enjoy seeing the world, and I have as many broad experiences as I can. I feel privileged to be able to be creative. But does it have a point? I don't know. It's not clear that it matters. I guess it's a kind of statement that I would never make. I figure, thinking in the small way that I think as a human being, well, okay why should it have a point? What point? It's just a physical system, what point is there?[4]

It is in fact quite exceptional to find scientists who publicly allow that the universe may have some 'point' to it, or that a transcendent purpose influences its evolution. In fact the majority of evolutionary biologists now think that neo-Darwinian science has decisively debunked the myth of purpose.[5] The Cornell Professor of Natural History, William Provine, summarizes what he takes to be the position of almost all biologists, and indeed of most other scientists today as well:

[Modern evolutionary biology] tells us (and I would argue that the same message flows in from physics, chemistry, molecular biology, astrophysics, and indeed from all modern science) that there is in nature no detectable purposive force of any kind. Everything proceeds purely by materialistic and mechanistic processes . . . modern science directly implies that the world is organized strictly in accordance with mechanistic principles. There are no purposive principles whatsoever in nature. There are no gods and no designing forces that are rationally detectable. The frequently made assertion that modern biology and the assumptions of the Judeo-Christian tradition are fully compatible is false.[6]

This view that the universe is 'pointless' may be called 'cosmic pessimism'. It is the academically founded belief that, since science and reason can offer us no unambiguously clear evidence of it, the cosmos has neither a transcendent origin nor a meaningful destiny. While the universe may include goal-oriented organisms and political animals such as ourselves, as a whole it is devoid of meaning. Hence the origins of life, consciousness and our inclination toward cultural creativity and political life as well, are themselves only the accidental, unplanned outcomes of an aimless evolutionary process made up of random variations filtered through an impersonal process of 'natural selection' over enormous spans of mindless temporal duration.

Such a generally grim sense of the universe, I suspect, continues to contextualize much scholarly discussion in our universities today, and the so-called postmodern approaches are no less, at least tacitly, tied to this background than are modern ways of thinking. Critically exploring the historical roots of cosmic pessimism, therefore, would be a very worthwhile pursuit.[7] However, instead of dwelling on the fascinating intellectual history that lies behind the modern expulsion of cosmic teleology, I would prefer here simply to ask about the ecological implications of our divesting nature of any aspect of inherent purpose. For it would seem, at least at first sight, that the academically sanctioned assumption that the evolving universe is either hostile or at best indifferent to life and our own existence, hardly provides strong reasons for respecting nature. Is a pointless universe, in other words, worth caring for? One of the main implications of the current ecological crisis is that it almost forces us to pay attention once again to the slippery old question of cosmic purpose.

I should point out, however, that even when cosmic pessimists entertain no prospects of a final meaning to the universe, this does not preclude a vigorous humanism, though, as we shall see, humanism itself can be ecologically problematic. Bertrand Russell, for example, used to say that this immense universe is not worthy of us and will eventually crush us, but that we can still gain a sense of our human dignity and even a degree of happiness by courageously resisting its mindless indifference.[8] And Albert Camus likewise claimed that we could find happiness only in the lucid acknowledgement of the universe's hostility.[9] Numerous other modern sceptics have argued that it is precisely the absence of objective cosmic meaning that allows us humans to grasp our own dignity as the sole authors of whatever meaning and value there is. Only in the apprehension of our astounding creativity, they argue, do we become fully aware of our human greatness. In fact, the presence of an objective cosmic meaning would only frustrate such an awareness. The American philosopher, E. D. Klemke, for example, remarks:

> From the standpoint of present evidence, evaluational components such as meaning or purpose are not to be found in the universe as objective aspects of it . . . Rather, we 'impose' such values upon the universe . . . An objective meaning – that is, one which is inherent within the universe or dependent upon external agencies – would, frankly, leave me cold. It would not be mine . . . I, for one, am glad that the universe has no meaning, for thereby is man all the more glorious. I willingly accept the fact that external meaning is non-existent . . . for this leaves me free to forge my own meanings.[10]

And the renowned palaeontologist Stephen Jay Gould, who has little patience for those of us who are too cowardly to embrace the utterly directionless universe that he finds in Darwinian science, has also stated that an objectively meaningless cosmos has the advantage of providing us with a neutral canvas on which to impose our own meanings, and thereby grasp the true glory of being human.[11]

It is of course true that new developments in twentieth-century science have seriously challenged the scientific materialism upon which so much modern despair about the universe and the reactionary forms of humanism have arisen. But a general sense of what I am calling cosmic pessimism still remains very much alive in the academic world, even where postmodern suspicions of modernity have arisen. My purpose here, therefore, is to ask just how plausible and integral an intellectual framework cosmic pessimism might be when it functions as the tacit background of our thinking today about global politics and ecology? Can a cosmological resignation to the suspicion that the whole universe is pointless ever allow people of the earth to reach a deep and sincere ethical consensus on the need to revere and preserve nature? I would argue that it cannot, and that today more than ever we may need to search for a scientifically tenable religious cosmology as the horizon of our global politics and our search for a sustainable ecological practice.

However, cosmic pessimism will prove to be a formidable obstacle to such a quest. For even though its divesting nature of any intrinsic value would appear to provide a rather flimsy foundation for ecological ethics, ironically it is often those very thinkers who renounce any notion of cosmic purpose who publicly exhibit the most fervent ethical and political commitment to ecological conservation today. It is scientific sceptics such as Carl Sagan, E. O. Wilson and Stephen Jay Gould who are among the most visible carriers of the banner of conservationism.

Obviously, then, many cosmic pessimists think the non-human natural world is eminently worth saving, and so it is important that those of us who prefer a religious grounding of ethics should carefully examine the sceptics' own reasons for extending such appreciation to nature. In the absence of any transcendent grounding of nature's value, what could possibly be the reasons for their ecological concern? On what grounds do the same scientifically enlightened intellectuals who see no 'point' to the universe, often so vigorously oppose the reckless destruction of our minuscule terrestrial portion of it? Cosmic pessimists are often the first to espouse ecological causes, and even while they explicitly deny any permanent meaning and value to the universe as a whole, they are nevertheless deeply committed to the conservation of the earth and its eco-systems. Even though the cosmic story as a whole is destined for the pit of nothingness, they insist that we should still work to preserve life on our planet as long as we can.

How does a cosmic pessimist justify such an ethical posture? One possible argument, even though it is an abomination to many ecologists, is to maintain that the non-human natural world is worth saving simply for the sake of human survival, or for the sake of perpetuating our social, political and cultural institutions and ideals. Accordingly, we are obliged to take care of nature because otherwise our own species and all that it has accomplished will tragically disappear forever.[12] While some ecologists protest that it is just this anthropocentrism that sadly opens nature to our abuse, pragmatically minded sceptics often insist that if there is no 'point' to the universe itself, and if there is no transcending religious reason for attributing intrinsic value to nature, anthropocentric motives are about the best we can come up with.[13] In view of the reigning academic assumptions about the cosmos as a whole, ethicists often find themselves forced to fall back on a purely humanistic grounding of ecological responsibility.

If you assume that the universe is 'pointless', however, a less anthropocentric and more captivating way of justifying ecological concern might be to argue that the very fragility of life on earth is what makes it so precious and worth saving. The indifference of the universe at large actually makes life in our small corner of it all the more worthy of our care. Within the deadness of a predominantly inanimate cosmic environment, whatever life eventually blossoms here on earth deserves a special regard. The very improbability of life ever appearing at all in a massively indifferent universe actually bestows on it a very special significance. The preciousness of life is therefore grounded in its precariousness, and this is enough on which to build our ecological ethics and activism.[14]

To the anticipated rejoinder that religion might provide much more permanent reasons for valuing nature, the cosmic pessimist will typically point out that the world's dominant religious traditions have actually tolerated ecological indifference. By positing an 'ultimate' or 'final' cosmic meaning, and by sometimes even looking forward to the dissolution of our immediate world, does not a sense of the eternal actually foster a lack of concern for the temporal welfare of nature here and now? Does not religious interest in the supernatural diminish our appreciation of the earth? And so, is not a pure naturalism, the view that purposeless nature is all there is to reality, sufficient to ground the ecological concern that our common quest for global order requires today?[15]

In response to these questions I would argue that scientific naturalism, with its attendant cosmic pessimism is, in the final analysis, incapable of providing adequate grounds for the global ecological concern the world needs today. Naturalism and cosmic pessimism, as I pointed out earlier, are not necessarily inconsistent with a human-centred ecological concern, and they may discover in the sheer perishability of the earth's eco-systems a reason for our cherishing them. But neither human survival nor the fragility of our eco-systems constitutes sufficient grounds for a global ethical consensus on ecological responsibility.

There is no need for us to dwell here on the problematic aspects of the anthropocentric or humanistic kind of ecological ethics. Let it suffice to say that making humanity and its cultural achievements either the only intrinsic value or the main pragmatic reason for our taking care of nature can easily lead us to devalue all that is non-human whenever it seems convenient to do so. A convincing case can be made that modern anthropocentrism is just as likely the cause as the cure for our ecological ills. Any ethical perspective that fails to discover intrinsic rather than purely instrumental value in nature will eventually prove to be ecologically unsatisfactory.

But what about the argument that we can value our eco-systems because, in an otherwise purposeless universe, they have a delicate fragility that sets them apart? Perhaps in a meaningless universe there is intrinsic value in life after all – simply by virtue of its being such a notable exception to the pervasive deadness and indifference of the rest of the cosmos. Accordingly, we should protect all of life on earth, and not just human existence, lest it be dissolved back into the inorganic banality of the senseless universe out of which it accidentally emerged.

This, it seems to me, is really the only serious argument the ecologically responsible cosmic pessimist can fall back on once the absurdity of the universe as a whole is accepted and the anthropocentric brand of environmental ethics is rightly rejected. But is the claim that nature's value consists in its perishability itself a coherent one? I would argue that it is not, and that we need to discover a much more substantive basis for valuing nature as a good in itself if we are ever to place ecological ethics on a sufficiently firm foundation.

Perishability as such can hardly be the quality that gives intrinsic worth to living beings. After all, does not perishability actually diminish their value? Is not the fact that living beings are perishable an argument against their inherent worth? How can their tendency toward non-being be the ground of their value?[16] Life on earth must possess something other than mere impermanence if it is to merit our ethical regard. But what is this 'something'?

Following the thought of mathematician and philosopher Alfred North Whitehead, I would suggest that we may locate the basis for life's intrinsic value not in its fragility, but in its *beauty*.[17] In a manner consistent with traditional philosophy's identifying beauty as one of the so-called 'transcendentals' (along with being, unity and truth), we may see the beauty of nature as intrinsically valuable, and therefore as an end in itself.

It is not uncommon, of course, to ground nature's value aesthetically. But most attempts to do so end up still thinking of beauty too anthropocentrically, that is, as a purely human creation, and consequently they render human subjectivity the only intrinsic value in the universe. But beauty, if we follow Whitehead, is not just in the eye of the human beholder. It is an objective aspect of all things in nature, even apart from us and our valuations. In fact beauty is the objective patterning that gives things their very actuality and definiteness. The very being of things *is* their beauty.

Beauty is the 'harmony of contrast' that gives definiteness and actuality to all things. Fragility or perishability, on the other hand, is the tendency of harmonized contrast to fall apart. Beauty, in our dynamic world-in-process, is the ordering of novelty, or the unifying of complexity, whereas fragility is the inclination toward disorder and chaos. What we value, therefore, is not the fragility but the beauty that is intrinsic to things.

Of course, we tend to cherish fragile entities and occurrences, things that delicately unify a wide variety of complexity, nuance or shades of diversity (such as a great work of art or the mammalian brain). But we appreciate these not because they are inclined to perish so much as because they subtly balance harmony with contrast, order with novelty, and unity with complexity. That is, we value them because of the inherent tension and balance that give them the quality of beauty. We respect living organisms and eco-systems, therefore, not simply because they are perishable (which of course they are), but because they are entities that temporarily synthesize an amazing variety of diversity into intensely beautiful unities of function and achievement.

Consequently, we may say that what gives our earth's ecology its inherent value is neither its precariousness, nor simply our own human valuations (though these too belong to the cosmic process). Rather, it is the objective fact that our eco-systems are unique and unrepeatable instances of intensely ordered novelty, or of delicately harmonized diversity, that is, of beauty. Certainly eco-systems are always in great danger of disintegrating, but it is not this instability that renders them inherently precious. For, like all instances of beauty, living beings and eco-systems are comprised of an exquisite balance of order and novelty, harmony and contrast, pattern and nuance. Whenever we encounter such syntheses we are intuitively appreciative of the fact that the novelty, complexity and nuance could easily have overwhelmed the order, harmony and pattern, and thus reduced them to the ugliness of chaos. And, at the same time, we sense how easily the order, harmony and unity may have flattened out all the nuance and subtlety, reducing things to the banality of homogeneity. There is always a degree of tension in any concrete instance of beauty, and it is this aesthetic tension that gives to our eco-systems the inevitable delicacy that renders them forever subject to disintegration. But, once again, it is not their precariousness as such that grounds the value we see in them. The precariousness is a derivative of the beauty.

Thus, our ecological concern can best be situated within an aesthetic rather than a pessimistic vision of the universe. Modern intellectual history, however, has divorced aesthetics almost completely from the objective natural world itself, attributing beauty's origin to us humans who remain fundamentally estranged from the inherently valueless cosmos out of which which we are said to have accidentally evolved.[18] Modernity, and some forms of postmodernity as well, have understood beauty – and all values for that matter – as nothing more than human concoctions, while the non-human natural world 'out there' remains inherently devoid of value and meaning. Ever since Descartes, modern philosophy, with its emphasis on the primacy of human subjectivity, has made it difficult if not impossible for us to see beauty and value as objective aspects of the universe. And so, having lost a sense of the universe, we have come to suspect that whatever value we see in nature has its origins in our own creative originality rather than in a cosmic process that is inherently good and beautiful even apart from us.

Every university in the Western world, Whitehead once observed, has organized itself along the lines of this dualistic, materialistic and pessimistic way of thinking about nature.[19] I suspect that today he would agree with those who now realize how much this modern myth has shaped our own ecologically problematic attitudes toward nature.[20] He would still wonder at the failure of our contemporary universities to acknowledge just how much their adherence to modernity's cosmic pessimism and its fatal alliance with humanistic mythology has contributed to the perpetuation of ecologically noxious ways of looking at the natural world.[21]

Where then can we find an ecologically responsible post-modernism? If we look to traditional religion and theology we are likely to be disappointed. For they have usually been quite anthropocentric themselves, and even when they are theocentric their preoccupation with the supernatural has sometimes led them to discredit and even despise the natural world. At best, our religious traditions seem ecologically ambiguous. Although Christian teachings about creation, incarnation and the sacramentality of nature are ecologically significant, by and large the churches and their theologians have until recently thought very little about their relevance for the welfare of nature. Is there anywhere, then, a genuinely 'postmodern' theological vision capable of connecting religious traditions to a wholesome ecological ethic in a scientifically enlightened and politically promising way?

Some early sparks of such a vision seem to me to be present in what is now known as 'process theology'. Using concepts of the philosopher Alfred North Whitehead and his followers, process theology provides, on the one hand, a religiously sensitive alternative to anthropocentrism, and, on the other, a scientifically informed alternative to modernity's cosmic pessimism.[22] In spite of its still undeveloped status, process theology deserves special attention today. It follows the most ecologically sophisticated philosophy of nature available today, and it also provides the most systematically rigorous attempt to ground the value of the natural world in a non-anthropocentric way.[23]

Process theology vigorously opposes the modern view that we humans are the sole source of the world's value, even though it allows that we certainly do contribute much to the importance of the cosmos. Instead, it accepts the evolutionary view according to which we humans are only lately emergent from a lengthy cosmic process that would have been inherently beautiful and intrinsically valuable even had it not produced us. For even without us there would still be harmony of contrast, or the ordering of novelty, in everything that exists. Indeed, any given entity could not exist at all without some internal patterning, for the very actuality of a thing is rooted in the internal ordering of its contrasting components, that is, its beauty. Thus, fact and value (beauty) are inseparable, even apart from our own creative, evaluating subjectivity.

However, since aesthetic value exists inherently in nature, and does not stem solely from us humans, it seems legitimate to ask what is the source of nature's intrinsic value if it is not us? In answer to this question process theology invites us to consider the possibility of a transcendent source of the order and novelty, the harmony and the contrast, the unity and complexity that make up the aesthetic actuality of all entities. It locates the ultimate source of the ever new forms of cosmic beauty in the God of religion. It is important to point out, however, that 'God' is understood here not only as the source of order (which was the emphasis in traditional theism), but also as the source of the novelty that makes evolution and a processive universe possible.

This distinction is of special relevance when we reflect upon the prospect of global order today. For as source of the novelty and not just the order in the universe, God is the ground of the world's constant urge toward evolution, and the impetus for its adventure toward deeper and wider aesthetic intensity. Thus, God is the ultimate ground not only of any global order we might achieve politically, but also a constant and unsettling source of disturbance of all forms of order that fall short of relevant aesthetic intensity. In other words, a global order that remains non-inclusive or which refuses to accommodate variety and diversity is, in the perspective of process thought, not a good to be desired, but an evil to be overcome.

In process theology God is understood as a persuasive rather than coercive power, luring the cosmos (at every stage of its evolution), in the manner of love rather than force, toward the instantiation of ever new and richer forms of order. Another way of saying this is that God wills the maximization of beauty in the universe.[24] And the role of humans in the universe is to participate with all of their moral and political energy in the maximization of the evolution toward wider cosmic beauty. Indeed the meaning of our lives, both individually and collectively, is to participate and promote the cosmic adventure toward beauty. We do so proximately, of course, through our cultural and political activities. But a process perspective encourages us not to lose sight of the fact that these activities are ultimately not just phenomena that take place on the face of the earth, but happenings that the earth and the cosmos are now seeking to accomplish through us.

This cosmic-centred theological vision has the advantage not only of allowing us to envisage God as the exemplar of our ecological concern (a role that hardly fits the rather apathetic, non-relational and stoical God of so much of our traditional theism), but it also thrusts us humans back so deeply into nature and its emergent beauty that we may no longer understand ourselves in modernity's sense as strangers in an indifferent universe and therefore as the sole originators of the world's value. Instead, we will gratefully acknowledge how our own existence and creativity have themselves emerged from a more fundamental and momentous cosmic process that has always aimed at ever deeper aesthetic intensification – long before our own very recent appearance. And we shall then more willingly accept our role as stewards of creation, not simply in the sense of conserving what has been present in creation from the beginning, but also as shepherds of an ongoing cosmic process that seeks ever new ways of sustaining its urge toward deeper beauty. We will grasp our vocation as sponsors of a creative cosmic impulse that seeks through us and in us to expand far beyond us.

Process theology, therefore allows us once again, in a truly postmodern way, to acknowledge the abiding presence of a kind of teleology in the cosmos, and it does so in a manner that should give no offence to scientists. As Whitehead puts it, the purpose of the cosmos is its aim toward beauty.[25] And to the extent that any process is orientated toward the realization of value (such as beauty) it may legitimately be called teleological or purposeful.

That the universe has already moved generically toward richer aesthetic intensity should be evident to anyone who is aware of contemporary science. The cosmos began in a hot and undifferentiated broth of radiation and it eventually evolved into the incredible complexity of life, mind and civilization. If we survey the cosmic story as presented by contemporary science, it is clear that the universe, at least over the long haul, has moved toward increasingly more intense forms of ordered novelty. Thus we can say that it does have at least a net directionality to it. In spite of the protests of Stephen Jay Gould and other naturalists who choose to see evolution only as a randomly branching bush, there can be little question that the cosmos now contains significantly more ordered novelty, for example, in the phenomena of life, consciousness and culture here on earth and perhaps elsewhere, than it did three minutes after the big bang. The new cosmic story, which dwarfs, contextualizes and relativizes all of our national histories on this small planet, tells of a restlessness in nature that is not content to remain stuck in triviality, but which over the course of fifteen billion years has clearly heightened the beauty and value of the universe.

It seems entirely appropriate to ask, then, why the universe has this adventurous character to it. The answer process theology gives is that the cosmos is responding to the influence of a supremely Persuasive Love that is never content with the *status quo*, and that seeks always to intensify the value of the world. The cosmos, however, is not compelled but only persuaded by this Supreme Love to appropriate the novel forms of order that can heighten its inherent beauty. It need not rush to embrace this invitation in a straightforward way, and so it may tend to experiment in a meandering manner with many kinds of ordered novelty. Terrestrial evolution is the story of one such set of experiments. So also are the political endeavours of nations of the earth.

In this cosmic vision God wills the independence of the world and promotes the self-creativity of all its constituents. Their inherent value is thus intensified by the fact that they are self-creative syntheses of order and novelty. The earth's eco-systems may be said to deserve our care, therefore, because they are especially intense actualizations of divinely inspired creativity and cosmic beauty. Humanity, in this vision, is not the only creative or intrinsically valuable aspect of the cosmos. Of course, as humanism rightly demands, in order to gain an appropriate sense of our human worth we need to become aware of our creative potential. But we do not have to do so by depriving the rest of nature of its own share in the creative process that modernity has associated so one-sidedly with human existence.

As in the case of beauty, we need not clasp creativity to ourselves as though it were completely absent from the non-human realms of cosmic process. Creativity is pervasive throughout the universe. It is a characteristic not only of God and humans, but of the whole cosmos. The universe clearly would not be the same without our own creative cultural contributions, but process theology allows that the universe in general and the earth's biosphere in particular would still be objectively valuable, beautiful and creative quite independently of our contingent emergence in evolution. Hence, we must divorce ourselves not from the cosmos, as modernity has encouraged, but from the modern bias that nature is a value-neutral canvas that remains completely vacuous until we have painted it over with our cultural and political inventions.

Finally, it is the conviction of process theology that what happens to our natural environment happens also to God. Unlike traditional theologies that emphasized God's apartness from the world, process theology maintains that the same God who seeks to maximize the world's beauty also assimilates the world-process, in its totality, into the divine life. This is not pantheism but *pan-en-theism*. God still transcends the universe as its ultimate stimulus to adventure, but God also feels and preserves everlastingly all the world's actual experiments with beauty, including its failures, tragedies and achievements. God, therefore, is internally affected by what happens in the entire cosmic process, in its natural as well as its political history. God is vulnerable to all that occurs in the world, including our ecological abuse. When nature suffers, God also suffers. At root, therefore, our ecological neglect deprives not only ourselves but also God of appropriately intense aesthetic enjoyment. What happens to our environment happens to God, our ultimate environment.

Such a vision of the cosmos, I think, provides us with a much more promising framework for thinking about politics, religion and ecology than does the still prevalent academic commitment to the purely naturalist assumptions of cosmic pessimism. It recaptures the ancient religious sense that we live in a meaningful and intrinsically valuable world and it does so in a manner entirely consonant with contemporary science.[26] Finally, it provides us with a basis for thinking about 'global order' that is deeply rooted in cosmology while remaining open to the insights of theology.

Notes

[1] Steven Weinberg, *The First Three Minutes* (New York, Basic Books, 1977), 144.

[2] Alan Lightman and Roberta Brawer, *Origins: The Lives and Worlds of Modern Cosmologists* (Cambridge, MA, Harvard University Press, 1990), 340.

[3] Ibid., 358.

[4] Ibid., 377.

[5] Biologist S. E. Luria, for example, writes: 'The essence of biology is evolution, and the essence of evolution is the absence of motive and purpose', *Life: The Unfinished Experiment* (New York, Charles Scribner's Sons, 1973), 148.

[6] 'Evolution and the foundation of ethics', in Steven L. Goldman (ed.), *Science, Technology and Social Progress* (Bethlehem, PA, Lehigh University Press, 1989), 261.

[7] One of the most thorough of such surveys remains John Hermann Randall's *The Making of the Modern Mind* (New York, Columbia University Press, 1976).

[8] Bertrand Russell, *Religion and Science* (New York, Oxford University Press, 1961).

[9] Albert Camus, *The Myth of Sisyphus and Other Essays*, trans. Justin O'Brien (New York, Knopf, 1955).

[10] E. D. Klemke, 'Living without appeal', in E. D. Klemke (ed.), *The Meaning of Life* (New York, Oxford University Press, 1981), 169–72.

[11] Stephen Jay Gould, *Ever Since Darwin* (New York, Norton, 1977), 12–13.

[12] Jonathan Shell makes a similar argument against the stockpiling of nuclear weapons in *The Fate of the Earth* (New York, Knopf, 1982).

[13] See the discussion by Bryan Norton, *Why Preserve Natural Variety* (Princeton, NJ, Princeton University Press, 1987).

[14] In view of recent astrophysics, the assumption that physical reality is fundamentally 'indifferent' or 'hostile' toward life needs to be questioned even on scientific grounds. For there is a growing consensus among scientists that physical reality in our cosmos has always favoured the emergence of life when there is no physical necessity that

it do so. See esp. John D. Barrow and Frank J. Tipler, *The Anthropic Cosmological Principle* (New York, Oxford University Press, 1986).

¹⁵ See, for example, John Passmore, *Man's Responsibility for Nature* (New York, Scribner, 1974), 184.

¹⁶ The cosmic pessimist might reply that, in the absence of anything eternal, permanent, holy or sacred, there can be no basis for anything's worth other than the delicacy inherent in its perishability. But to say that something, such as a living species, is perishable means that it has a tendency toward non-being. If you attempt to introduce anything other than perishability as the ground of its value, then this would, logically speaking, have to be something imperishable. For example, you might say that a thing's simply 'being' is what gives it its value. But by introducing the notion of 'being' you have already brought in something logically distinct from 'non-being', that is, something that by definition partakes of the imperishable or the eternal.

¹⁷ I have summarized Whitehead's position more fully in my books, *The Cosmic Adventure* (Mahwah, NY, Paulist Press, 1984) and *The Promise of Nature* (New York, Paulist Press, 1993). See also Alfred North Whitehead, *Adventures of Ideas* (New York, The Free Press, 1967), 252–96.

¹⁸ The classic distinction of primary from secondary qualities contributes to the sense that nature 'in itself' is valueless while the value of 'inherently' valueless nature comes from the presence of creative human subjects.

¹⁹ Alfred North Whitehead, *Science and the Modern World* (New York, The Free Press, 1967), 54–5.

²⁰ See, for example, Carolyn Merchant, *The Death of Nature* (San Francisco, Harper & Row, 1980).

²¹ David W. Ehrenfeld, *The Arrogance of Humanism* (Oxford, Oxford University Press, 1978), 202.

²² I do not subscribe to every aspect of process theology. What I find most appealing, however, is its ecological conception of nature and its vision of a God who is truly related to the world.

²³ For an introduction to process theology see John B. Cobb and David Griffin, *Process Theology: An Introductory Exposition* (Philadelphia, The Westminster Press, 1976). For the best discussion of the environmental implications of process theology see Charles Birch and John B. Cobb, Jr., *The Liberation of Life* (Cambridge, Cambridge University Press, 1981).

²⁴ Alfred North Whitehead, *Adventures of Ideas* (New York, The Free Press, 1967), 252–96.

²⁵ Ibid., 265.

²⁶ See my book *Science and Religion: From Conflict to Conversation* (New York, Paulist Press, 1995).

Index